T0227862

LogiQL

A QUERY LANGUAGE
FOR SMART DATABASES

EMERGING DIRECTIONS IN DATABASE SYSTEMS AND APPLICATIONS

Series Editor
Sham Navathe
Professor
Georgia Institute of Technology
College of Computing
Atlanta, Georgia, U.S.A.

Linked Data Management, by Andreas Harth, Katja Hose, and Ralf Schenkel

Automated Physical Database Design and Tuning, Nicolas Bruno

Patterns of Data Modeling, Michael Blaha

LogiQL: A Query Language for Smart Databases, Terry Halpin and Spencer Rugaber

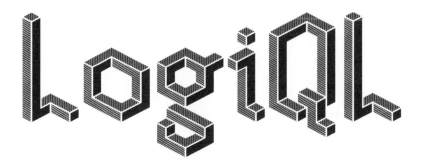

A QUERY LANGUAGE
FOR SMART DATABASES

Terry Halpin

INTI International University
Malaysia

Spencer Rugaber

College of Computing
Georgia Institute of Technology
USA

CRC Press
Taylor & Francis Group
Boca Raton   London   New York

CRC Press is an imprint of the
Taylor & Francis Group, an **informa** business

A CHAPMAN & HALL BOOK

CRC Press
Taylor & Francis Group
6000 Broken Sound Parkway NW, Suite 300
Boca Raton, FL 33487-2742

First issued in hardback 2017

ISBN 13: 978-1-138-41654-3 (hbk)
ISBN 13: 978-1-4822-4493-9 (pbk)

Library of Congress Cataloging-in-Publication Data

Halpin, T. A.
    LogiQL : a query language for smart databases / Terry Halpin, Spencer Rugaber.
        pages cm
    Includes bibliographical references and index.
    ISBN 978-1-4822-4493-9 (paperback)
    1. LogiQL (Computer program language) 2. Query languages (Computer science) 3. Querying (Computer science) 4. Databases. I. Rugaber, Spencer. II. Title.

QA76.73.L62H35 2015
005.74'1--dc23   2014027305

Visit the Taylor & Francis Web site at
http://www.taylorandfrancis.com

and the CRC Press Web site at
http://www.crcpress.com

Contents

Preface

THE PURPOSE OF THIS book is to introduce you to programming in LogiQL. This includes the syntax of the language, the structure of programs, and how to express your understanding of a problem in terms of the major language elements: constraints, derivation rules, and facts. The book is not intended to provide a complete and precise language specification; for that purpose, you should refer to the LogicBlox 4.0 Reference Manual.* In particular, there may be situations in which this book intentionally omits certain advanced details in order to better focus on introductory concepts. It is assumed throughout that you at least have a basic background in computer programming.

LogiQL is a declarative logic programming language developed by LogicBlox, Inc. to harness the power of first-order logic to support access to databases. It has been influenced by two other logic languages, Prolog and Datalog.

Prolog is a popular logic programming language initially implemented in France in 1972. Both Prolog and LogiQL are built on first-order logic and provide elegant support for deductive inferences, including recursive rules. Unlike Prolog, LogiQL programs are guaranteed to terminate. This useful property is achieved by placing further syntactic restrictions on what kinds of rules may be formulated.

Datalog was also developed in the 1970s with a specific emphasis on providing access to deductive databases. Unlike Datalog, LogiQL has been designed to handle large quantities of data stored in industrial-strength databases. Hence, it can be thought of as a query language for such databases. In fact, the name "LogiQL" combines "logic" with "QL," which is shorthand for "query language."

---

* https://developer.logicblox.com/content/docs4/core-reference/webhelp

This book is structured as a series of chapters, each broken into units. Each unit presents a small set of related concepts ending with some simple exercises. The exercises give you a chance to test your understanding. You should try each exercise before looking at the answer that follows. At the end of a chapter, some more substantial problems are provided to help you consolidate the concepts introduced in that chapter.

The text contains numerous examples of LogiQL code, expressed using Courier font. In addition, you are occasionally referred to external files. These might contain programs for you to modify, data to test against, or scripts to run. These files are available to you online at https://developer. logicblox.com/documentation/logiqlbook/. On this page, you will see a further link to an archive file containing the resources. After you have downloaded and opened the archive, you will see directories (folders) for the book's chapters. Files associated with units are contained in further subdirectories called resources/U#, where # is the number of the unit referring to the file. For files referred to in Consolidation Exercises, there are subdirectories called resources/CE.

As you work through the units in a chapter, you may come across terms that are **boldfaced**. Definitions for these terms are collected in a separate Glossary. Appendices describe the stylistic conventions used, provide basic instructions for running and testing your programs, and summarize LogiQL syntax, constraints, and built-in libraries. Other appendices compare LogiQL to SQL and to mathematical logic and provide you guidance for improving the performance of your LogiQL programs.

Many of the units in the book contain examples taken from an interesting problem area—historical data about the British monarchy. Much more information on this topic can be found in related Wikipedia articles. If you are interested, you might start with the Wikipedia article "List of British Monarchs."

In order to use this book, you should already have access to the LogiQL software. Information about obtaining this access can be found at http:// developer.logicblox.com. In addition to access to the software, there are several things you should have already learned before going forward: (1) You should know how to use an editor to construct text files to contain the programs you write to answer the exercises; (2) you should know how to display a window into which you can enter commands to the operating system on your machine; and (3) you should know the basic syntax of the command language that you enter into this window.

For the purposes of this book, your primary means of using LogiQL is through the `lb` command, which enables you to build workspaces, load and execute programs, and query results. A short introduction to `lb` is given in Appendix A, which you should take a look at before you begin answering the exercises.

At the time of this writing, the coding examples were tested using LogiQL version 4.0. It is anticipated that this document will be updated as newer versions of LogiQL are released.

Acknowledgment

T HE AUTHORS WISH TO thank LogiBlox, Inc. and its technical staff for their support in the development of this book.

Authors

Terry Halpin is a professor in computer science at INTI International University, Malaysia, and a data modeling consultant. He previously held senior faculty positions in computer science at the University of Queensland (Australia) and Neumont University (Salt Lake City, Utah). He spent many years in data modeling technology at Asymetrix Corporation, InfoModelers Inc., Visio Corporation, Microsoft Corporation, and LogicBlox. His doctoral thesis formalized object-role modeling (ORM/NIAM), and his current research focuses on conceptual modeling and rule-based technology. He has authored more than 200 technical publications and seven books, and has co-edited nine books on information systems modeling research. He is a regular columnist for the *Business Rules Journal*, and is a recipient of the DAMA International Achievement Award for Education (2002) and the IFIP Outstanding Service Award (2006).

Spencer Rugaber is a computer scientist who has worked both in industry and in academia as well as serving as program director for the Software Engineering and Languages program at the U.S. National Science Foundation. His research interests are in the area of software engineering, human–computer interaction, and cognitive science. He is the author of the article on program understanding included in the *Encyclopedia of Computer Science and Technology* and of numerous software engineering articles appearing in technical journals and conference proceedings. He is currently an adjunct faculty member at the Georgia Institute of Technology (Atlanta, Georgia).

Key LogiQL Concepts

L OGIQL AND ITS ASSOCIATED execution engine provide you with a powerful way to address your computational needs. Its power arises from its ability to efficiently deal with large amounts of data while avoiding many of the low-level implementation details found in other languages.

The language contains a number of intertwined features, and some connections between concepts might not be immediately obvious as you read sequentially through this book. To ease your way, this section provides a brief introduction to the language's key concepts that you will learn about in subsequent chapters. Each of the mentioned concepts is highlighted in bold and also appears in the Glossary to this book. Be aware that many of these terms have other senses. Further clarification is provided when the concepts are discussed in the chapters.

WORKSPACES

LogiQL programs manage **workspaces** (also called *databases*) that contain both your program and your data. In particular, workspaces hold collections of facts, each of which is concerned with a predicate. In logic, **predicates** are either properties that may be held by individual things or relationships that may apply to multiple things. In a workspace, a collection of facts associated with a predicate is called that predicate's *population*. Sometimes the distinction between the logical predicate and its population is glossed over by referring to the stored predicate population simply as a *predicate*.

You can think of a stored predicate as a named table. The **facts** of a predicate population correspond to table rows, and each row comprises a tuple of **data elements**. There are two types of data elements stored in LogiQL workspaces. Built-in **primitive types** include strings, numbers, and datetimes. In addition, programmers can define their own entity types, elements of which are guaranteed to be distinct. Moreover, an entity

TABLE 1   British Monarchy
houseOf Predicate

Monarch	House
Anne	Stuart
George I	Hanover
George II	Hanover
George III	Hanover
George IV	Hanover
William IV	Hanover
Victoria	Hanover
Edward VII	Saxe-Coburg and Gotha
George V	Windsor
Edward VIII	Windsor
George VI	Windsor
Elizabeth II	Windsor

type may have a corresponding programmer-visible reference scheme (**refmode**) that can be used to identify the individual elements of that type.

All of the tuples in a predicate population have the same length (*arity*). Thinking again in terms of tables, this says that all rows in a given table have the same number of data elements. Hence, a column in a table consists of all of the data elements occupying the corresponding position in the facts of the predicate. Moreover, all of the elements of a column are of the same type. The data elements in a particular column of a predicate are said to fill that column's **role** in the predicate.

Table 1 contains an example that you will see again in Chapter 1. It illustrates the houseOf predicate relating British monarchs to their houses. Monarch and House are entity types referenced by their names, which are elements of type string.

There are 12 facts in this predicate, and each fact fills two roles in the predicate population, one for the monarch and one for the house. A LogiQL program could be used to add these facts to the houseOf predicate and store the results in a workspace.

LOGIC PROGRAMS

To manipulate the predicates in a workspace, you write logic programs. A **logic program** is a set of **clauses**, each of which makes a claim about the facts in a predicate. There are three kinds of clauses: fact assertions/retractions (facts), constraints, and derivation rules (*rules*). A **fact assertion** is used to add a fact to a predicate's population, and a **fact retraction** is used to delete a fact from a predicate's population. **Constraints** can be used to declare predicates or limit the facts that can populate them. **Derivation rules** are used for programmatically altering a workspace, typically by deriving new facts.

A clause comprises a *head* and/or a *body*, both of which contain atoms, possibly combined by operators. An **atom** consists of a predicate name and a parenthesized list of arguments, each of which corresponds to one of the predicate's roles. In addition, an atom may be adorned with a *delta modifier* to control changes to the contents of the corresponding predicate.

LogiQL's syntax enables a programmer to specify two key properties of each rule: whether or not the predicate that the rule computes is an intensional database (IDB) predicate or an extensional database (EDB) predicate, and whether or not the rule computes an aggregation. EDB predicates are populated either by fact assertions, which have an empty body and a head containing only delta-modified atoms, or *delta rules*, that specify existing contributing predicates in their bodies. A program's *delta logic* comprises its fact assertions/retractions and its delta rules. IDB predicates, in contrast, are populated by *IDB rules*, in which neither head nor body atoms may be delta modified. *Aggregation rules* have their own syntax that includes mention of one of the built-in functions for aggregating data.

Here are some examples of how these concepts are expressed in LogiQL. The first example illustrates how you could declare the Monarch entity type, along with its hasMonarchName refmode.

```
Monarch(m), hasMonarchName(m:s) -> string(s).
```

Here is how you can assert the existence of a specific Monarch entity:

```
+Monarch("George VI").
```

If you wished to ensure that each such monarch must belong to a house, you could specify the following constraint, using "_" to mean "something."

```
Monarch(m) -> houseOf[m] = _.
```

If you wanted the LogiQL engine to automatically add facts about grandparents every time you added facts about parents, you could use the following IDB rule to derive the isGrandParentOf predicate.

```
isGrandparentOf(p1, p2) <- isParentOf(p1, p3),
    isParentOf(p3, p2).
```

Alternatively, if you wished to manage the isGrandParent predicate yourself, you could use the following delta rule:

```
+isGrandparentOf(p1, p2) <-
    +isParentOf(p1, p3), isParentOf(p3, p2) ;
    isParentOf(p1, p3), +isParentOf(p3, p2).
```

Finally, here is an aggregation rule you could use to compute the number of monarchs:

```
nrMonarchs[] = n <- agg<<n = count()>> Monarch(_).
```

WORKSPACE ORGANIZATION AND MANAGEMENT

A LogiQL program manipulates two kinds of predicates—EDB predicates and IDB predicates. *EDB predicates* normally are used to hold the facts that you explicitly enter into the workspace with fact assertions or facts you wish to manage yourself using delta rules. The term *extensional database (EDB)* is used to describe the set of all EDB predicate populations. In contrast, the facts populating IDB predicates are computed for you by your logic program with its IDB rules. The *intensional database (IDB)* is the set of IDB predicates stored in a workspace.

The logic program in a workspace comprises a set of **blocks**, each of which, in turn, is a set of related clauses residing in a source file. The process of loading a block into a workspace is called **installation**, and when you install a block you can designate it as *active* or *inactive*. Active blocks are used to automatically update the predicates in a workspace, whereas inactive blocks are available for on-demand use.

Program evaluation is broken into atomic units called *transactions*, each of which has two stages. The *initial stage* is used for processing queries and for on-demand evaluation of inactive blocks. This is typically the stage at which fact assertions/retractions are applied. During the *final stage*, active blocks are evaluated by continually interpreting all active program rules until a fixed point is reached; that is, until no further changes to the workspace occur. If at any time during evaluation a constraint is violated, the current transaction aborts and the content of the workspace reverts to its state before the transaction began. When a non-aborting transaction completes, it is said to *commit*.

Here is an example of a short LogiQL program consisting of two blocks. The first, an active block, provides a schema declaring the `Person` entity type and the `isParentOf` and `isAncestorOf` predicates. It also includes a constraint disallowing a person from being an ancestor of himself or herself.

```
Person(p), hasPersonName(p:n) -> string(n).
isParentOf(p1, p2) -> Person(p1), Person(p2).
isAncestorOf(p1, p2) -> Person(p1), Person(p2).
isAncestorOf(p1, p2) <- isParentOf(p1, p2).
isAncestorOf(p1, p2) <- isParentOf(p1, p3),
    isAncestorOf(p3, p2).
!isAncestorOf(p, p).
```

The second, inactive, block is responsible for populating the `isParentOf` predicate with three facts:

```
+isParentOf("Doctor Who", "Doc Brown").
+isParentOf("Doc Brown", "Merlin").
+isParentOf("Merlin", "Doctor Who").
```

The above program will not run as expected. Can you tell why? It is because the given facts and rules determine that Doctor Who is an ancestor of himself, but the constraint expressed in the schema disallows this. If you try to run this program, it will print an error message and abort.

PROGRAMMING IN LOGIQL

The first step in writing a LogiQL program is, of course, to understand the problem that you are trying to solve. Usually, the problem consists of inputting a data file into a workspace, where rules are applied to derive new facts that you can later query. You express your understanding of the problem by devising a schema in the form of a set of predicate declarations and accompanying constraints. Then you specify the rules you intend to use to compute the required results. You may also need to do some work preparing your input data for entry into the workspace. Naturally, you should also devise tests to ensure your program computes the correct result and performs efficiently. Hopefully, this book you are about to work through will prepare you to successfully accomplish these steps.

Quick Start

LOGIQL IS A POWERFUL language containing many features to be described in the upcoming chapters. The text includes numerous embedded examples and exercises that you are encouraged to try out for yourself. There are several ways to actually run your programs including a Web-based interpreter, a sophisticated middleware interface, and the one we choose to use in this book, a command-line interface, called lb.

The lb command and its subcommands are described in Appendix A, but in this section, we will take you through a short example so you can quickly get started using LogiQL. The example covers how you use lb and LogiQL to declare predicates and constraints, define rules, enter data, and query the results. In particular, it computes for each member of the British monarchy those other monarchs who were his or her ancestors.

The first thing you need to do for any application is to create a workspace that will contain your data and program. The lb create command can do this for you as follows:

```
lb create royalty
```

Here we give the name to our workspace. The system should respond with the message `created workspace 'royalty'` indicating that the workspace has been successfully created.

As with most programming languages, in LogiQL you need to declare the properties of the data with which you will be working. Our example concerns the British monarchy, so it is natural to declare a data type to represent them. A declaration to do this looks like the following:

```
Monarch(m), hasMonarchName(m:s) -> string(s).
```

The declaration says that a new predicate called Monarch exists and that Monarch entities will be referred to using their names via the hasMonarchName predicate, where the monarch name itself is represented internally with a LogiQL string value.

To install this declaration into the royalty workspace, you can use the addblock subcommand of the lb command as follows:

```
lb addblock royalty 'Monarch(m), hasMonarchName(m:s)
   -> string(s).'
```

The command indicates that a new block of code is being added to the royalty workspace. Note the use of apostrophes so that the command shell you are using will ignore any character that has special meaning to it. Then the system responds with the message added block 'block_1Z1I6CCX' where block_1Z1I6CCX is the internal name that the system has given to your program segment.

The data with which your program is concerned has to do with parenthood facts. So you can now declare a predicate to hold this information:

```
lb addblock royalty 'parentOf[m1] = m2 -> Monarch(m1),
   Monarch(m2).'
```

That is, parentOf is a predicate that when given a Monarch argument (m1) responds with another Monarch (m2) that is m1's parent.

In a similar manner, you can add constraints preventing your data from containing some mistakes, such as someone being their own parent:

```
lb addblock royalty '!parentOf[m1] = m1.'
```

Now that you have declared your predicates and a constraint, you can actually enter the data into the workspace. This time you will use the exec subcommand of lb as follows:

```
lb exec royalty '
  +parentOf["George II"]      = "George I".
  +parentOf["George IV"]      = "George III".
  +parentOf["William IV"]     = "George III".
  +parentOf["Edward VII"]     = "Victoria".
  +parentOf["George V"]       = "Edward VII".
  +parentOf["Edward VIII"]    = "George V".
  +parentOf["George VI"]      = "George V".
  +parentOf["Elizabeth II"]   = "George VI".
'
```

In the case of the exec subcommand, no feedback is given to you for successful completion. However, if you wish to see the contents of the parentOf predicate in the workspace, you can use the print subcommand, as follows: lb print royalty parentOf.

Your results should look like the following, where the numbers within square brackets are internal identifiers for each of the Monarch entities in the workspace:

```
[10000000001] "George II"    [10000000006] "George I"
[10000000002] "George V"     [10000000005] "Edward VII"
[10000000003] "George IV"    [10000000000] "George III"
[10000000004] "Edward VIII"  [10000000002] "George V"
[10000000005] "Edward VII"   [10000000012] "Victoria"
[10000000007] "Elizabeth II" [10000000013] "George VI"
[10000000013] "George VI"    [10000000002] "George V"
[10000000015] "William IV"   [10000000000] "George III"
```

You are now ready to write a rule to compute ancestors. An ancestor is either a parent or the ancestor of a parent. This relationship can be expressed in LogiQL with the following code:

```
lb addblock royalty '
  ancestorOf(m1, m2) -> Monarch(m1), Monarch(m2).
  ancestorOf(m1, m2) <- parentOf(m1, m2).
  ancestorOf(m1, m2) <- parentOf(m1, m3),
      ancestorOf(m3, m2).
  '
```

To see the results, you can use the lb query subcommand. A LogiQL query looks much like a rule, except that the name of the predicate being defined begins with an underscore, such as in the following. (Note, we have also used lb echo to dress up the output a bit.)

```
lb echo "Ancestors of British monarchs who were also
monarchs"
lb query royalty '
  _(s1, s2) <-
      ancestorOf(m1, m2),
      hasMonarchName(m1, s1),
      hasMonarchName(m2:s2).
  '
```

Here are the results you should expect to see:

```
"Ancestors of British monarchs who were also monarchs"
/- - - - - - - - _- - - - - - - -\
"Edward VII"     "Victoria"
"Edward VIII"    "Edward VII"
"Edward VIII"    "George V"
"Edward VIII"    "Victoria"
"Elizabeth II"   "Edward VII"
"Elizabeth II"   "George V"
"Elizabeth II"   "George VI"
"Elizabeth II"   "Victoria"
"George II"      "George I"
"George IV"      "George III"
"George V"       "Edward VII"
"George V"       "Victoria"
"George VI"      "Edward VII"
"George VI"      "George V"
"George VI"      "Victoria"
"William IV"     "George III"
\- - - - - - - - _- - - - - - - -/
```

Finally, to clean up when you are done, you can delete the workspace using lb delete royalty. You should then expect to see the following message: deleted workspace 'royalty'.

You have now completed a very quick run through the basic process of entering and executing a LogiQL program. The details of the language constructs and the situations in which you should use them are described in detail in the chapters to follow. Enjoy!

Basics

CONTENTS

THE GOAL OF THE first chapter is to quickly get you started writing LogiQL programs. Such a program tries to model aspects of a real-world **domain** inside a computer. The program is written in the LogiQL programming language, a member of the Datalog family of languages, and relevant data are stored in a LogiQL database.

By the end of this chapter, you will have built a working LogiQL program. Your program will include constraints, derivation rules, and fact assertions, and this chapter introduces you to all of these aspects. The program is used to record and derive information of interest about the British monarchy. In writing this program, you should obtain a feel for the structure of LogiQL programs, the basic syntax of the language, and how your program is processed. Later chapters will go into further detail on these topics and introduce you to many other interesting and powerful features of LogiQL.

UNIT 1.1: DATABASES, PREDICATES, AND FACTS

LogiQL is a programming language for accessing logic databases. The data stored in these databases consist of predicates—named collections of related facts. Each fact in a predicate relates the same fixed number of values. For example, the fact bought("Jim","car") relates two string values, "Jim" and "car" via the bought predicate. The number of values in each fact of a predicate is that predicate's *arity*. For example, bought has arity two.

Predicates can be thought of as tables, where each row in the table is a fact, and the number of columns in the table is the predicate's arity. Each column in the table plays a *role* in the predicate. For example, the first column in the bought table plays the purchaser role, and the second column plays the product role. For each role, all data values in that column have the same datatype.

There are many different kinds of predicates found in LogiQL programs. An *entity* predicate asserts the existence of a set of elements in the problem domain that the program is modeling. The assertion of an entity can be expressed using either of two other kinds of predicates. A *refmode* predicate associates a unique primitive identifying value, such as a string or a number, with each entity. For example, the vehicle identification number of a car serves to uniquely identify it. Alternatively, a *constructor* predicate asserts the existence of an entity as a function of a tuple of values.

Entity predicates often are accompanied by property predicates. A *property* predicate associates a typed value with each entity. For example, an integer age predicate might be associated with a Person entity predicate to hold data about people's ages.

The most general class of predicate is the *relation*, which can be used to hold information that associates a typed tuple of values. For example, a relation might assert that particular university courses meet in particular rooms at particular times. A useful kind of relation comprises the functional predicates. A *functional predicate* is a relation in which a subset of the predicate's roles serve as a *key* or index into the predicate's facts. Usually, values of the keys' roles are used to look up the values of the other roles in a predicate's facts. Functional predicates have their own syntax that makes apparent which values serve as the key.

File predicates are one means by which a program can perform input and output (I/O) operations. An input file predicate provides predicate access to the contents of an input file. That is, the facts in the predicate correspond to the contents of the file. Similarly, an output file predicate ensures that the contents of an output file reflect the facts in the predicate.

One final category of predicate contains the *system* or *built-in* predicates. These predicates are provided by the LogiQL runtime engine because they are generally useful, because the engine can compute them more efficiently than can the program, or because they involve LogiQL's primitive datatypes.

Exercise 1: For each of the following descriptions, select the type of predicate most appropriate for expressing it:

1.	the square root function	a.	constructor predicate
2.	data imported from a spreadsheet application	b.	entity predicate
3.	Social Security Numbers of U.S. citizens	c.	file predicate
4.	purchases of cars by individuals	d.	functional predicate
5.	the ages of famous generals when they died	e.	property predicate
6.	descriptions of sports teams in terms of their cities and leagues	f.	refmode predicate
7.	the states of Australia	g.	relation predicate
8.	the year U.S. presidents were elected	h.	system predicate

UNIT 1.2: DECLARING ENTITY TYPES AND REFMODES

Many of the examples in this book are concerned with the British monarchy. In writing programs about a domain like this, you need to make decisions about the data that your program deals with. A key early choice you should think about is which elements of the domain you express as **entities** and which you express as **values**. Roughly speaking, a value is represented in LogiQL using a literal of a built-in datatype, such as a character string (e.g., "Germany" or "Windsor"). An entity is a concrete object or abstract concept, which you describe with one or more values (e.g., the actual country Germany or the royal house Windsor). Also, most entities can change their state over time. For example, a country may change its average temperature over time, but the string "Germany" never changes, even if the country changes its name.

To get started, let's consider how to describe the key entities in the British monarchy domain, the monarchs themselves. In LogiQL, you use an **entity type** declaration to designate a set of similar entities. **Declarations** specify what kinds of entities and facts are of interest and how they are represented in the computer. For example, the Monarch entity type could be declared as follows:

```
Monarch(m) -> .          // Monarch is an entity type.
```

Syntactically, a LogiQL **logic program** comprises a set of clauses, and a declaration is an example of one kind of clause called a *constraint*. A declaration consists of two parts, separated by a right arrow. On the left is a predicate name, giving the name of the entity type, Monarch. A predicate denotes a named collection of facts. In this case, the facts indicate the monarchs we refer to in our program.

Predicate names can be followed by a list of arguments, and in this case, there is a single argument, denoted by the identifier m, which ranges over individual Monarch entities. The combination of a predicate name and its argument terms is called an **atom** (e.g., Monarch(m)).

In this example, there is nothing after the right arrow other than a period, which signifies the end of the declaration. That is, there is no information given about how monarch entities are represented in the computer. In fact, the LogiQL engine will handle the internal representation automatically, keeping track of each Monarch entity subsequently introduced. The text starting with the two slashes is a comment, which does not have any effect on how the program is evaluated. In the examples, comments are used to suggest how you can verbalize the commented program text.

The above approach for describing monarchs is fairly abstract, and you would normally want to provide some way for people to identify the monarchs rather than relying on artificial internal identifiers created by the system. In database modeling, you would define a *key* in similar situations. In LogiQL, refmodes can be used in circumstances such as this, and a refmode predicate is normally declared at the same time you declare an entity type. For example, here is how you could declare monarchs that are identified by their names:

```
Monarch(m), hasMonarchName(m:s) -> string(s).
/* Monarch is an entity type, and hasMonarchName is a
   refmode predicate for it. A monarch name is
   represented in the computer as a string. */
```

The text on the left of the arrow has several interesting aspects. First, it contains two atoms, separated by a comma (',') denoting the logical *and* operator. **Formulas** that connect parts by using *and* operators are called **conjunctions**. Second, the two arguments of hasMonarchName, m (the monarch entity) and s (the monarch name), are separated by a colon. Third, each atom declares a predicate, and the two predicates hasMonarchName and Monarch share an argument, m. Together, these syntactic elements indicate that a special kind of relationship exists between monarchs and their names, in particular that each monarch entity must have exactly one name and that no two monarchs have the same name. Relationships like these not only express actual properties of the domain, but they also give the compiler advice helping it to detect data typing violations and to improve performance.

In the `hasMonarchName` example, there is text to the right of the arrow, `string(s)`. The additional text tells us that s is represented in the computer as a string.

Finally, the text following the declaration illustrates a multi-line comment. Multi-line comments start with "/*", span one or more lines, and end with "*/". This kind of comment enables you not only to provide multiple lines of commentary but also to easily comment out a large block of program text.

Note that in this book, we conventionally use uppercase letters to begin the names of entity types and lowercase letters to start the names of non-entity predicates. Also, if the name of any identifier comprises multiple words, we capitalize the first letter of all subsequent words. This convention is called *camelCase*. Be aware that the LogiQL compiler is sensitive to case. That is, `Monarch(m)` is different from `monarch(m)`, and you will see error messages from the compiler if you inadvertently misuse the shift key in typing an identifier's name. These and other conventions are collected in Appendix F.

Tip: When constructing a LogiQL program, for each different kind of entity of interest in the domain, declare an entity type and a refmode.

Tip: Use comments to relate programming elements to the domain elements they represent.

Tip: LogiQL is case sensitive, so be sure to be consistent in your choice of uppercase or lowercase letters when you write a predicate name.

Exercise 2: Members of the British monarchy belong to houses, such as the current house of Windsor. Prepare a LogiQL declaration for the `House` entity type and a corresponding refmode predicate, `hasHouseName`, for the house's name. Do this now before looking at the answer at the end of the chapter.

UNIT 1.3: ENTERING FACTS

Now that we have introduced entity types and refmodes, we can populate a database with actual facts about the British monarchy. For example, we might want to add the fact that George VI was a monarch. We can express this in LogiQL, as follows:

```
+Monarch(m), +hasMonarchName(m:"George VI").
// Add the fact that there is some monarch m,
// where m has the monarch name "George VI"
// (i.e. there is a monarch named "George VI").
```

Note the plus sign ('+') before each predicate name in the above conjunction. This symbol is a **delta modifier** that indicates that the denoted fact should be added to the set of asserted facts. The set of asserted facts for a program is called its **extensional database**, often abbreviated as *EDB*.

There is a shorter way to express the existence of an entity that has a refmode. Instead of the above conjunction, we may simply assert the following:

```
+Monarch("George VI").
// There is a monarch with the monarch name "George VI".
```

The LogiQL compiler reads the above and recognizes that Monarch's argument is a literal string rather than a variable. It also knows that Monarch has a refmode that is represented by a string. It therefore realizes that a shortcut is being taken and substitutes the longer formula given above.

Either of the above approaches asserts facts to the EDB. Those facts are associated with the two predicates Monarch and hasMonarchName. The former is a unary predicate that is populated by a set of invisible (system-provided) values that denote, within the context of that predicate, the monarchs for whom a fact has been asserted. The latter is a binary predicate relating the specific monarch-name strings with the system-provided values. In both cases, the predicate is said to be an **EDB predicate**.

Tip: Enter facts into the EDB to express what you know about domain entities.

Exercise 3: Prepare LogiQL fact assertions for each of the houses in the British monarchy (Stuart, Hanover, Saxe-Coburg and Gotha, and Windsor).

UNIT 1.4: EXPRESSING DOMAIN RELATIONSHIPS WITH PREDICATES

We have seen in earlier units how to declare entities and to express simple facts about them. Using LogiQL, it is possible to describe more general relationships among the domain elements. For example, in the British monarchy domain, monarchs may be identified by their monarch name (e.g., "Elizabeth II"), but they were also given names at birth, one of which was chosen as the basis of their monarch name. As you can see from Table 1.1, a monarch may have many given names, and the same given name may be used by many monarchs. This association between monarchs and given names is an example of a *many-to-many relationship*. In order to express the facts represented in this table, it's best to first verbalize some of them in natural language. How would you verbalize the information indicated by the predicate fragment shown in Table 1.2?

Because we are familiar with the domain, we can see that the two column entries are related to each other. Assuming that we are not interested in the order of the given names, we might verbalize this connection as follows:

The monarch named "George I" has the given names "George" and "Louis."

Note, however, that the above sentence is really expressing two facts. In general, you should ensure that the facts you assert are atomic, in the sense that they cannot be expressed as conjunctions of smaller facts without losing information. This makes it easier to avoid redundancy and

TABLE 1.1 Given Names of British Monarchs

Monarch	Given Names
Anne	Anne
George I	George, Louis
George II	George, Augustus
George III	George, William, Frederick
George IV	George, Augustus, Frederick
William IV	William, Henry
Victoria	Alexandrina, Victoria
Edward VII	Albert, Edward
George V	George, Frederick, Ernest, Albert
Edward VIII	Edward, Albert, Christian, George, Andrew, Patrick, David
George VI	Albert, Frederick, Arthur, George
Elizabeth II	Elizabeth, Alexandra, Mary

TABLE 1.2 Given Names for George I

Monarch	Given Names
George I	George, Louis

make changes later on. Because the above statement is compound rather than atomic, it should be rephrased as the following two facts:

The monarch named "George I" has the given name "George."

The monarch named "George I" has the given name "Louis."

We may declare facts of this sort in the following way:

```
hasGivenName(m, gn) -> Monarch(m), string(gn).
// If m has the given name gn
// then m is a Monarch and gn is a string.
```

Note that when you declare a **many-to-many predicate** like hasGiven-Name, its arguments are enclosed in parentheses and separated by a comma, unlike refmode predicate declarations where the arguments are separated by a colon. Informally, we sometimes refer to predicates like hasGivenName as **property predicates**, to distinguish them from entity predicates and refmode predicates. Intuitively, property predicates are used to indicate properties of known entities.

Once we have declared the hasGivenName predicate, we can express the facts about George I's given name as follows:

```
+hasGivenName("George I", "George"),
    +hasGivenName("George I", "Louis").
// George I has given name George and
// George I has given name Louis.
```

Note that if you assert either of these facts about George I's given names, there is no need to explicitly assert the following fact, because it can be inferred from the given name fact and the type declaration for the has-GivenName predicate.

```
+Monarch("George I").
```

Tip: Express many-to-many relationships with many-to-many predicates.

Exercise 4: hasGivenName is an example of a many-to-many predicate. This means both that monarchs may have many given names and that a single given name may belong to many monarchs.

Exercise 4A: Have a look at the table of given names at the start of this unit, and determine which monarch has the most given names.

Exercise 4B: Have a look at the table of given names at the beginning of this unit, and determine which given name belongs to the most monarchs.

UNIT 1.5:. CONSTRAINING THE DATA

Unit 1.4 discussed how to declare predicates to model facts about the British monarchy. The entity types were modeled as the unary predicates Monarch(m) and House(h), and their instances were identified using the refmode predicates hasMonarchName(m:s) and hasHouseName(h:s). Relationships between monarchs and their given names were modeled using the many-to-many predicate hasGivenName(m,gn). However, there are restrictions on the above data that have not yet been expressed. For example, each monarch must have at least one given name. If we were entering monarchy data ourselves or importing monarchy data from an external source, we would want to make sure that the imported data does not violate this restriction. In this unit we discuss how to explicitly represent such restrictions using constraints.

The following code shows how to declare the constraint that each monarch has a given name:

```
Monarch(m) -> hasGivenName(m, _).
// If m is a monarch then m has some given name.
```

Syntactically, a constraint looks like a declaration. The left-hand side indicates the predicate being constrained, and the right-hand side indicates the properties that facts about the corresponding entity must obey.

In this constraint, the **anonymous variable**, depicted by an underscore (' _ '), is read as "something." We use the anonymous variable, because in this example, we do not care what the given name is, only that it must exist.

The above constraint is an example of a simple **mandatory role constraint**, since it declares that the role of having a given name is mandatory for each monarch. We use the term **role** to mean a part played in a relationship. For example, a binary predicate has two roles, one for each argument position.

With this constraint in place, if you try to add a monarch without any given names you will get a constraint violation error, for example,

```
+Monarch("George I").          // Error!
// George I is a monarch, but no given name is declared.
```

Note that, in this example, even though King George I was given a monarch name, there is no explicit given name asserted.

Tip: If you wish to place a specific restriction on how non-refmode predicates may be populated with data, then declare a constraint to express that restriction.

Tip: Refmode predicates are understood to be mandatory for their entity type, so there is no need to separately code a mandatory role constraint for them.

Tip: If you do not care what value a variable holds and it is only used once, use the anonymous variable ('_').

Exercise 5A: Assume that a predicate isOfHouse(m,h) is used to record membership of monarchs in royal houses. Prepare a LogiQL mandatory role constraint guaranteeing that each monarch is a member of some royal house.

Exercise 5B: Add a constraint to the isOfHouse(m,h) predicate to ensure that each monarch belongs to at most one house. *Hint 1:* If two facts both assert that a given monarch belonged to a house, the two houses must be the same. *Hint 2:* To indicate that the values of two variables are the same in LogiQL, the *equals* operator ('=') can be used. *Note:* In the next unit, we discuss an easier way to express this constraint.

UNIT 1.6: DECLARING FUNCTIONAL PREDICATES

To date, there have been 12 British monarchs belonging to four houses. Unit 1.2 discussed how to declare the Monarch and House entity types and the refmode predicates used to identify their instances. Unit 1.3 showed how to add instance data about these entities. Exercises 5A and 5B showed one way to relate the monarchs to their houses. In this unit we'll see an alternative way to declare a predicate that can express the house membership facts. The predicate is written using LogiQL's **functional notation**.

As you can see from the data in Table 1.3, although many monarchs may belong to the same house, each monarch may belong to only one house. This association between monarchs and their houses is said to be *functional*, because the house can be determined from the monarch.

TABLE 1.3   British Monarchy houseOf Predicate

Monarch	House
Anne	Stuart
George I	Hanover
George II	Hanover
George III	Hanover
George IV	Hanover
William IV	Hanover
Victoria	Hanover
Edward VII	Saxe-Coburg and Gotha
George V	Windsor
Edward VIII	Windsor
George VI	Windsor
Elizabeth II	Windsor

If a predicate is functional and not a refmode predicate, its arguments should be declared using LogiQL's functional notation, in which the arguments that functionally determine the final argument (the **keyspace**) are placed in square brackets, followed by the *equals* operator and the final argument. Those arguments not in the keyspace of a predicate are said to form its **valuespace**. In the case of the houseOf predicate, the first argument, m, a Monarch entity, is the only member of the keyspace, and the result, h, a House entity, comprises the valuespace.

For example, the house membership predicate may be declared as follows:

```
houseOf[m] = h -> Monarch(m), House(h).
// If the house of m is h
// then m is a monarch and h is a house.
// Each monarch m is of at most one house.
```

The square brackets in the above declaration indicate the functional nature of the relationship between a monarch and his/her house. The use of the word Of in the name of the predicate emphasizes the connection between a monarch and that monarch's house.

Similarly to how we asserted facts about entities in the previous unit, we can assert facts for functional predicates. For example, we can indicate that William IV belonged to the House of Hanover as follows:

```
+houseOf["William IV"] = "Hanover".
// William IV is of the house of Hanover.
```

Although the functional, square-bracket notation should be used in the program code for the functional predicate, if you prefer you may use the semantically equivalent parenthesis notation as an alternative when adding data, for example,

```
+houseOf("William IV", "Hanover").
// William IV is of the house of Hanover.
```

Contrast the functional approach described here to that of Exercises 5A and 5B, in which house membership is declared using a parenthesized argument list as follows:

```
isOfHouse(m, h) -> Monarch(m), House(h).
// If m is of house h
// then m is a monarch and h is a house.
```

Note that although isOfHouse and houseOf appear to serve the same purpose, there is a subtle difference. Implicit in the monarch domain is the constraint that no monarch can belong to two houses. To express this constraint with isOfHouse, we would have to explicitly add the following constraint:

```
isOfHouse(m, h1), isOfHouse(m, h2) -> h1 = h2.
// If m is of house h1 and m is of house h2 then h1
// and h2 are the same.
```

With the functional notation, however, this constraint is implicit. That is, because we used the functional notation, the predicate's functional nature is automatically declared.

Tip: Use functional notation to express functional associations.

Exercise 6: Consider another property of monarchs, their genders. Table 1.4 expresses this information for the British monarchs, using the gender codes "M" (for male) and "F" (for female).

Exercise 6A: Declare an entity predicate (Gender) and a refmode predicate for it (hasGenderCode) that represent the gender code by a string.

TABLE 1.4   Genders of British Monarchs

Monarch	Gender
Anne	Female (F)
George I	Male (M)
George II	M
George III	M
George IV	M
William IV	M
Victoria	F
Edward VII	M
George V	M
Edward VIII	M
George VI	M
Elizabeth II	F

Exercise 6B: Declare a constraint guaranteeing that each monarch is either male or female. *Hint 1:* Recall from Unit 1.5 how to use anonymous variables to indicate that a constraint holds for all monarchs. *Hint 2:* In situations like the above, where there are two possibilities, you can use the *inclusive-or* operator, denoted by a semicolon (';'). Such situations are called **disjunctions**.

Exercise 6C: Declare a functional predicate `genderOf[m]=g` reporting the gender g for monarch m.

Exercise 6D: Provide explicit facts asserting that Anne I is a monarch with monarch name "Anne I," that there is a gender code "F," and that Anne I has that gender.

Exercise 6E: Use the shortened form of fact entry described in Unit 1.3 to assert that George I is a male monarch.

UNIT 1.7: DECLARING DERIVATION RULES

In a typical application, some facts are simply asserted to be true, using the delta modifiers presented in Unit 1.3, while other facts are computed by applying a derivation rule to facts that are already known. For example, if we assert the length and breadth of a window, we can derive the window's area by multiplying its length by its breadth.

In the current unit, we discuss how to express some basic derivation rules in LogiQL. As a simple example, recall that earlier we represented gender data for monarchs using the functional, binary predicate genderOf[m]=g. Instead, we might have declared unary predicates to express the same information as follows:

```
isMale(m) -> Monarch(m).
// If m is male then m is a monarch.

isFemale(m) -> Monarch(m).
// If m is female then m is a monarch.
```

Choosing this approach has a subtle implication. Recall that genderOf is a functional predicate. This means that for each value of argument m, there can be at most one g such that genderOf[m]=g. In other words, no monarch can have two genders.

Because isMale and isFemale are separate, unary predicates, we have to explicitly eliminate the possibility of someone being both male and female at the same time. We can indicate this kind of mutual exclusion by using an **exclusion constraint**. Here is one way to express this:

```
isMale(m) -> !isFemale(m).
// If m is male then m is not female.
```

Note the use of the exclamation mark ('!') for the logical *not* operator. Note also that there is no need to add the following constraint, since it is implied by the above constraint:

```
isFemale(m) -> !isMale(m).
// If m is female then m is not male.
```

Because the same information is being expressed by genderOf and the new predicates, we should be able to derive isMale and isFemale facts from genderOf data. For example, if we assert the following fact:

```
+genderOf["Edward VII"] = "M".
```

we should be able to derive the fact

```
isMale("Edward VII").
```

To do this we can declare a simple rule that can perform this kind of derivation for all the male gender facts as follows:

```
isMale(m) <- genderOf[m] = "M".
// m is male if m has the gender with gender code "M".
```

Note that the direction of the arrow in rules is opposite to what we have seen before. An arrow directed to the right is used in constraints, whether its purpose is to declare a predicate or to limit the facts that can populate one. To visually distinguish rules, their arrows point leftward. Both arrows indicate a conditional dependency that may be expressed using a phrase containing the words "if" and "then." That is, "if" the formula that comes after the arrow is true, "then" the formula before the arrow will also be true.

The formula on the left-hand side of "<-" is called the **rule head**, and the formula on the right-hand side of "<-" is called the **rule body**. The rule specifies the following: for each value of m where genderOf[m] has the value "M", the following fact is derived: isMale(m).

From a programming point of view, the above rule searches for gen-derOf facts having the string "M" in the value role. For each such fact found, a corresponding isMale fact is derived. Predicates computed from rules, like isMale, which are explicity asserted are called **IDB predicates** to distinguish them from EDB predicates like genderOf.

A more complex derivation rule can be demonstrated using the parent-hood graph shown in Figure 1.1. If a monarch is a parent of another monarch, this is shown as a line connecting the parent to the child below it.

Because this graph is confined to the 12 British monarchs, at most one parent is shown for each monarch. We can assert the eight parenthood facts conveyed by this graph using the functional predicate parentOf, which may be declared as follows:

```
parentOf[m1] = m2 -> Monarch(m1), Monarch(m2).
// If the parent of m1 is m2, then m1 and m2 are
// monarchs.
```

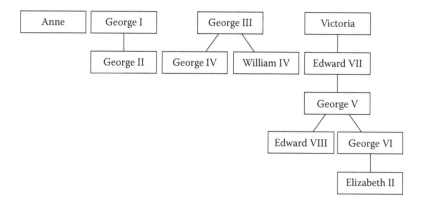

FIGURE 1.1   Parenthood relationship among British monarchs.

Note that in a wider domain where both of a person's parents may be recorded, parenthood would instead be modeled as an *m:n* predicate such as hasParent(p1,p2) or isParentOf(p1,p2).

Now consider a rule to derive the sibling relationship. Two different people are siblings of each other if they share a parent. For example, George IV and William IV are siblings. Because it is possible for a monarch to have more than one sibling monarch, we express the siblinghood relationship as an *m:n* predicate rather than as a functional predicate, using the following rule:

```
isSiblingOf(m1, m2) -> Monarch(m1), Monarch(m2).
isSiblingOf(m1, m2) <- parentOf[m1] = m3,
    parentOf[m2] = m3, m1 ! = m2.
// m1 is a sibling of m2 if there is some m3 such that
// m1 and m2 have m3 as a parent, and m1 is not the
// same as m2.
```

Note that in this rule, the rule body introduces a new variable, m3, that does not occur in the head of the rule. Occurrences of variables in the rule body that do not appear in the rule head are treated specially. In particular, variables that occur only in the body are assumed to have at least one existing instance. In this example, m3 is such a variable. It is as if the phrase "there is some m3 such that" is inserted before the conjunction of three conditions in the rule body.

In the above example, inequality is expressed using the *not-equals* operator ('!='). If we omitted the final check that uses it (m1 != m2), then each monarch would be his/her own sibling!

One other thing to observe about the isSiblingOf example is that it does not include atoms, such as Monarch(m1), limiting isSibling Of's arguments. In this case, the LogiQL compiler is able to infer the types of m1 and m2 because of their use in the parentOf atoms in the rule's body. The compiler is able to make such inferences for derivation rules in most cases. However, if you see an unexpected error message from the compiler, it is always okay to include an explicit mention of the type for the arguments of the predicate in the derivation rule.

One final example shows how a derivation rule may use an IDB predicate in its body. The following rule invokes two derived predicates to derive a third:

```
isBrotherOf(m1, m2) <- isSiblingOf(m1, m2), isMale(m1).
// m1 is a brother of m2 if m1 is a sibling of m2 and
// m1 is male.
```

Recall that for any given application domain, the set of facts that are simply asserted is known as the extensional database (EDB). In contrast, the set of facts that are inferred from other facts via derivation rules is called the intensional database (IDB). Whereas asserted facts must be explicitly managed (i.e., retracted, updated, etc.) by the programmer, derivation rules are automatically invoked whenever a workspace change affects predicates in the rules' bodies.

Tip: Use derivation rules to express computed domain relationships.

Exercise 7A: Compose LogiQL fact assertions to express the parenthood data illustrated in Figure 1.1.

Exercise 7B: Write a derivation rule to derive `isFemale` from `genderOf`.

Exercise 7C: Write a derivation rule to derive `fatherOf[m1]=m2`.

Exercise 7D: Write a derivation rule to derive `isSisterOf(m1,m2)`.

Exercise 7E: Write a derivation rule for a predicate named `hasNoMonarchSibling` to derive those monarchs who have no monarchs as siblings. Use the parenthood data you entered for **Exercise 6A** to determine which monarchs satisfy this rule.

Exercise 7F: For which pairs of monarchs is the predicate `isBrotherOf` true?

UNIT 1.8: QUERYING A WORKSPACE

Once you have written your program, loaded it into a workspace, and entered relevant facts, you will want to see the results. The `lb` command, described more completely in Appendix A, provides several ways for accessing this information. For example, the following `lb` command prints out the contents of the *predicateName* predicate:

```
lb print workspaceName predicateName
# Print out the current contents of the predicate
# named in the workspace named.
```

Sometimes, we may want to find out about information in the workspace that relates to more than one predicate. You can do this by issuing a **query**.

A query to lb makes use of the exec option, but instead of asking lb to execute the contents of a file, you can supply a LogiQL rule. In this case, the rule you provide indicates that a new predicate, occurring on the left-hand side of the arrow, should be populated with all facts satisfying the right-hand side of the rule.

Conventionally, the predicate on the left-hand side is an **anonymous predicate**, designated with an underscore (' _ '), optionally followed by other characters allowed in an identifier. Note that this use of underscore indicates an anonymous predicate, where earlier we used it to indicate an anonymous variable. Because predicates are followed by arguments, you can always tell which use of underscore is intended.

Here is how lb can be used to express a query:

```
lb exec workspaceName '_(args) <-
    predicateName(args, "someString").'
# Using the workspace named workspaceName, locate
# those facts in the predicate named predicateName
# whose final role is filled with the literal value
# "someString" and print out the corresponding
# values that fill the other roles.
```

Tip: Use the '.logic' filename extension to name your LogiQL program and fact files.

Tip: Use an anonymous predicate to construct workspace queries.

Exercise 8A: Create a new workspace named ws. *Hint:* Refer to Appendix A if needed.

Exercise 8B: Add the rules in the file base.logic to this workspace. The file contains the rules we have seen thus far in the chapter.

Exercise 8C: Add the facts in the baseData.logic to this workspace. The file contains the facts we have seen thus far in the chapter.

Exercise 8D: Use lb to print out the names of the houses in the British monarchy.

Exercise 8E: Execute a query on this workspace to list each female monarch and her royal house.

Exercise 8F: Execute a query on this workspace to list each monarch who has either "George" and/or "William," but not "Albert" as a given name.

Exercise 8G: Execute a query on this workspace to list each monarch who has at least three given names.

UNIT 1.9: CONSOLIDATION EXERCISE 1

Thus far, you have been introduced to LogiQL via a series of small examples—individual declarations, facts, constraints, rules, and queries—but applications are not only larger than this, their pieces are more interdependent. This unit asks you to integrate what you have learned so far to produce a comprehensive program for providing information about the British monarchy.

The exercise begins with what you have done already. The file base. logic contains the declarations, constraints, and rules that were introduced during the course of Chapter 1; the file baseData.logic contains the facts. In this exercise you will add to these files using a text editor and test them using lb, as described in Unit 1.8 and Appendix A. At this point, please create a new workspace called ws, load in base.logic, and execute baseData.logic.

During the course of this exercise, you will be asked to prepare new declarations, rules, constraints, and facts. You should place these into appropriately named files using a text editor and then use lb to include them in the workspace you have created. You should use lb addblock for new rules and constraints, and for new facts you should use lb exec. Depending on the specific task you are asked to perform, you may need to recreate your workspace and reload your code. You should be particularly careful to do this if your previous test resulted in an error. Another situation to be aware of is when you add a constraint to the program installed in your workspace that requires certain facts to pertain, but you have not yet asserted those facts.

PART 1: COUNTRY OF BIRTH

The first extension that we would like to consider is information about the countries in which the British monarchs were born: It turns out that two of them were actually born in Germany! The relevant data is shown in Table 1.5.

Q1a: Extend the program in base.logic by declaring the entity predicate Country(c), the refmode predicate hasCountryCode(c:cc), and the property predicate birthCountryOf[m]=c to enable facts to be stored about monarch birth countries. Also include a constraint to

TABLE 1.5   Birth Countries of British Monarchs

Monarch	Birth Country
Anne	Great Britain (GB)
George I	Germany (DE)
George II	DE
George III	GB
George IV	GB
William IV	GB
Victoria	GB
Edward VII	GB
George V	GB
Edward VIII	GB
George VI	GB
Elizabeth II	GB

ensure that each monarch was born in some country. The answer can be found in the file `Q1Answera.logic`.

Q1b: Use `1b` to add the information in the above table as new facts to `baseData.logic`. The answer can be found in file `Q1Answerb.logic`.

Q1c: You should now be able to write a query to determine which monarchs were not born in Britain. The answers can be found in file `Q1Answerc.logic`.

PART 2: BIRTH AND DEATH DATES

More interesting and more ambitious than incorporating monarchs' birth countries is keeping track of important dates for them, such as their birth and death dates. Table 1.6 (available in `birthDeathData.logic`) provides this data for the British monarchs.

Using the techniques that we have already seen, we could encode these dates as `strings`. This approach would prove difficult, however, once we started doing computations on the dates, such as determining how old the monarchs were when they died. Fortunately LogiQL has a way around this difficulty using the `datetime` primitive datatype.

Using `datetime`, we can declare a predicate expressing the information in the second column of the table as follows:

```
birthdateOf[m] = d -> Monarch(m), datetime(d).
// If m was born on d then m is a monarch
// and d is a datetime value.
```

TABLE 1.6   Birth and Death Dates of British Monarchs

Monarch	Born	Died
Anne	February 6, 1665	August 1, 1714
George I	May 28, 1660	June 11, 1727
George II	October 30, 1683	October 25, 1760
George III	June 4, 1738	January 29, 1820
George IV	August 12, 1762	June 26, 1830
William IV	August 1, 1765	June 20, 1837
Victoria	May 24, 1819	January 22, 1901
Edward VII	November 9, 1841	May 6, 1910
George V	June 3, 1865	January 20, 1936
Edward VIII	June 23, 1894	May 28, 1972
George VI	December 14, 1895	February 6, 1952
Elizabeth II	April 21, 1926	—

Here is a corresponding constraint that guarantees that every monarch has a birthday:

```
Monarch(m) -> birthdateOf[m] = _ .
```

Additionally, we can assert Anne's date of birth as follows:

```
+birthdateOf["Anne"] = #02/06/1665#.
// Anne was born on 6 February, 1665.
```

Note that literal `datetime` values are surrounded by hash symbols ('#'). In particular, in this example, dates are expressed using the format #mm/dd/yyyy#, where *mm* is the month number, *dd* is the day number, and *yyyy* is the year number. Be aware that the order of these three values is different from the order in which they were presented in the above table.

If you run the above code, you may see a warning message from the LogiQL compiler indicating that timezone information is missing from the `datetime` literals. If you wish to suppress the display of this warning, include the following line of code in your source file:

```
lang:compiler:disableWarning:DATETIME_
  TIMEZONE[] = true.
```

Q2a: Declare a predicate `deathdateOf` indicating the `datetime` of a monarch's death, and assert Anne's date of death. The answer can be found in the file `Q2Answera.logic`.

Q2b: Using the *less than or equal to comparison* operator ('<='), add a constraint to require that a monarch's death date must come no earlier than the monarch's birth date. (Note that from here on out, we will not be specifically reminding you to run 1b, but good coding practice says you should always test your results.) The answers can be found in the file Q2Answerb.logic.

Note that in **Q2**, you were not asked to provide a constraint guaranteeing that each monarch has a date of death. Can you see why doing so would be a problem?

Of course, it's because Queen Elizabeth II is very much alive!

Given this difference between the birthdateOf and deathdateOf predicates, we might like to know, for a given monarch, if that monarch is dead.

Q3: Write a derivation rule, isDeadMonarch, to determine whether a monarch is dead. The answer can be found in Q3Answer.logic.

If we can determine if a monarch is dead using isDeadMonarch, it is natural to ask the inverse question—is a monarch alive? We can do this as follows:

```
isLiveMonarch(m) <- Monarch(m), !isDeadMonarch(m).
// m is a live monarch if m is a monarch and m is not
// dead.
```

Would it be acceptable to shorten this rule as follows?

```
isLiveMonarch(m) <- !isDeadMonarch(m).
```

No! This shorter rule implies that anything that does not have a death date is a live monarch. For example, the house of Tudor would be a live monarch. So you need to be careful when using negation to properly constrain the objects under discussion to the entity types that you intend.

PART 3: AGE AT DEATH

As a more complex derivation example, we may compute the age at death for monarchs from their dates of birth and death. The derivation rule for death ages is complicated by the need to consider not just the year, but the month and day values. Think for a moment how you would go about expressing this rule.

As you probably determined, you can derive the death age by subtracting the birth date from the death date, extracting the number of years, and then compensating for monarchs who died during a year before having had their birthday that year.

Table 1.7 illustrates the possibilities.

Note that Anne was born in February and died in a later month (August). Her age at death can be easily computed by subtracting her birth year, 1665, from her death year, 1714, resulting in an age at death of 49. Edward VII, however, died in May, well before his birth month of November. If we tried to simply subtract 1841 from 1910, we would erroneously compute 69. Instead we have to recognize this situation and compensate by subtracting an additional year.

The problem is even worse than indicated so far. Consider the data for George II shown in Table 1.8.

Note that he was born and died in the same month, October. Hence, we have to look to see when in the month these two events took place. Of course, we could go further and look at the time of day or even the time zone in which the monarchs were born and died. But, for this exercise, we will be satisfied with the above degree of precision.

To perform the age-at-death computation, we have to be able to extract the month and day information from datetime values. Fortunately, LogiQL has built-in functions for working with datetime data. For example, the datetime:part function can be used to extract the day, month, and year parts of a date, and the datetime:offset function may be used to return the difference between two dates in a specified duration unit. By the way, the names of these two functions share a common prefix, "datetime:", suggesting that the two functions are members of a group of related functions. Note also that this use of the colon is distinct from its use declaring refmode predicates that we saw in Unit 1.2.

TABLE 1.7   Ages at Death of British Monarchs

Monarch	Born	Died	Age at Death
Anne	February 6, 1665	August 1, 1714	49
Edward VII	November 9, 1841	May 6, 1910	68

TABLE 1.8   Age at Death of George II

Monarch	Born	Died	Age at Death
George II	October 30, 1683	October 25, 1760	76

While the whole process of computing the age at death could be formulated as a single derivation rule, the solution is easier to construct and understand if we break the problem into smaller steps, using intermediate predicates to help with deriving later ones. Hence, we begin by extracting the month-of-the-year information from a datetime value. In particular, here is a derivation rule for determining the number (from 1 to 12) of the month in which a person was born:

```
birthMonthNrOf[m] = n <-
    birthdateOf[m] = d,
    datetime:part[d, "month"] = n.
// The birth month number of monarch m is n if m was
// born on the date d, and the month part of d is n.
```

The datetime:part function has two arguments. The first is a datetime value and the second is a string, in this case "month," specifying which part of the datetime value is to be returned.

Q4: Formulate derivation rules for deathMonthNrOf, birthDayNrOf, and deathDayNrOf. *Hint:* For the last two, you should use "day" as the second argument to datetime:part. The answers can be found in Q4Answer.logic.

Our next step is to determine whether a person's calendar day of death occurs before his/her calendar day of birth. This is true if one of the following conditions holds: (a) the death month number precedes the birth month number (like George IV); (b) the death and birth month numbers match, but the death day number precedes the birth day number (like George II).
    We can express these conditions using our newly defined rules as follows:

```
hasDeathdayBeforeBirthday(m) <-
    (deathMonthNrOf[m] < birthMonthNrOf[m]) ;
    ((deathMonthNrOf[m] = birthMonthNrOf[m]),
    (deathDayNrOf[m] < birthDayNrOf[m])).
// Monarch m has deathday before birthday if either
// m's deathmonth number is less than m's birthmonth
// number or the two numbers are equal and m's
// deathday number is less than m's birthday number.
```

Note the parentheses on the right-hand side of the above rule. They are used to ensure that the two requirements of the second alternative are both met.

We can now make use of the `datetime:offset` function to estimate the age at death. This function takes three arguments. The first two are `datetime` values, and the third is a `string` indicating the unit of duration we are interested in. In our case, this is `"years"`. The result is an estimate, however, because we may have to adjust the value if indicated by `hasDeathdayBeforeBirthday`.

```
approxDeathAgeOf[m] = n <-
    birthdateOf[m] = d1, deathdateOf[m] = d2,
    datetime:offset[d1, d2, "years"] = n.
// Monarch m's approximate death age is n if m was born
// on datetime d1 and died on datetime d2, and the
// offset between these two values was n years.
```

We can express the derivation rule that computes the age at death using `approxDeathAgeOf` and adjusting the computed value, if necessary, by `hasDeathdayBeforeBirthday`. Specifically, if a person's calendar day of death is before his/her calendar day of birth, then the death age is the approximate age minus one year. Otherwise, the death age is the approximate death age. This rule has the form *if p then q else r*, where *p*, *q*, and *r* are assertions. In LogiQL, such rules are expressed in the following way:

```
q <- p.      // q if p (i.e., if p then q)
r <- !p.     // r if not p (i.e., if not p then r).
```

Applying that rewrite for the current case, we finalize the computation by the following two rules:

```
deathAgeOf[p] = n - 1 <-
    approxDeathAgeOf[p] = n,
    hasDeathdayBeforeBirthday(p).
// person p has an age at death equal to n-1
// if p's approximate death age is equal to
// n, and p's deathday is before p's birthday

deathAgeOf[p] = n <-
    approxDeathAgeOf[p] = n,
    !hasDeathdayBeforeBirthday(p).
// person p has an age at death equal to n
// if p's approximate death age is equal to
```

```
// n, and it is not the case that p's deathday is
// before p's birthday.
```

Q5: The rules and constraints we have developed to this point in the exercise are available in file `birthDeath.logic`. The corresponding data for the British monarchs is available in the file `birthDeathData.logic`. Use `lb` to add the former and execute the latter. Then construct an `lb` query to display the age-at-death values. The answers can be seen in file `Q5Answer.logic`.

PART 4: REIGNS AND ANCESTRY

To complete this exercise, you are asked to answer the following questions on your own.

Q6a: Declare the predicates `reignStartOf[m] = d` and `reignEndOf[m] = d` to store facts about the start and end of monarch reigns.

Q6b: Add a constraint to ensure that each monarch started some reign.

Q6c: Add a constraint to ensure that no reign ended before it began.

Q6d: Add a single constraint to ensure both that no dead monarch reigned before he/she was born and that no monarch reigned after he/she died. The answers can be found in file `Q6Answer.logic`. The data from the table itself can be found in the file `reignData.logic`.

Q7a: Add a rule to derive the predicate `daughterOf[m1]=m2` to indicate that monarch m2 is a daughter of monarch m1. Note that in a wider domain where a monarch might have multiple daughters who are monarchs, a functional predicate would not work.

Q7b: Add a rule to derive the predicate `isGrandParentOf(m1,m2)` to indicate that monarch m1 is a grandparent of monarch m2.

Q7c: Enter a query to print out the `isGrandParentOf` predicate. The answers can be found in file `Q7Answer.logic`.

Q8: Write a query to list each monarch who is the parent of at least two monarchs. The answer can be found in file `Q8Answer.logic`.

Q9: Add a rule to derive the predicate `isFirst(m)` indicating who is the first monarch. After installing, query this predicate to display its result. *Hint:* LogiQL does not allow rule bodies to include negated conjunctions if one of the conjuncts is the anonymous variable. So first declare the rule `isLater(m)` to derive the monarchs who reigned later (i.e., after the first monarch), then use that rule to help you derive `isFirst(m)`. The answer can be found in file `Q9Answer.logic`.

ANSWERS TO EXERCISES

Answers to Exercise 1:

1. h—provided by the built-in math library

2. c—file predicates import data from external files

3. f—how person entities are uniquely referred to

4. e—a relation between car entities and person entities

5. d—each general had exactly one age at death; hence, a functional predicate is appropriate

6. a—"the Detroit National Football league team" is an implicit way of describing a team entity

7. b—one entity for each state

8. g—a property of each president; note that some presidents were elected more than once

Answer to Exercise 2:

```
House(h), hasHouseName(h:s) -> string(s).
/* House is an entity type, and hasHouseName is a
   refmode predicate for it. House names are
   represented in the computer as strings. */
```

Answer to Exercise 3:

```
+House("Stuart").  // "Stuart" is the name of a house
+House("Hanover").  // "Hanover" is the name of a
    house
+House("Saxe-Coburg and Gotha").
// "Saxe-Coburg and Gotha" is the name of a house
+House("Windsor").  // "Windsor" is the name of a
    house.
```

Answer to Exercise 4A:

Edward VIII had seven given names!

Answer to Exercise 4B:

`"George"` (the given name George is shared by seven monarchs).

Answer to Exercise 5A:

```
Monarch(m) -> isOfHouse(m, _).
// If m is a monarch then m is of some house.
```

Answer to Exercise 5B:

```
isOfHouse(m, h1), isOfHouse(m, h2) -> h1 = h2.
// Each monarch belongs to at most one house.
```

Answer to Exercise 6A:

```
Gender(g), hasGenderCode(g:gc) -> string(gc).
// g is a gender, identified by its gender code.
// Gender codes are stored as strings.
```

Answer to Exercise 6B:

```
hasGenderCode(_:gc) -> gc = "M" ; gc = "F".
// If some gender has a gender code
// then that code is either "M" or "F".
```

This kind of constraint is called a **value constraint** because it constrains the possible values used for the specified role. Here the anonymous variable is used to indicate any arbitrary gender. Note the use of the semicolon (';') for the *inclusive-or* operator.

Answer to Exercise 6C:

```
genderOf[m] = g -> Monarch(m), Gender(g).
// If m has gender g, then m is a monarch and g is a
// gender.
// Each monarch has at most one gender.
```

Answer to Exercise 6D:

```
+Monarch(m), +hasMonarchName(m:"Anne"), +Gender(g),
+hasGenderCode(g:"F"), +genderOf[m] = g.
// "Anne" is a monarchName for Monarch m.
// "F" is a genderCode for a Gender g.
// Monarch m has gender g.
```

Answer to Exercise 6E:

```
+genderOf ["George I"] = "M".
// George I has gender with genderCode "M".
```

Answer to Exercise 7A:

```
+parentOf ["George II"] = "George I".
+parentOf ["George IV"] = "George III".
+parentOf ["William IV"] = "George III".
+parentOf ["Edward VII"] = "Victoria".
+parentOf ["George V"] = "Edward VII".
+parentOf ["Edward VIII"] = "George V".
+parentOf ["George VI"] = "George V".
+parentOf ["Elizabeth II"] = "George VI".
```

Answer to Exercise 7B:

```
isFemale (m) <- genderOf [m] = "F".
// m is female if m has the gender with gender code
// "F".
```

Answer to Exercise 7C:

```
fatherOf [m1] = m2 -> Monarch (m1), Monarch (m2).
fatherOf [m1] = m2 <- parentOf [m1] = m2, isMale (m2).
// The father of m1 is m2 if the parent of m1 is m2
// and m2 is male.
```

Answer to Exercise 7D:

```
isSisterOf (m1, m2) -> Monarch (m1), Monarch (m2).
isSisterOf (m1, m2) <- isSiblingOf (m1, m2),
    isFemale (m1).
// m1 is a sister of m2 if m1 is a sibling of m2,
// and m1 is female.
```

Answer to Exercise 7E:

```
hasNoMonarchSibling (m) -> Monarch (m).
hasNoMonarchSibling (m) <- Monarch (m),
    !isSiblingOf (m, _).
// m has no monarch as a sibling if
```

```
// m is a monarch and it is not the case that
// m is the sibling of another monarch.
```

Why do not we also have to say that !isSiblingOf(_, m)?
The following monarchs have no monarchs as siblings:

Elizabeth II

George V

Edward VII

Victoria

George III

George II

George I

Why isn't Anne on this list? How would you fix the problem?

Answer to Exercise 7F:

```
"George IV", "William IV"
"Edward VIII", "George VI"
"William IV", "George IV"
"George VI", "Edward VIII"
```

Answer to Exercise 8A:

```
lb create ws
#  Create a new workspace with name "ws".
```

Answer to Exercise 8B:

```
lb addblock -f base.logic ws
#  Add the program in file base.logic to the
#  workspace ws.
```

Answer to Exercise 8C:

```
lb exec -f baseData.logic ws
#  Add facts from the file baseData.logic to the
#  workspace ws.
```

Answer to Exercise 8D:

```
lb print ws House
# Print out the current contents of the predicate
# named House in the workspace ws.
```

Results:

```
Windsor
Saxe-Coburg and Gotha
Hanover
Stuart
```

Answer to Exercise 8E:

```
lb exec ws '_(m, h) <- isFemale(m), houseOf[m] = h.'
# Retrieve names and houses of all female monarchs
# from workspace ws.
```

Results:

```
Elizabeth II, Windsor
Victoria, Hanover
Anne, Stuart
```

Answer to Exercise 8F:

```
lb exec ws '
_(m) <-
    (hasGivenName(m, "George") ; hasGivenName(m,
    "William")),
    !hasGivenName(m, "Albert").
'
# Retrieve names of monarchs with given names "George"
# or "William" but not "Albert" from workspace ws.
```

Note that the parentheses are required to group the two atoms in the disjunction.

Results:

```
William IV
George IV
```

```
George III
George II
George I
```

Answer to Exercise 8G:

```
lb exec ws '
_(m) <-
    hasGivenName(m, n1),
    hasGivenName(m, n2),
    hasGivenName(m, n3),
    n1 ! = n2, n1 ! = n3, n2 ! = n3.
'

    #  Using the workspace ws, retrieve the names of
    #  monarchs with at least three given names.
```

Results:

```
Elizabeth II
George VI
Edward VIII
George V
George IV
George III
```

What would happen if the tests on the last line of the query were left off?

Intermediate Aspects

CONTENTS

THIS CHAPTER BUILDS ON the basic concepts and syntax of LogiQL considered in the previous chapter and introduces some more advanced features of the language. Although the British monarchy remains the primary domain from which examples and exercises are constructed, we begin to introduce other, more business-oriented domains to demonstrate the breadth of applicability of LogiQL.

The first unit considers inverse-functional predicates, which are binary predicates where the first argument is a function of the second argument. The second unit discusses predicates that have more than two arguments and also surveys the various kinds of numeric datatypes available in LogiQL. The next unit covers some constraints that apply to two or more predicate arguments. We then learn how to use subtyping, where a type is contained in a larger type (e.g., Woman is a subtype of Person), as well as some simple subset constraints. The following unit then examines recursion, one of LogiQL's most powerful features, and discusses constraints that often apply to predicates used in recursive rules. The final unit introduces two of LogiQL's aggregation functions (count and total), useful for computing properties of a set of facts in the database. The consolidation exercise gives you an opportunity to test your mastery of the new concepts and syntax considered in the chapter.

UNIT 2.1: INVERSE-FUNCTIONAL PREDICATES

Table 2.1 repeats some details about British monarchs discussed in Chapter 1. The Monarch, House, and Gender entity types were declared using the unary predicates Monarch(m), House(h), and Gender(g), and the refmode predicates hasMonarchName(m:s), hasHouseName(m:s), and hasGenderCode(g:gc) were declared to provide a natural way to refer to their instances. The facts about their given names, royal houses, and genders

TABLE 2.1   Facts about British Monarchs

Monarch	Given Names	House	Gender
Anne	Anne	Stuart	F
George I	George, Louis	Hanover	M
George II	George, Augustus	Hanover	M
George III	George, William, Frederick	Hanover	M
George IV	George, Augustus, Frederick	Hanover	M
William IV	William, Henry	Hanover	M
Victoria	Alexandrina, Victoria	Hanover	F
Edward VII	Albert, Edward	Saxe-Coburg and Gotha	M
George V	George, Frederick, Ernest, Albert	Windsor	M
Edward VIII	Edward, Albert, Christian, George, Andrew, Patrick, David	Windsor	M
George VI	Albert, Frederick, Arthur, George	Windsor	M
Elizabeth II	Elizabeth, Alexandra, Mary	Windsor	F

Note: M, male; F, female.

TABLE 2.2   Gender Codes and Names

Gender	
Code	**Name**
F	Female
M	Male

were captured using the many-to-many predicate `hasGivenName(m,gn)`, and the many-to-one predicates `houseOf[m]=h` and `genderOf[m]=g`.

This unit concerns inverse-functional predicates. As an example, let's revisit our modeling of genders via gender *codes*. Suppose now that we wish to also store gender *names*, as indicated in Table 2.2, so that these can be displayed to users unfamiliar with the codes. This is a very simple example of a two-column lookup table. Lookup tables are often used to store lists of codes and/or names for countries, states, currencies, and so on.

Given our decision to standardly refer to genders by their codes, we may verbalize the association between entries in the two columns:

The gender with gender code "F" has the gender name "Female."

The gender with gender code "M" has the gender name "Male."

To store these facts, we declare the `genderNameOf` predicate. Because each gender has at most one name (i.e., gender name is a function of gender), we use LogiQL's functional notation.

```
genderNameOf[g] = gn -> Gender(g), string(gn).
// If g has gender name gn
// then g is a gender and gn is a string.
// Each gender has at most one gender name.
```

Note also that each gender name relates to at most one gender (i.e., gender is a function of gender name). So the genderNameOf predicate is also functional in the inverse direction (from right argument to left argument). Hence, the genderNameOf predicate is said to be an **inverse-functional predicate**. As there is no special notation for this in LogiQL, we declare this inverse-functional constraint as follows:

```
genderNameOf[g1] = gn, genderNameOf[g2] = gn ->
    g1 = g2.
// For each gender name, at most one gender has that
// gender name.
```

The binary predicate genderNameOf has two roles, one played by gender instances (e.g., g1) and one by gender name instances (gn). The functional constraint that each *gender* occurs at most once in the population of the genderNameOf predicate is said to be a **uniqueness constraint** on the gender role. In this case, it is a *simple* uniqueness constraint because only one role is involved. Similarly, the inverse-functional constraint that each *gender name* occurs at most once in the population of the genderNameOf predicate is a simple uniqueness constraint on the gender name role. Because the genderNameOf predicate is both functional and inverse-functional, it is said to be a **one-to-one predicate**.

An additional constraint is that the genderNameOf predicate is mandatory for Gender, that is,

```
Gender(g) -> genderNameOf[g] = _.
// If g is a gender then it has some gender name.
```

A 1:1 relationship that is mandatory for all instances of its first argument is said to be *injective*. Hence, the genderNameOf predicate is injective. Refmode predicates are always understood to be injective in this sense, so the colon used to separate arguments of refmode predicates constrains them to be mandatory and 1:1. This colon syntax is used only for refmode predicates, so if a non-refmode predicate is injective, this must be declared explicitly, as shown above for genderNameOf.

Just as a 1:1 predicate can have an inverse, the inverse of a **many-to-one predicate** is said to be a **one-to-many predicate** (or *1:n predicate*). For example, isMotherOf(p1,p2) is a 1:*n* predicate because a single person may be the mother of many persons, even though each person has at most one mother. Both 1:*n* and 1:1 predicates are inverse-functional predicates, and a 1:1 predicate is also functional. If you declare a 1:*n* predicate, you need to declare its uniqueness constraint separately. For example,

```
isMotherOf(p1, p2) -> Person(p1), Person(p2).
// If p1 is mother of p2, then p1 and p2 are persons.

isMotherOf(p1, p), isMotherOf(p2, p) -> p1 = p2.
// Each person has at most one mother.
```

Note that if you have a 1:*n* predicate, in most cases, it's better to replace it by its inverse, which you can declare as an *n*:1 predicate simply by using the functional notation. For example,

```
motherOf[p1] = p2 -> Person(p1), Person(p2).
// If p1 has mother p2, then p1 and p2 are persons.
// Each person has at most one mother.
```

Table 2.3 summarizes the four kinds of binary predicates we have discussed. Each type of predicate relates instances of the first argument role with instances of the second argument role. The rows in the Table 2.3 indicate how many instances of the first argument may be related to a number of instances of the second type. For example, an *n:1* predicate may contain multiple (*n*) facts with different instances of the first argument pertaining to a single (*1*) instance of the second argument. For the motherOf predicate, multiple children (p1) may have the same mother (p2).

TABLE 2.3　Types of Predicate Cardinalities

Predicate Type	Example	Functional	Inverse-Functional Constraint Needed
m:n	hasGivenName(p,gn)	No	No
n:1	motherOf[p1] = p2	Yes	No
1:1	genderNameOf[g] = gn	Yes	Yes
1:*n*	isMotherOf(p1,p2)	No	Yes

Tip: If you have a 1:*n* predicate, consider replacing it by, or deriving it from, its inverse *n*:1 predicate.

Exercise 1A: Declare the predicate `isFatherOf` over person pairs and constrain it to be inverse-functional.

Exercise 1B: Declare the functional predicate `fatherOf`, as well as a rule to derive `isFatherOf` from it.

UNIT 2.2: *N-ARY PREDICATES*

Consider Table 2.4 as discussed in Chapter 1. Earlier, we modeled the relationship between monarchs and their given names with the *m:n* predicate `hasGivenName(m,gn)`. This is fine, so long as we are not interested in recording the *order* of a monarch's given names. Now suppose we are interested in this order (e.g., we want to know that George I had "George" as his first given name and "Louis" as his second given name). How would you express this?

One way to model this requirement is to use multiple given name predicates, one for each position (Table 2.4), for example,

```
firstGivenNameOf [m]  = gn
secondGivenNameOf [m] = gn
thirdGivenNameOf [m]  = gn
...
```

TABLE 2.4   Given Names for British Monarchs

Monarch	Given Names
Anne	Anne
George I	George, Louis
George II	George, Augustus
George III	George, William, Frederick
George IV	George, Augustus, Frederick
William IV	William, Henry
Victoria	Alexandrina, Victoria
Edward VII	Albert, Edward
George V	George, Frederick, Ernest, Albert
Edward VIII	Edward, Albert, Christian, George, Andrew, Patrick, David
George VI	Albert, Frederick, Arthur, George
Elizabeth II	Elizabeth, Alexandra, Mary

This is reasonable if a monarch may have just a few given names. However, Edward VIII (the only British monarch so far to abdicate) had seven given names. Because of this large number and the problem of setting a limit on how many given names a monarch may be assigned, it's far better to use a predicate that includes a position to indicate the place of the given name. For example, we could verbalize the facts about George I's given names informally; thus,

George I, in position 1, has the given name "George."

George I, in position 2, has the given name "Louis."

To indicate the position, we use the LogiQL integer (abbreviated as "int") primitive datatype. It is specified in the form int(p), where p is the name of the variable holding the position. Hence, we can now declare the relevant predicate as shown in the following code:

```
inPositionHasGivenName[m, n] = gn -> Monarch(m),
   int(n), string(gn).
/* If m in position n has given name gn, then m is a
   monarch, n is an 8 bit unsigned integer, and gn is
   a string. For each monarch and position, there is
   at most one given name. */
```

The inPositionHasGivenName predicate has three arguments (two within the square brackets and one to the right of the equals sign), so it is an example of a *ternary predicate*. In general, if a predicate has *n* arguments, and *n* > 2, we call it an *n-ary predicate*.

Note the use of the functional notation, with the variables *m* and *n* in square brackets, to express the *compound* uniqueness constraint that for a given monarch and position in the monarch's given name list there is at most one given name. That is, the combination of monarch and position functionally determines the given name. Analogous to the notion of primary key in a relational database table, the arguments in square brackets comprise the keyspace of the functional predicate (or *compound key*). For a predicate that is not functional (e.g., a many-to-many predicate), the collection of all of its arguments also comprise a keyspace, since each instance in the population of the predicate is unique. Such predicates are called *all-key*.

To ensure that given name positions start at 1 rather than 0, we can declare the following value constraint on the position argument. Notice the use of anonymous variables for the other arguments.

```
inPositionHasGivenName[_, n] = _ -> n > 0.
// If something in position n has some given name
// then n is greater than 0.
```

Note that in this example, there were two uses of anonymous variables—one for monarchs and one for given names. Be aware that even though the same symbol (' _ ') was used for both, these represent different variables.

If you look at the table of monarch names, you should see that there is another uniqueness constraint on this ternary predicate. For each monarch, each given name occurs in at most one position. For example, no monarch would be given the names "George, George." This compound uniqueness constraint needs to be declared separately, because the functional syntax can be used for only one choice of keyspace. The unit exercise challenges you to code this constraint in LogiQL.

Just as a binary predicate may be *m:n* and hence all-key, it is possible that an *n*-ary predicate is all-key. Here is an example of a many-to-many-to-many, ternary predicate taken from a business domain—keeping track of retail products. In the example, we declare the following predicate to record what products are available at what stores in what seasons:

```
productAvailability(p, st, se) -> Product(p),
    Store(st), Season(se).
/* If p is available for st during se, then p is a
   product, st is a store and s is a season. */
```

The keyspace of an *n*-ary functional predicate typically has *n*–1 arguments, with the final argument being a function of the previous arguments. As an example of a functional predicate to record the number of units sold for a given product in a given store in a given season, we might declare the following predicate (assuming Product, Store, and Season are also declared):

```
productStoreSeasonUnitsSold[p, st, se] = nrSold ->
    Product(p), Store(st), Season(se), int(nrSold).
// If p is sold in st during se in amount nrSold, then
// p is a product, st is a store, se is a season, and
// nrSold is an int.
```

Typically, any asserted predicate should be *atomic* (i.e., not equivalent to a conjunction of smaller predicates). For this reason, it is rare to use predicates with more than five arguments. By restricting asserted predicates to be atomic, we capture the information as simply as possible, avoid the need to deal with missing or inapplicable values, and facilitate subsequent changes to the model.

Tip: Make sure that your asserted predicates are all atomic.

Exercise 2A: Modify the value constraint given above for positions in given name lists (`inPositionHasGivenName`) to ensure that each position number is in the range 1..9 (i.e., at least 1 and at most 9).

Exercise 2B: Code the constraint that for each monarch, each given name occurs in at most one position.

Exercise 2C: Write a derivation rule, `sharesGivenName(m1, m2)`, that derives pairs of `Monarchs` that share a given name.

Exercise 2D: Your solution to **Exercise 2C** likely listed both the pair (`"George I"`, `"George II"`) and the pair (`"George II"`, `"George I"`). Write another rule, `sharesGivenName2(m1,m2)`, that derives pairs of `Monarchs` that share a given name without including this form of redundancy. *Hint:* Only include a `Monarch` pair if the monarch name of the first monarch is alphabetically less than the monarch name of the second.

UNIT 2.3: INCLUSIVE-OR AND EXTERNAL UNIQUENESS CONSTRAINTS

A previous unit considered the genders of the British monarchs as presented in Table 2.5, where the gender codes "M" and "F" denote male and female genders. The following code shows the way we model this information in LogiQL, using a binary, functional `genderOf` predicate. We include a value constraint to limit the possible gender codes and a simple mandatory constraint to ensure that each monarch has a gender:

```
Monarch(m) , hasMonarchName(m:n) -> string(n) .
Gender(g) , hasGenderCode(g:gc) -> string(gc) .
genderOf[m] = g -> Monarch(m) , Gender(g) .
genderOf[_] = g -> g = "M" ; g = "F" .
Monarch(m) -> genderOf[m] = _ .
```

TABLE 2.5   Genders of British Monarchs

Monarch	Gender
Anne	F
George I	M
George II	M
George III	M
George IV	M
William IV	M
Victoria	F
Edward VII	M
George V	M
Edward VIII	M
George VI	M
Elizabeth II	F

Note: M, male; F, female.

As an alternative way to model the information, we briefly considered using the unary isMale and isFemale predicates:

```
Monarch(m), hasMonarchName(m:n) -> string(n).
isMale(m) -> Monarch(m).
isFemale(m) -> Monarch(m).
isMale(m) -> !isFemale(m).
// No monarch is both male and female.
```

The exclusion constraint on the fourth line captures the functional nature of the genderOf predicate (each monarch has at most one gender), but to ensure that each monarch has a gender, we need to add the following **inclusive-or constraint** that each monarch is either male or female:

```
Monarch(m) -> isMale(m) ; isFemale(m).
// Each monarch is either male or female.
```

In this example, the isMale and isFemale disjuncts are also mutually exclusive. The combination of the inclusive-or and exclusion constraints is known as an *exclusive-or* constraint. Unlike Latin, LogiQL does not have two varieties of the *or* operator, one inclusive and one exclusive. So you need to code an exclusive-or constraint as two constraints, one for the inclusive-or aspect and one for the exclusive aspect, as done above.

In the second approach just described, the isMale and isFemale predicates were asserted, not derived. In this case, any constraints on the predicates need to be explicitly declared. However, suppose that in addition to using the gender0f predicate to assert the gender facts, we also derive the isMale and isFemale predicates, using the following derivation rules:

```
isMale(m)   <- gender0f[m] = "M".
isFemale(m) <- gender0f[m] = "F".
```

In this case, there is no need to assert the inclusive-or and exclusion constraints on the isMale and isFemale predicates, because these constraints are implied by the constraints declared for the gender0f predicate.

Inclusive-or constraints may apply to two or more roles of predicates of any arity, so long as the roles are played by instances of compatible types. For example, suppose that in our business domain, each product p included in a sale must satisfy at least one of the following requirements: p is a discontinued product; p is a loss leader; or p was nominated by a marketing analyst. Assuming SaleProduct and MarketingAnalyst are already declared, we could code this situation as follows:

```
isDiscontinued(p) -> SaleProduct(p).
isLossLeader(p)  -> SaleProduct(p).
wasNominatedBy[p] = m -> SaleProduct(p),
    MarketingAnalyst(m).
SaleProduct(p) ->
    isDiscontinued(p) ; isLossLeader(p) ;
    wasNominatedBy[p] = _.
// Each sale product is discontinued or is a loss
// leader or was nominated by a marketing analyst.
```

For simplicity, the only products of interest in this example are sales products.

Now consider Table 2.6, an extract from a table used by a particular business to record the major cities where the company has offices. In this business domain, cities are primarily identified by city numbers, since these provide a simple, rigid identifier that remains valid even if the city changes its name (e.g., consider Constantinople and St. Petersburg). States are identified using state codes (e.g., "ME" for Maine and "OR" for Oregon). Since many users of the information system might not know the city numbers, the combination of city name and state provides an alternative reference scheme to enable them to easily refer to the cities.

TABLE 2.6   Locations of Company Offices

City Number	City Name	State
1	Portland	Maine
2	Portland	Oregon
3	Eugene	Oregon
...	...	...

The basic structure (*schema*) and data for this example may be coded as shown below, using techniques already discussed:

```
// Schema
City(c), hasCityNr(c:n) -> int(n).
State(s), hasStateCode(s:sc) -> string(sc).
cityNameOf[c] = cn -> City(c), string(cn).
stateOf[c] = s -> City(c), State(s).
City(c) -> cityNameOf[c] = _.
City(c) -> stateOf[c] = _.

// Data
+cityNameOf[1] = "Portland", +stateOf[1] = "ME".
+cityNameOf[2] = "Portland", +stateOf[2] = "OR".
+cityNameOf[3] = "Eugene", +stateOf[3] = "OR".
```

What is missing from this code is a constraint to ensure that each combination of city name and state refers to only one city. This constraint may be coded as follows:

```
cityNameOf[c1] = cn, stateOf[c1] = s,
    cityNameOf[c2] = cn, stateOf[c2] = s ->
    c1 = c2.
// Each combination of city name and state refers to
// at most one city.
```

This is called an *external* uniqueness constraint, since the uniqueness applies to roles from multiple predicates rather than being internal to a single predicate. As a check that the constraint is enforced, if you try to execute the following fact assertions on the above schema, you will get a runtime error indicating that a constraint has been violated:

```
+cityNameOf[4] = "Seattle", +state[4] = "WA". // Error!
+cityNameOf[5] = "Seattle", +state[5] = "WA". // Error!
```

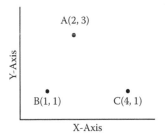

FIGURE 2.1   Company location grid.

Constraint violation errors are detected only after the compiler has checked that there are no syntax errors, such as writing "stateOf(c1) = s" in the program code or omitting the "+" in a data assertion.

Tip: Add relevant constraints to predicates to prevent them being populated with data that is inconsistent with the application domain.

Exercise 3A: A given company identifies its employees by employee numbers but also requires each employee to have either an identifying Social Security Number or an identifying passport number. Express this situation in LogiQL, using strings to store the identifying numbers.

Exercise 3B: The neighborhoods in which a company has stores are identified by (single-character) names. Each store can also be referenced by the combination of its *x* and *y* map coordinates, as shown in Figure 2.1. Express this situation in LogiQL using integers for the coordinates, and issue a query to list the label and coordinates of each store.

UNIT 2.4: SUBTYPING AND SUBSETTING

Types are an important concept in most programming languages, and LogiQL is no exception. The built-in (primitive) datatypes include boolean, numbers of various sorts (int, float, and decimal), string, and datetime. In addition, as described in Chapter 1, programmers can declare their own entity types. This unit discusses an additional, powerful feature of types called *subtyping*. Subtyping is a way of indicating that a set of the entities of one type, the **subtype**, must be a subset of the entities of another type, the **supertype**. To illustrate the possibilities, we consider King and Queen as subtypes of Monarch in the British royalty as presented in Table 2.7.

TABLE 2.7   Another Representation of
Monarch Genders

Monarch	King	Queen
Anne		✓
George I	✓	
George II	✓	
George III	✓	
George IV	✓	
William IV	✓	
Victoria		✓
Edward VII	✓	
George V	✓	
Edward VIII	✓	
George VI	✓	
Elizabeth II		✓

Subtypes

Table 2.7 lists the British monarchs, indicating the kings and queens by
a check mark (✓) in the relevant column. For now, let us assume that the
genderOf predicate discussed in earlier units is not declared. If we wish
to think of kings and queens as entities, we may declare the entity types
King and Queen as follows:

```
Monarch(m), hasMonarchName(m:n) -> string(n).
King(m) -> Monarch(m).
// If m is a king, then m is a monarch.
lang:isEntity[`King] = true.
// King is an entity type.
Queen(m) -> Monarch(m).
// If m is a queen, then m is a monarch.
lang:isEntity[`Queen] = true.
// Queen is an entity type.
```

Here, the constraints indicate that each king and queen is also a monarch,
making King and Queen subtypes of Monarch. Equivalently, Monarch
is a supertype of King and Queen. The **metapredicate** lang:isEntity
is used to declare that the predicate in parentheses after the grave accent
character ('`') is an entity predicate.

The King and Queen subtypes inherit the properties of their
supertype Monarch, including its refmode identification scheme.

For example, we may assert that Anne is a queen and that George I is a king as follows:

```
+Queen("Anne"), +King("George I").
```

Because of the declarations for King and Queen, the compiler is able to infer that Anne and George I are also monarchs—that is, Monarch("Anne") and Monarch("George I"). There is no need to include +Monarch("Anne") and +Monarch("George I") assertions. Here, King and Queen are said to be *asserted subtypes* because we simply assert their instances rather than derive them from other facts.

To complete the example, we should add the following constraints to ensure that King and Queen form a partition (disjoint union) of Monarch:

```
Monarch(m) -> King(m) ; Queen(m).
// Each monarch is a king or a queen.
King(m) -> !Queen(m).
// No king is a queen.
```

Because they have not been declared supertypes of other types, King and Queen are said to be *leaf* subtypes. Leaf predicates without lang:isEntity declarations are treated as simple property predicates rather than entity predicates. In such situations, if you really do not want to think of them as entity predicates, it's better to name the predicates using verb phrases (e.g., isaKing, isaQueen) rather than noun phrases.

Now suppose that instead of the above approach of asserting subtype entities, we chose to explicitly indicate the gender of each monarch using the genderOf predicate and to define kings and queens in terms of their gender. Table 2.8 and the code that follows it represent this new situation.

```
Monarch(m), hasMonarchName(m:n) -> string(n).
Gender(g), hasGenderCode(g:gc) -> string(gc).
genderOf[m] = g -> Monarch(m), Gender(g).
Monarch(m) -> genderOf[m] = _.
hasGenderCode(_:gc) -> gc = "M" ; gc = "F".
King(m) -> Monarch(m).
King(m) <- genderOf[m] = "M".
Queen(m) -> Monarch(m).
Queen(m) <- genderOf[m] = "F".
```

TABLE 2.8   Combined Gender Presentation

Monarch	Gender	King	Queen
Anne	F		✓
George I	M	✓	
George II	M	✓	
George III	M	✓	
George IV	M	✓	
William IV	M	✓	
Victoria	F		✓
Edward VII	M	✓	
George V	M	✓	
Edward VIII	M	✓	
George VI	M	✓	
Elizabeth II	F		✓

Note: M, male; F, female.

In this case, you might expect King and Queen to be subtype entities that had been derived from Monarch. However, the absence of the lang:isEntity declarations for King and Queen requires LogiQL to treat them as property predicates rather than entity predicates (which we should really have emphasized by beginning their names with lowercase letters). Moreover, note that there is no need to declare the inclusive-or and exclusion constraints used above to ensure that King and Queen partition Monarch, because the King and Queen predicates are derived, and these partition constraints are implied by the functional, mandatory, and value constraints on the predicates used to define them.

Alternatively, if you explicitly declare the types of the King and Queen predicates, then you may declare them to be entity predicates as shown below. In this case, King and Queen may be properly viewed as *derived subtypes* because their instances are determined using rules rather than being simply asserted:

```
Monarch(m), hasMonarchName(m:n) -> string(n).
Gender(g), hasGenderCode(g:gc) -> string(gc).
genderOf[m] = g -> Monarch(m), Gender(g).
Monarch(m) -> genderOf[m] = _.
hasGenderCode(_:gc) -> gc = "M" ; gc = "F".
King(m) -> Monarch(m). // Type declaration
   lang:isEntity[`King] = true.
King(m) <- genderOf[m] = "M".
```

```
Queen(m) -> Monarch(m). // Type declaration
lang:entity[`Queen] = true.
Queen(m) <- genderOf[m] = "F".
```

The above derivation rules for the King and Queen predicates are trivially based purely on gender because in our current application domain the only people are monarchs. Suppose we now expand our universe of discourse to include any royal family member of interest, where each can be identified by a "royal name" such as "Elizabeth II" or "Prince William." Even though, historically, there has been more than one royal family member named "Prince William," let us assume there is only one of these of interest in our domain, in this case, the Prince William of Wales born in 1982.

We could now record the gender of each royalty, assert who are monarchs, and derive who is a king and who is a queen using the following schema. Here we use *royalty* in the singular sense, and use the variable p in the sense of *person*:

```
Royalty(p), hasRoyalName(p:n) -> string(n).
Gender(g), hasGenderCode(g:gc) -> string(gc).
genderOf[p] = g -> Royalty(p), Gender(g).
Royalty(p) -> genderOf[p] = _.
hasGenderCode(_:gc) -> gc = "M" ; gc = "F".
Monarch(p) -> Royalty(p). // Asserted subtype
King(p) -> Monarch(p).
lang:isEntity[`King] = true.
King(p) <- Monarch(p), genderOf[p] = "M".
// Derived subtype
Queen(p) -> Monarch(p).
lang:isEntity[`Queen] = true.
Queen(p) <- Monarch(p), genderOf[p] = "F".
// Derived subtype
```

In this code, Monarch is an asserted subtype of Royalty, while King and Queen are derived subtypes of Monarch. Because subtyping is **transitive**, this means that King and Queen are also (indirect) subtypes of Royalty. If you run this program with the following data, the compiler will infer that Anne is a queen, George I is a king, and all three persons are royalty:

```
+genderOf["Anne"] = "F", +Monarch("Anne").
+genderOf["George I"] = "M", +Monarch("George I").
+genderOf["Prince William"] = "M".
```

Note that we did not bother declaring that Monarch is an entity predicate, because Monarch is no longer a leaf subtype. The compiler is able to infer that Monarch is an entity predicate because it appears on the right-hand side of the type declaration for King (or Queen), which have themselves been explicitly declared to be entity types. Nevertheless, because King and Queen are leaf subtypes, explicit entity declarations are required.

The subtyping examples discussed so far are all examples of *single inheritance*, where each subtype has at most one direct supertype. If a subtype has more than one direct supertype, this is called *multiple inheritance*. For example, we might define Queen and DeadMonarch as separate but overlapping subtypes of Monarch, and define DeadQueen as a subtype of both Queen and DeadMonarch. Be aware that LogiQL does not properly support multiple inheritance, and you can easily generate inconsistent results if you try to use it.

Subset Constraints

Subtyping constrains one entity type to be a subtype of another. Similarly, for property predicates, we can constrain the population of one property predicate to always be a subset of the population of another property predicate. This is known as a **subset constraint**. As a simple example of a subset constraint between two property predicates, consider the following code. Here hasGardenCenter and sellsLawnMowers are property predicates of the Store entity type. The final line of code, just above the comment, declares a subset constraint from the hasGardenCenter predicate to the sellsLawnMowers predicate:

```
Store(s), hasStoreNr(s:n) -> int(n).
hasGardenCenter(s) -> Store(s).
sellsLawnMowers(s) -> Store(s)
    hasGardenCenter(s) -> sellsLawnMowers(s).
// If store s has a garden center, then s sells lawn
// mowers.
```

Here is another example, this time of a subset constraint between role pairs (the s and p arguments of purchased and storeProductNr-Sold), to ensure that stores sell only those products that they have already purchased:

```
Store(s), hasStoreNr(s:n) -> int(n).
Product(p), hasProductCode(p:pc) -> string(pc).
```

```
purchased(s, p) -> Store(s), Product(p).
storeProductNrSold[s, p] = n -> Store(s), Product(p),
    int(n).
storeProductNrSold[s, p] = _ -> purchased(s, p).
// If store s sold product p in some quantity
// then store s purchased that product p.
```

Tip: Use a noun phrase to name an entity predicate, and use a verb phrase to name a unary property predicate.

Tip: If a leaf subtype is intended to be an entity type, declare this explicitly using a lang:isEntity declaration.

Tip: Avoid multiple inheritance.

Tip: Although the LogiQL subtyping mechanism enables you to define new entity types, it does not allow you to define subtypes of primitive types, such as defining a type of string comprising the names of the months. To do this, you should use subset constraints instead.

Exercise 4A: The following program is used to record information about companies. Some companies (dealers) sell products, while others provide services. Extend the program to include derived subtypes for Dealer (companies that sell products), NonDealer (all other companies), and IPhoneDealer (companies that sell iPhones). Then install the program, execute the data, and query the Store, Dealer, NonDealer, and IPhoneDealer predicates:

```
// Schema
Company(c), hasCompanyName(c:n) -> string(n).
Product(p), hasProductName(p:n) -> string(n).
carries(c, p) -> Company(s), Product(p).

// Data
+Company("Target"), +Company("KMart"),
+Company("Sears").
+carries("Target", "Blackberry").
+carries("Sears", "IPhone").
```

Exercise 4B: Extend the following program with a subset constraint to ensure that bookstores own the coffee shop(s) that they provide:

```
BookStore(s), hasStoreName(s:n) -> string(n).
CoffeeShop(c), hasShopName(c:n) -> string(n).
provides(s, c) -> BookStore(s), CoffeeShop(c).
owns(s, c) -> BookStore(s), CoffeeShop(c).
```

UNIT 2.5: RECURSIVE RULES AND RING CONSTRAINTS

In Chapter 1, the `isGrandparentOf` predicate was introduced to express the grandparenthood relationship between monarchs in terms of the parenthood relationship. We could have also defined other variants, such as `isGreatGrandparentOf`. What we could not have done with the concepts available at that time was define the more general relationship of *ancestry*.

Recursion

The problem is that if one person is an ancestor of another there may be any number of intermediate parents. Expressing this imprecision requires the more powerful notion of **recursion**. Roughly speaking, recursion is the use of a concept in its own definition. In LogiQL, recursion can be used in derivation rules and constraints.

For generality, we will now consider people other than monarchs, so that ancestorhood is a many-to-many relationship between two persons. Let's see how we could specify an `isAncestorOf` derivation rule using recursion. If we were to verbalize the rule, we might say the following:

> *Person p1 is an ancestor of person p2 if either p1 is a parent of p2 or p1 is a parent of some ancestor of p2.*

Note the two uses of "ancestor" in the above definition. The first gives the term being defined, while the second is part of the definition.

The use of "or" in the above description indicates that the corresponding derivation rule is disjunctive. A disjunctive rule can be expressed directly using the *or* operator ('`;`'), or it can be replaced by multiple non-disjunctive rules, one for each disjunct. Let's use the latter approach. The first disjunct in the above ancestor rule can be expressed by a non-recursive rule as follows, assuming that the `isParentOf` *m:n* predicate is defined between two monarchs:

```
isAncestorOf(p1, p2) <- isParentOf(p1, p2).
// If p1 is a parent of p2 then p1 is an ancestor of p2.
```

The second part is nearly as simple once you realize that you can use `isAncestorOf` on the right-hand side:

```
isAncestorOf(p1, p2) <- isParentOf(p1, p3),
    isAncestorOf(p3, p2).
// If p1 is a parent of some p3 and p3 is an ancestor
// of p2 then p1 is an ancestor of p2.
```

The `isAncestorOf` predicate was defined in two parts, which is typical of recursive definitions. The first rule, known as a *basis clause*, deals with the *ground* case where there is no recursion—that is, where ancestorhood is simply parenthood. The second rule, known as a *recursive clause*, derives an ancestorhood fact from a parenthood fact and an ancestorhood derivation that is one step shorter. Repeated applications of this rule eventually spiral into a case where only one step is left, and this case is satisfied by the basis clause.

Any derivation rule that includes the same predicate in both the head and body of the rule is a **recursive rule**. Recursion is a powerful capability, and the elegant and efficient way in which LogiQL supports recursion is one of its most attractive features. In general, when you have a predicate, such as `isParentOf`, that you wish to apply an indefinite number of times to compute a new predicate (`isAncestorOf`), you should use recursion. Such situations compute what is called the **transitive closure** of the original predicate, and rules to compute transitive closures are needed in many applications.

Recursion can also be applied to constraints. We will use the genealogy graph for the current Prince George going back through four generations to illustrate several constraints, including one that is recursive, as shown in Figure 2.2.

In Figure 2.2, each node in the graph denotes a person, using rectangles for males and rounded rectangles for females. Line segments that connect nodes represent biological parenthood relationships, read from left to right. For example, Prince Charles and Princess Diana are the parents of Princes William and Harry.

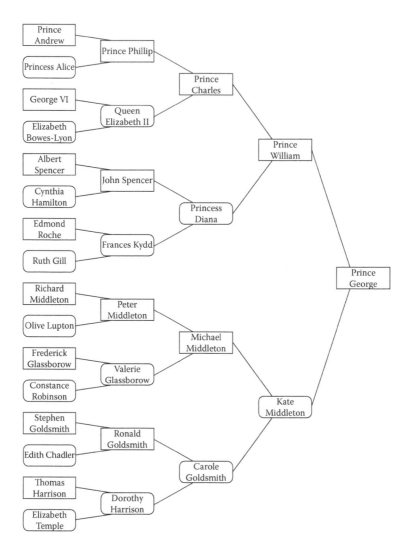

FIGURE 2.2   Genealogy for Prince George.

Treating each of the royalty simply as a person and their identifiers in the graph nodes as person names, we may use the following basic schema to encode the gender and parenthood facts. Because a person may have up to two parents listed, and some have more than one child, the parenthood predicate is many-to-many:

```
Person(p), hasPersonName(p:n) -> string(n).
Gender(g), hasGenderCode(g:gc) -> string(gc).
```

```
genderOf[p] = g -> Person(p), Gender(g).
isParentOf(p1, p2) -> Person(p1), Person(p2).
Person(p) -> genderOf[p] = _.
hasGenderCode(_:gc) -> gc = "M" ; gc = "F".
```

Ring Constraints

Notice that both arguments of the `isParentOf` predicate are of type `Person`. A binary predicate whose arguments are of the same type is called a **ring predicate**. Typically, ring predicates need to be constrained in various ways to prevent them being populated with bad data. For example, we should constrain the parenthood predicate to be **irreflexive** (i.e., no instance may participate in the relationship with itself) by adding the following constraint:

```
!isParentOf(p, p).
// No person is a parent of his/her self.
// Note that there is no head nor arrow on this
// constraint.
```

If you add this constraint to the above program, compile it, and try to assert the following data, you will get an error because the second line of data violates the above irreflexive constraint:

```
+genderOf["George V"] = "M".
+isParentOf("George V", "George V"). // Error!
```

The file containing the correct data for the figure is available as `PrincesData.logic`.

Logical constraints on two type-compatible arguments of a predicate are called **ring constraints**. An irreflexive constraint is just one of many kinds of ring constraint. We now discuss some other varieties of ring constraints.

A ring predicate is **asymmetric** if it works in one direction only. For example, the `isParentOf` predicate is asymmetric, and we can constrain it to be so by adding the following *asymmetry constraint*:

```
isParentOf(p1, p2) -> !isParentOf(p2, p1).
// If p1 is a parent of p2, then p2 cannot be a parent
// of p1.
```

For example, if you try to assert that George V is a parent of George VI and also assert that George VI is a parent of George V, you will violate this constraint. If a predicate is asymmetric, it must be irreflexive, so if you include the asymmetric constraint above, there is no need to include the irreflexive constraint given above.

A ring predicate R is *intransitive* if and only if, given any x, y, and z, if $R(x, y)$ and $R(y, z)$ are true, then $R(x, z)$ must be false. Assuming no incest, the parenthood relationship is intransitive, and we may constrain it to be so by adding the following *intransitive constraint*:

```
isParentOf(p1, p2), isParentOf(p2, p3) ->
    !isParentOf(p1, p3).
// If p1 is a parent of p2, and p2 is a parent of p3
// then p1 cannot be a parent of p3.
```

Note that if a binary predicate is both functional and irreflexive, it must be intransitive.

A ring predicate R is **acyclic** if and only if no object may cycle back to itself by one or more applications of R. Ignoring the possibility of reincarnation, the parenthood relationship is acyclic. Since there is no restriction on how many times the R predicate is applied, we need to use recursion to express an acyclic constraint.

To ensure that a ring predicate R is acyclic, we first recursively derive a predicate T that captures all pairs of arguments resulting from one or more applications of R. That is, T is the transitive closure of R. We then constrain T to be irreflexive. With our current example, R is the isParentOf predicate, and T is the isAncestorOf predicate. Hence, we can specify the acyclic constraint on parenthood by constraining ancestorhood to be irreflexive as follows:

```
!isAncestorOf(p, p).
// No person is an ancestor of himself/herself.
```

If you look back at Figure 2.2, you should be able to see that this prevents any cycles appearing in the graph of parenthood facts (i.e., parenthood is acyclic).

Note that acyclicity implies asymmetry. So if you constrain a predicate to be acyclic there is no need to also declare it to be asymmetric (or irreflexive).

Hard and Soft Constraints

LogiQL constraints are checked at runtime when new data is added to the workspace, either by fact assertion or by derivation from a rule. If a constraint is violated, program execution is stopped, and an error reported to the user. For many types of constraints, this is exactly the behavior that we want. For example, if two facts are asserted, one stating that Queen Anne is a female and one that she is a male, we want to be told immediately, so we can correct the data. Such constraints are called **hard constraints** and indicate what conditions must necessarily hold for the application domain.

Sometimes, however, there are constraints that could be violated in the domain of interest, even though they ought to be obeyed. For example, the above intransitive constraint on parenthood could be violated if incest occurs. These are examples of **soft constraints**. Ideally, we would like violations of soft constraints to be handled differently from how hard constraints are handled. In particular, our programs should be able to detect them, take appropriate action, such as issuing a warning message, and continue processing. Unfortunately, LogiQL does not support this capability. Instead, if we know that parenthood is intransitive in the domain being modeled (as in this royal ancestry domain), then it may be declared as a hard constraint.

Tip: If a predicate has two arguments of the same type, consider which ring constraints apply to it.

Exercise 5A: The ancestry program discussed is accessible as the file `Ancestry.logic`, and the ancestral data depicted in Figure 2.2 is accessible as the file `PrincesData.logic`. Compile the program, execute the data file, and then issue a query to list all the ancestors of Prince William.

Exercise 5B: A typical business application of recursion is a bill-of-materials report. The following schema and data are used to record which products directly contain which other products in what quantities. Since the first two arguments of the direct containment predicate are `Products`, one or more ring constraints might apply. Extend the schema to express the predicate `contains(p1,p2)`, which indicates which product contains which product (directly or indirectly). Use `contains` to constrain direct containment to be acyclic. Then query this predicate to provide information about all instances of direct and indirect containment:

```
// Schema
Product(p), hasProductCode(p:pc) -> string(pc).
directlyContainsIn[p1, p2] = qty -> Product(p1),
    Product(p2), int(qty).

// Data
+directlyContainsIn("A", "B", 1).
+directlyContainsIn("A", "C", 2).
+directlyContainsIn("B", "C", 1).
+directlyContainsIn("B", "D", 1).
+directlyContainsIn("B", "E", 2).
+directlyContainsIn("C", "E", 2).
+directlyContainsIn("C", "F", 2).
```

Exercise 5C: Assuming no incest, the parenthood predicate is not just intransitive, but *strongly* intransitive, so that no person can be a parent of any of his/her non-direct descendants. Code a constraint to ensure that parenthood is strongly intransitive.

UNIT 2.6: THE count AND total FUNCTIONS

This unit considers the first two of the four most important **aggregation functions** supported by LogiQL: count, total, max, and min. Each of these four functions operates on a collection of facts and returns a single value. Aggregation functions are invoked using a special agg<<...>> syntax. Hence, rules referring to aggregation functions are called **aggregation rules** to distinguish them from other kinds of derivation rules. Inside the double-angle brackets, a variable is assigned the result of applying the indicated aggregation function to facts satisfying a filtering condition that follows the closing double-angle bracket.

Computing Counts

To invoke the count function, the following pattern is used:

```
agg<<n = count()>> condition
// n is the number of instances where condition is true.
```

Intermediate Aspects ■ 61

TABLE 2.9   Genders of British
Monarchs

Monarch	Gender
Anne	F
George I	M
George II	M
George III	M
George IV	M
William IV	M
Victoria	F
Edward VII	M
George V	M
Edward VIII	M
George VI	M
Elizabeth II	F

Note: M, male; F, female.

As our first example, we'll use the count function to derive the number of British monarchs, as listed in Table 2.9. The code below provides the basic schema for this domain, as discussed in Chapter 1:

```
Monarch(m), hasMonarchName(m:n) -> string(n).
Gender(g), hasGenderCode(g:gc) -> string(gc).
genderOf[m] = g -> Monarch(m), Gender(g).
genderOf[_] = g -> g = "M" ; g = "F".
Monarch(m) -> genderOf[m] = _.
```

Let us use the predicate nrMonarchs[]=n to denote the number of monarchs. Because this function takes no key arguments, you may also think of it as a variable whose value at any given moment of time is the number of Monarch entities. Note that to be able to hold the result of the count function, the value argument of nrMonarchs[] must be of type int. The following code uses the count function to derive the number of monarchs:

```
nrMonarchs[] = n -> int(n).
nrMonarchs[] = n <- agg<<n = count()>> Monarch(_).
// nrMonarchs = number of monarchs.
```

The count function, written as count(), returns the number of instances satisfying the condition specified after the double-angle brackets. In this case it counts the number of facts where some object (denoted by the anonymous variable) is a monarch.

If you install the program with the monarchy data shown above and then print or query the nrMonarchs predicate, you will get 12 as the result.

In the above example, we declared the nrMonarchs predicate along with a derivation rule using it. You may also use the count function in ad hoc queries, using an anonymous predicate ('_ [] ') for the query result. For example, you could query for the number of kings using the following query string:

```
_[] = n <- agg<<n = count()>> Monarch(m),
    genderOf[m] = "M".
// Return the number of kings (male monarchs).
```

Unlike the earlier use of count, the condition to be satisfied here is a conjunction. Be aware however that disjunctions are not allowed in such situations. For the data shown, this query returns the value 9.

Dealing with Empty Predicates

There is a subtle issue raised if the condition for the count function is never satisfied. You might expect that count would return a value of zero. In this case, however, the query is considered to have failed, and no value is assigned to the function result. For example, the following query has a condition that can never be satisfied, so the query result is simply empty, instead of being the number 0:

```
_[] = n <- agg<<n = count()>> Monarch(m), !Monarch(m).
```

Although this example is silly, there are situations where you would like to see a value of zero. As a simple example, consider Table 2.10.

TABLE 2.10   Descendants of Princess Diana and Prince Charles

Person	Children
Princess Diana	Prince William, Prince Harry
Prince Charles	Prince William, Prince Harry
Prince William	Prince George
Prince Harry	
Catherine, Duchess of Cambridge	Prince George

We may code this report as follows. (Strictly speaking, we should add the ring constraints on parenthood discussed previously, but for simplicity let's ignore these for now.)

```
// Schema
Person(p), hasPersonName(p:n) -> string(n).
isParentOf(p1, p2) -> Person(p1), Person(p2).

// Data
+isParentOf("Princess Diana", "Prince William").
+isParentOf("Princess Diana", "Prince Harry").
+isParentOf("Prince Charles", "Prince William").
+isParentOf("Prince Charles", "Prince Harry").
+isParentOf("Prince William", "Prince George").
+isParentOf("Catherine, Duchess of Cambridge",
    "Prince George").
```

Now suppose we want to use the count function to derive, for each person, how many children that person has. To begin, we might try adding the following code to the schema:

```
nrChildrenOf[p] = n -> Person(p), int(n).
nrChildrenOf[p] = n <- agg<<n = count()>>
    isParentOf(p, _).
// The number of children of person p =
// the count of parenthood facts for person p.
```

If you run the program with the data shown and then print the Person and nrChildrenOf predicates, you get the following results:

```
/- - start of Person facts- -\
    Prince Charles
    Prince Harry
    Prince William
    Princess Diana
    Prince George
    Catherine, Duchess of Cambridge
\- - end of Person facts- -

/- - start of nrChildrenOf facts- -\
    Prince Charles,                  2
    Princess Diana,                  2
```

```
    Prince William,                           1
    Catherine, Duchess of Cambridge,  1
\- - end of nrChildrenOf facts- - /
```

As expected, we see that Prince Charles and Princess Diana each have two children and that Prince William and "Princess Kate" have one. However, Prince Harry and Prince George are excluded from the nrChildrenOf output because they do not play the parent role in any parenthood facts. We might instead want to include them with a value of zero for their number of children. One way to do this is to split the nrChildrenOf rule into two pieces—one to handle the case of parents with children and another to deal with people who do not have children.

To implement the first part of this strategy, we rename the nrChildrenOf predicate to positiveNrChildrenOf to deal with the case where the number of children is greater than zero:

```
positiveNrChildrenOf[p] = n -> Person(p), int(n).
positiveNrChildrenOf[p] = n <- agg<<n = count()>>
    isParentOf(p, _).
// The positive number (i.e. number above 0) of
// children of person p = the count of parenthood
// facts for person p.
```

We can then derive the nrChildrenOf predicate using two rules, one for this case and one for the case of no children, as shown below:

```
nrChildrenOf[p] = n -> Person(p), int(n).
nrChildrenOf[p] = 0 <- Person(p), !isParentOf(p, _).
nrChildrenOf[p] = positiveNrChildrenOf[p] <-
    isParentOf(p, _).
// The number of children of p = 0
// if p is a person who is not a parent of someone,
// else it's the positive number of children of p.
```

With this change, a print of the nrChildrenOf predicate displays the intended results:

```
/- - start of nrChildrenOf facts- -\
    Princess Diana,            2
    Prince William,            1
```

```
    Prince Charles,                     2
    Catherine, Duchess of Cambridge, 1
    Prince Harry,                       0
    Prince George,                      0
\- - end of nrChildrenOf facts- - /
```

Be aware that there is a subtle performance cost to taking the above approach. For each `Person` entity, both of the `nrChildrenOf` rules must search the `isParentOf` predicate, even though we know that the `Person` cannot satisfy both rules (a person cannot both be a parent and not be a parent). In Appendix J, we will revisit this example to show how this extra cost can be avoided.

Computing Totals and Averages

This section discusses the `total` function, as well as how it can be used together with the `count` function to compute averages. The `total` function operates on a collection of facts and returns a single value; but unlike the `count` function, `total` requires an individual variable as a key argument. If x and y are individual variables and Cx denotes a condition in which x is a variable, then the following syntax is used to assign the value of `total(x)` to y when the condition Cx is true:

```
agg<<y = total(x)>> Cx // y = total(Cx) where Cx is true.
```

The `total` function sums numeric values, and therefore `total(x)` is legal only if x is a numeric variable. Table 2.11 lists the numeric datatypes supported by LogiQL.

For floating-point numbers that include an exponent, "E" precedes the power of 10. For example, the universal gravitational constant 6.67×10^{-11} may be written `6.67E-11.f`. Note that to distinguish literal values of types `float`, an explicit suffix `f` is required. Literals of type `decimal` may optionally include the suffix `d`.

TABLE 2.11   LogiQL Numeric Datatypes

Numeric Datatype	LogiQL Syntax	Examples
Integer	int	−3, 0, 35
Floating Point	float	0.0f, 31.555f, 2.9979E8f, 6.67E-11f
Decimal	decimal	0.0, 567.99d

TABLE 2.12   Expense Report

Item	Expense (US$)
Travel	300.50
Accommodation	300.50
Meals	100.20
Total	701.20

There are also built-in predicates for converting among types. The format for usage is that the names of the two types precede the name `convert`, as in the following example that converts a `string` literal to `decimal`:

```
+a[] = string:decimal:convert["52.43"].
```

As another example of the `total` function, consider the expense report presented in Table 2.12. Currently, LogiQL allows the `total` function only on numeric values and has no built-in support for units of measure, so we represent U.S. dollar amounts simply by numeric values. We use the `decimal` datatype to encode expense amounts. A basic schema and input data for the report is shown below:

```
// Schema
Item(i), hasItemName(i:n) -> string(n).
expenseOf[i] = e -> Item(i), decimal(e).
Item(i) -> expenseOf[i] = _.
// Each item has an expense.

// Data
+expenseOf["Travel"] = 300.50.
+expenseOf["Accommodation"] = 300.50.
+expenseOf["Meals"] = 100.20.
```

To derive the total expense, we add the following code to the schema, using the function `totalExpense[]` to store the derived total, and using the `total` function to sum over each expense amount:

```
totalExpense[] = t -> decimal(t).
totalExpense[] = t <- agg<<t = total(e)>>
    expenseOf[_] = e.
// The total expense is the sum of the item expenses.
```

TABLE 2.13 Multiple Expense Claims

Expense Claim	Item	Expense (US$)	Total (US$)
1	Travel	300.50	
	Accommodation	300.50	
	Meals	100.20	701.20
2	Travel	55.05	
	Meals	30.10	85.15

Note that 300.50 appears twice in the expense column of the above table. When the `total` function is applied to the asserted facts, it adds each of the two duplicate values just like any other value. So if you compile the program with the data shown and then print or query the `totalExpense` predicate, you get the correct value 701.2 (not 400.7) as the result.

Note also that LogiQL requires the result datatype for the `total` function to be the same as the input datatype of the component being summed. For example, changing the datatype of `totalexpense` in the above code to be `float` results in an error.

Now consider the report in Table 2.13 that deals with multiple expense claims, where we wish to total the expenses for each claim.

Using the ternary predicate `claimItemExpense[c,i]=e` to indicate that claim `c` for item `i` has expense `e` and the expression `totalExpenseOf[c]=t` to indicate that claim `c` has a total expense of `t`, we may code this report as follows:

```
Claim(c), hasClaimNr(c:n) -> int(n).
Item(i), hasItemName(i:n) -> string(n).
claimItemExpense[c, i] = e -> Claim(c), Item(i),
    decimal(e).
Claim(c) -> claimItemExpense[c, _] = _.
// Each claim has an item with an expense.
totalExpenseOf[c] = t -> Claim(c), decimal(t).
totalExpenseOf[c] = t <-
    agg<<t = total(e)>> claimItemExpense[c, _] = e.
// The total expense of claim c is the sum of
// the item expenses on claim c.
```

The input data for the report may be asserted as follows:

```
+claimItemExpense[1, "Travel"] = 300.50.
+claimItemExpense[1, "Accommodation"] = 300.50.
+claimItemExpense[1, "Meals"] = 100.20.
```

```
+claimItemExpense[2, "Travel"] = 55.05.
+claimItemExpense[2, "Meals"] = 30.10.
```

If you run the program with the data shown, and then print the `total ExpenseOf` predicate, you get the following:

```
/- - start of totalExpenseOf facts- -\
   2, 85.15
   1, 701.2
\- - end of totalExpenseOf facts- - /
```

Now consider Table 2.14 containing estimated IQs for some famous people (for more listings, see www.kids-iq-tests.com/famous-people.html). Suppose we wish to compute the average IQ of those listed. LogiQL does not include a function to compute averages, but we can use the `total` function to sum the IQs, and the `count` function to count the number of IQs, and then divide the sum by the count to compute the average IQ.

As a first attempt, we could try the following, using `iqOf[p]` = `iq` to mean the IQ of person p is `iq`. Assuming all IQs are positive and none exceeds 255, we treat IQ values as `int`s and add constraints on the maximum and minimum IQ:

```
// Schema
Person(p), hasPersonName(p:n) -> string(n).
iqOf[p] = iq -> Person(p), int(iq).
iqOf[_] = iq -> 0 < = iq, iq <= 255.
// Each IQ > = 0 and <= 255.
Person(p) -> iqOf[p] = _.        // Each person has an IQ.
nrPersons[] = n -> int(n).
nrPersons[] = n <- agg<<n = count()>> Person(_).
totalIQ[] = t -> int(t).
totalIQ[] = t <- agg<<t = total(iq)>> iqOf[_] = iq.
avgIQ[] = n -> int(n).
avgIQ[] = n <- n = totalIQ[]/nrPersons[].

// Data
+iqOf["Hillary Clinton"] = 140.
+iqOf["Albert Einstein"] = 160.
+iqOf["Bill Gates"] = 160.
```

If you run the program with the data shown and print or query the `avgIQ` predicate, you get 153, which omits the fractional part. This is because

TABLE 2.14   IQs of Famous People

Person	IQ
Hillary Clinton	140
Albert Einstein	160
Bill Gates	160

avgIQ is obtained by dividing one integer into another, and the *division* operator ('/') is then treated as integer division not floating-point division. If you wish to include the fractional part in the result of dividing one integer term x by another integer term y, you may instead use a conversion function (i.e., int:float:convert). For example, if you replace the derivation rule for avgIQ given above by the following line of code, declare avgIQ to be of type float, and then recompile the program and print or query the avgIQ predicate, you get 153.33333333333334, which includes the fractional part:

```
avgIQ[] = n <- n =
avgIQ[] = n <-
    n = int:float:convert[totalIQ[]]/
    int:float:convert[nrPersons[]].
```

Note that if the terms in the division are already typed as floating point (e.g., float instead of int), floating-point division is automatically performed when using "/" for the *division* operator. Also note that any attempt to divide by zero fails to return a result.

Tip: When using the count function, decide whether or not to return 0 if there are no facts to be counted.

Tip: When using the total function, ensure that the datatype of the numbers being summed is large enough to hold the final sum.

Tip: When using division, decide whether integer, decimal, or floating-point division is intended, and use the appropriate datatype.

Exercise 6A: Extend the program found in countMonarchs. logic with code to derive the predicate nrQueens[]=n to count the

TABLE 2.15   Products and Accessories

Product	Accessories
Paperback book	
Kindle	Cover, light, wireless

TABLE 2.16   Student Course Credits

Student Number	Course	Credit	Total Credit
101	CS100	5	
	MA100	5	
	PH101	4	14
202	CS100	5	
	JP100	4	9

number of queens. Then compile and run your program with the data in genderOfData.logic and print nrQueens[]. Include code to return 0 if there are no queens.

Exercise 6B: Write and test a program to record the facts in Table 2.15 and display the number of accessories (possibly 0) available for each product.

Exercise 6C: The report in Table 2.16 is used to maintain details about course credits obtained by students for the courses they have passed. A stub of a program for this report is shown here, as well as the relevant data. The stub can be found in credits.logic, and the data can be found in creditsData.logic. Extend the program to compute the total credit obtained by each student and print the results:

```
// Schema
Student(s), hasStudentNr(s:n) -> int(n).
Course(c), hasCourseCode(c:cc) -> string(cc).
hasCredit[c] = n -> Course(c), int(n).
passedCourse(s, c) -> Student(s), Course(c).

// Data
+hasCredit["CS100"] = 5, +hasCredit["MA100"] = 5.
+hasCredit["PH101"] = 4, +hasCredit["JP100"] = 4.
+passedCourse(101, "CS100"), +passedCourse(101,
    "MA100"), +passedCourse(101, "PH101").
+passedCourse(202, "CS100"), +passedCourse(202,
    "JP100").
```

Exercise 6D: The expense claim program and data discussed in this unit are stored as the files `expenses.logic` and `expensesData.logic`. Extend the program to compute the average expense of items on each of the two expense claims.

UNIT 2.7: CONSOLIDATION EXERCISE 2

This exercise gives you a chance to test how well you have mastered the topics covered in this chapter. The application domain is adapted from a previously published example by one of the authors.* The universe of discourse concerns a fragment of an information system used by a book publisher to maintain details about its books and personnel. Your task is to model this domain in LogiQL.

PART 1: BOOKS

One requirement of the information system is to produce reports about books that are either already published by the publisher or are under consideration for publication. Each of these books is identified by an International Standard Book Number (ISBN). For any given title, the publisher also has a policy of publishing at most one book with that title in any given year; for example, only one book published by the company in 2010 may be titled *Informatics*. It is possible that a book is directly translated from another book written in a different language. A sample extract of this report is shown in Table 2.17.

TABLE 2.17   Book Publication Details

ISBN	Title	Language	Published	Translated from
1-33456-012-3	*Mizu no Kokoro*	Japanese	2009	
2-55860-123-6	*Mind Like Water*	English	2010	1-33456-012-3
3-540-25432-2	*Informatics*	English	2010	
4-567-12345-3	*Semantics*	English	2011	
5-123-45678-5	*Informatics*	English	2011	
6-246-80246-8	*Geist wie Wasser*	German	2011	2-55860-123-6
7-345-10267-4	*Geest als Water*	Dutch		6-246-80246-8
8-543-21012-3	*Mens quasi Aquam*	Latin		2-55860-123-6

---

* T. Halpin. "Fact-Oriented Modeling: Past, Present and Future." *Conceptual Modelling in Information Systems Engineering*, Springer, 2007, pp. 19–38.

The predicate declarations and some constraints for this report are shown below:

```
Book(b), hasISBN(b:n) -> string(n).
bookTitleOf[b] = t -> Book(b), string(t).
Language(lang), hasLanguageName(lang:ln) -> string(ln).
languageOf[b] = lang -> Book(b), Language(lang).
publicationYearOf[b] = yr -> Book(b), int(yr).
translationParentOf[b1] = b2 -> Book(b1), Book(b2).
Book(b) -> bookTitleOf[b] = _, languageOf[b] = _.
// Each book has a title and is written in a language.
```

The file and data for this program are accessible as Q1.logic and Q1Data.logic.

Q1: Extend the program with code to express the following external uniqueness constraint: For each book title and year, at most one book of that title is published in that year. Also, add code to capture the following exclusion constraint: If a book is directly translated from another book, its language must differ from that of the other book. The answers can be found in the file Q1Answer.logic.

Q2: Extend the program to derive the predicate isaTranslationOf (covering direct and indirect book translations) representing the transitive closure of translationParentOf. Constrain the direct translation predicate to be acyclic. Test your code by trying to add data that violates the constraint. Explain why there is no need to add an intransitivity constraint. The answers are in Q2Answer.logic and Q2Counterexample.logic.

Q3: Write a query to compute the number of books that are translated (directly or indirectly) from the book titled *Mizu no Kokoro* that was published in 2009. The answer is in Q3Answer.logic.

Q4: Write a query to list the ISBN and title of each book that is translated (directly or indirectly) from the book with ISBN 1-33456-012-3. The answer is in Q4Answer.logic.

PART 2: BOOK SALES

A report is also maintained on sales of published books. The extract from this report in Table 2.18 shows the sales figures for those published books in the previous report for which sales figures are available.

TABLE 2.18   Book Sales Information

ISBN	Year	Number Sold	Cumulative Sales	Best Seller?
1-33456-012-3	2009	5000		
	2010	6000		
	2011	5000	16000	Yes
2-55860-123-6	2010	3000		
	2011	4000	7000	No
3-540-25432-2	2010	1000		
	2011	2000	3000	No

The publisher considers any book that has sold at least 10,000 copies to be a best seller.

Q5: Write a program to model this report. Extend the file Q5.logic by introducing PublishedBook as a derived subtype of Book. Use the ternary predicate yearlySales[b,yr]=n to record the number of copies sold for a given book in a given year, ignoring books with no sales. Use cumulativeSalesOf[b]=n for computing the total number of copies sold to date for a given book with sales. Use the unary predicate isaBestSeller to derive whether a published book is a best seller. For testing purposes, you may use the associated data file Q5Data.logic. The answer is in the file Q5Answer.logic.

Q6: Add a rule to derive nrSalesYearsOf[b], which computes for each sold book b, the positive number of years that book has sales figures. Then add a rule to derive avgYearlySalesOf[b], which computes, for each book b with sales figures, the average number of copies sold per year. The answer is in Q6Answer.logic.

PART 3: PERSONNEL

Reports are also maintained on persons who perform work for the company as employees and/or authors and/or translators. The publisher identifies such persons by a personnel number (PNr). If a person has a Social Security Number (SSN), this is also recorded. Table 2.19 is an extract from a personnel report.

The predicate declarations and some constraints for this report are shown below. The applicableGenderOf predicate is used to indicate which person titles are restricted to which genders. For example, "Mr" is restricted to males and "Mrs" to females, while "Dr" has no such restriction.

TABLE 2.19   Personnel Information

PNr	Name	SSN	Title	Gender
1	John Smith	123-45-6789	Mr.	M
2	Don Bradchap	246-80-2468	Sir	M
3	Sue Yakamoto		Mrs.	F
4	Yoko Oya		Dr.	F
5	Isaac Seldon		Dr.	M
6	Fumie Mifune	678-90-1234	Dr.	F
7	John Smith	789-01-2345	Mr.	M
8	Ann Jones		Ms.	F
9	Selena Most		Mrs.	F
10	Julius Antony	100-01-2345	Mr.	M
11	Bernhard Schmidt		Dr.	M
12	Herman van Reit		Dr.	M

Note: M, male; F, female.

Though not required, we declared the `PersonTitle` predicate with a `string` refmode, instead of simply using `string` in its place, since this better explains the use of the `applicableGenderOf` predicate. However, doing this requires that we populate the `PersonTitle` predicate explicitly with data:

```
Person(p), hasPNr(p:n) -,> int(n).
Gender(g), hasGenderCode(g:gc) -> string(gc).
PersonTitle(pt) -> string(pt).
personNameOf[p] = pn -> Person(p), string(pn).
ssnOf[p] = ssn -> Person(p), string(ssn).
personTitleOf[p] = pt -> Person(p), PersonTitle(pt).
genderOf[p] = g -> Person(p), Gender(g).
applicableGenderOf[pt] = g -> PersonTitle(pt),
    Gender(g).
Person(p) -> personNameOf[p] = _,
personTitleOf[p] = _, genderOf[p] = _.
hasGenderCode(_:gc) -> gc = "M" ; gc = "F".
```

The program and data are accessible as `Q7.logic` and `Q7Data.logic`:

Q7: Add constraint code to ensure that the `ssnOf` predicate is inverse-functional (i.e., each SSN applies to at most one person). Also add constraint code to enforce the following subset constraint: If a person has a person title that applies only to a specific gender, then that person must be of that gender. The answer is in `Q7Answer.logic`.

TABLE 2.20   Personnel Roles

ISBN	Author PNrs	Translator PNrs	Reviewer PNrs
1-33456-012-3	3		1, 4
2-55860-123-6		3	
3-540-25432-2	5		1, 7
4-567-12345-3	5, 8		7, 11
5-123-45678-5	7		5, 8
6-246-80246-8		11	
7-345-10267-4		12	
8-543-21012-3		10, 12	

The report in Table 2.20 indicates who plays what roles (author, translator, reviewer) for what books. If a book is a translation of another book, then its author(s) is/are not explicitly recorded.

There are many different ways to model this report, but let us choose to use the three predicate declarations shown below. The full program up to this point, including the previous code and these new predicate declarations, is accessible as the file Q8.logic. The associated data file is Q8Data.logic:

```
authored(p, b)      -> Person(p), Book(b).
translatedFor(p, b) -> Person(p), Book(b).
reviewed(p, b)      -> Person(p), Book(b).
```

Q8: Without introducing any more subtypes, add code to the above to enforce the following constraints: **Q8a:** the subset constraint that each book with a translator is translated from another book (use the predicate translationParentOf); **Q8b:** the subset constraint that each reviewed book has an author; **Q8c:** the *inclusive-or* constraint that each book is either authored or translated, ignoring the exclusive aspect; **Q8d:** the exclusion constraint that no person may author and review the same book. The answer is in Q8Answer. logic.

Q9: Write a query to list each book that is a translation of another book, as well as the PNr and name of the original author(s). *Hint:* Make use of the isaTranslationOf predicate. The answer is in Q9Answer. logic.

ANSWERS TO EXERCISES

Answer to Exercise 1A:

```
isFatherOf (p1, p2) -> Person (p1), Person (p2).
// If p1 is father of p2, then p1 and p2 are
// persons.

isFatherOf (p1, p), isFatherOf (p2, p) -> p1 = p2.
// Each person has at most one father.
```

Answer to Exercise 1B:

```
fatherOf [p1] = p2 -> Person (p1), Person (p2).
// If the father of p1 is p2, then p1 and p2 are
// persons. Each person has at most one father.

isFatherOf (p1, p2) <- fatherOf [p2] = p1.
// p1 is father of p2 if the father of p2 is p1.
```

Answer to Exercise 2A:

```
inPositionHasGivenName [_, n] = _ -> n > 0, n < 10.
// If something in position n has some given name
// then the integer n is at least 1 and at most 9.
```

Note: The constraint may also be written as follows:

```
inPositionHasGivenName [_, n] = _ -> n > = 1,
    n < = 9.
```

Answer to Exercise 2B:

```
inPositionHasGivenName [m, n1] = gn,
inPositionHasGivenName [m, n2] = gn -> n1 = n2.
// Each given name of a monarch appears in only one
// position in that monarch's list of given names.
```

Note the occurrence of multiple atoms on the left-hand side of this constraint.

Answer to Exercise 2C:

```
sharesGivenName(m1, m2) -> Monarch(m1), Monarch(m2).
sharesGivenName(m1, m2) <-
  hasGivenName(m1, n), hasGivenName(m2, n),
  m1 ! = m2.
// Monarchs m1 and m2 share a given name if they are
// different monarchs and there is a given name n
// that both of them have.
```

Answer to Exercise 2D:

```
sharesGivenName2(m1, m2) -> Monarch(m1), Monarch(m2).
sharesGivenName2(m1, m2) <-
    hasGivenName(m1, n), hasGivenName(m2, n),
    hasMonarchName(m1:n1), hasMonarchName(m2:n2),
    n1 < n2.
// Monarchs m1 and m2 share a given name if there is a
// given name n that both of them have and if the
// first Monarch name is less than the second's.
```

Answer to Exercise 3A:

```
Employee(e), hasEmpNr(e:en) -> string(en).
ssnOf[e] = ssn -> Employee(e), string(ssn).
passportNrOf[e] = ppn -> Employee(e), string(ppn).

ssnOf[e1] = ssn, ssnOf[e2] = ssn -> e1 = e2.
// Each Social Security Number is for only one
// employee.

passportNrOf[e1] = ppn, passportNrOf[e2] = ppn ->
    e1 = e2.
// Each passport nr is for only one employee.

Employee(e) -> ssnOf[e] = _ ; passportNrOf[e] = _.
// Each employee has a Social Security Number
// or a passport number.
```

Answer to Exercise 3B:

```
// Schema
Store(s), hasNeighborhood(s:name) -> string(name).
```

```
xCoordinateOf[s] = x -> Store(s), int(x).
yCoordinateOf[s] = y -> Store(s), int(y).

// Each (x, y) coordinate pair applies to only one
// store.
xCoordinateOf[s1] = x, yCoordinateOf[s1] =
    y, xCoordinateOf[s2] = x,
    yCoordinateOf[s2] = y -> s1 = s2.

// Data
+xCoordinateOf["A"] = 2, +yCoordinateOf["A"] = 3.
+xCoordinateOf["B"] = 1, +yCoordinateOf["B"] = 1.
+xCoordinateOf["C"] = 4, +yCoordinateOf["C"] = 1.

// Query
_(s, x, y) <- xCoordinateOf[s] = x,
    yCoordinateOf[s] = y.
```

Result:

```
C, 4, 1 B, 1, 1 A, 2, 3
```

Answer to Exercise 4A:

```
Company(c), hasCompanyName(c:n) -> string(n).
Product(p), hasProductName(p:n) -> string(n).
carries(c, p) -> Company(c), Product(p).
Dealer(c) -> Company(c).
Dealer(c) <- carries(c, _).
NonDealer(c) -> Company(c).
NonDealer(c) <- Company(c), !Dealer(c).
// Instead of !Dealer(c) you may use !carries(c, _).
IPhoneDealer(c) -> Dealer(c).
IPhoneDealer(c) <- carries(c, "IPhone").
```

Results:

```
Company:       Sears, Target, KMart
Dealer:        Sears, Target
NonDealer:     KMart
IPhoneDealer:  Sears
```

Answer to Exercise 4B:

```
provides(s, c) -> owns(s, c).
```

Answer to Exercise 5A:

```
_(p) <- isAncestorOf(p, "Prince William").
```

Results:

```
Prince Charles
Princess Diana
John Spencer
Frances Kydd
Elizabeth II
Prince Phillip
Edmond Roche
Ruth Roche
Albert Spencer
Cynthia Spencer
Prince Andrew
Princess Alice
George VI
Elizabeth Bowes-Lyon
William Gill
Ruth Gill
James Roche
Frances Work
James Hamilton
Rosalind Hamilton
Charles Spencer
Margaret Baring
Prince Louis
Princess Victoria
George I of Greece
Olga Constantinovna
Claude Bowes-Lyon
Cecilia Bowes-Lyon
George V
Mary of Teck
```

Answer to Exercise 5B:

```
// Schema
Product(p), hasProductCode(p:pc) -> string(pc).
directlyContainsIn[p1, p2] = qty -> Product(p1),
    Product(p2), int(qty).
```

```
contains(p1, p2) <- directlyContainsIn[p1, p2] = _ .
contains(p1, p2) <- directlyContainsIn[p1, p3] = _,
    contains(p3, p2).
    !contains(p, p).

// Query
_(p, q) <- contains(p, q).
```

Results:

```
B, C
A, C
C, F
B, F
A, F
C, E
B, E
A, E
A, B
B, D
A, D
```

Answer to Exercise 5C:

```
isParentOf(p1, p2), isAncestorOf(p2, p3) ->
    !isParentOf(p1, p3).
```

Answer to Exercise 6A:

```
nrQueens[] = n -> int(n).
nrQueens[] = n <- agg<<n = count()>> Monarch(m),
    genderOf[m] = "F".
// nrQueens = count of female monarchs.
```

Result: 3

Answer to Exercise 6B:

```
positiveNrAccessoriesOf[p] = n -> Product(p), int(n).
positiveNrAccessoriesOf[p] = n <-
agg<<n = count()>> features(p, _).
nrAccessoriesOf[p] = 0 <- Product(p), !features(p, _).
```

```
nrAccessoriesOf[p] = positiveNrAccessoriesOf[p] <-
    features(p, _).
```

Answer to Exercise 6C:

```
Student(s), hasStudentNr(s:n) -> int(n).
Course(c), hasCourseCode(c:cc) -> string(cc).
hasCredit[c] = n -> Course(c), int(n).
passedCourse(s, c) -> Student(s), Course(c).
totalCreditOf[s] = t -> Student(s), int(t).
totalCreditOf[s] = t <-
    agg<<t = total(n)>> passedCourse(s, c),
    hasCredit[c] = n.
// The total credit of student s is the sum of
// the credit points of the courses passed by s.
```

Result:

```
/- - start of totalCreditOf facts- -\
202, 9
101, 14
\- - end of totalCreditOf facts- - /
```

Answer to Exercise 6D:

```
Claim(c), hasClaimNr(c:n) -> int(n).
Item(i), hasItemName(i:n) -> string(n).
claimItemExpense[c, i] = e -> Claim(c), Item(i),
    decimal(e).
Claim(c) -> claimItemExpense[c, _] = _.
// Each claim has an item with an expense.
totalExpenseOf[c] = t -> Claim(c), decimal(t).
totalExpenseOf[c] = t <-
    agg<<t = total(e)>> claimItemExpense[c, _] = e.
// The total expense of claim c is the sum of
// the item expenses on claim c.
nrItemsOf[c] = n -> Claim(c), int(n).
nrItemsOf[c] = n <-
    agg<<n = count()>> claimItemExpense[c, _] = _.
avgExpenseOf[c] = a -> Claim(c), decimal(a).
avgExpenseOf[c] = avgExp <-
    avgExp = totalExpenseOf[c]/nrItemsOf[c].
```

Result:

```
/- - start of avgExpenseOf facts- -\
  2, 42.575
  1, 233.733
\- - end of avgExpenseOf facts- - /
```

Diving Deeper

CONTENTS

THIS CHAPTER BUILDS ON the concepts and syntax of the LogiQL language considered in the previous chapters, introducing some more advanced features of the language and describing how programs are executed by the LogiQL engine. The first unit discusses aggregation functions for computing minima and maxima. We then identify some safety conditions to ensure that rules and queries execute in a finite time. After this, a description is given of how derivation rules are processed. Then come two units relating to the handling of changes to the EDB. The first examines how delta rules and pulse predicates may be used to make changes to the database, and the second provides a simple explanation of how transactions are supported in LogiQL. The final unit considers some further built-in operators and functions (scalar or aggregation) that can be useful. The consolidation exercise at the end gives you an opportunity to test your mastering of the new concepts and syntax considered in the chapter.

UNIT 3.1: THE max AND min FUNCTIONS

This unit discusses two additional aggregation functions, max and min, that are used to find the minimum or maximum value that satisfies a specified condition. They are applied using the same syntax that we have seen previously: If x and y are individual variables, f denotes one of the max or min functions, and Cx denotes a condition in which x is used as a variable, then the following syntax is used to assign the value of f(x) to y when the condition Cx is true:

```
agg<<y = f(x)>> Cx // y = f(x) where Cx is true
```

TABLE 3.1	IQs of Famous People
Person	**IQ**
Hillary Clinton	140
Albert Einstein	160
Bill Gates	160

As a simple example, consider Table 3.1 of proposed IQs, which we coded earlier using the following predicate declarations:

```
Person(p), hasPersonName(p:n) -> string(n).
iqOf[p] = iq -> Person(p), int(iq).
```

Using maxIQ[] to denote the maximum IQ and minIQ[] for the minimum IQ, we can use the max and min functions in aggregation rules to derive these values as follows:

```
maxIQ[] = n -> int(n).
maxIQ[] = n <- agg<<n = max(iq)>> iqOf[_] = iq.
// maxIQ equals the maximum IQ of any person.

minIQ[] = n -> int(n).
minIQ[] = n <- agg<<n = min(iq)>> iqOf[_] = iq.
// minIQ equals the minimum IQ of any person.
```

If you run the program with the data shown and then print or query the maxIQ and minIQ predicates, you will get 160 and 140, respectively.

Unlike the total function, which applies only to numeric values, the max and min functions may be used with values of any ordered datatype (e.g., where the *less than* operator ('<') is defined). For example, character strings may be ordered alphabetically using <, so we may derive the maximum (sorted last, alphabetically) person name as follows:

```
maxPersonName[] = n -> string(n).
maxPersonName[] = n <- agg<<n = max(pn)>>
    hasPersonName(_:pn).
// maxPersonName is the person name that is last
// when person names are ordered alphabetically.
```

For the data shown, querying maxPersonName returns "Hillary Clinton".

Now that maxIQ[] has been derived, we may use it to derive who are the brightest people (in the sense of having the highest IQ), as follows:

```
isBrightest(p) -> Person(p).
isBrightest(p) <- iqOf[p] = maxIQ[].
// Person p is brightest if the IQ of p is the maximum
// IQ.
```

For the data shown, printing the isBrightest predicate returns the following:

```
/- - start of isBrightest facts- -\
   Bill Gates
   Albert Einstein
\- - end of isBrightest facts- - /
```

Now consider Table 3.2, which is an extended report on IQs based on the same Web site used earlier, which adds gender details.

To include the gender facts, we extend the previous program with the following code:

```
Gender(g), hasGenderCode(g:gc) -> string(gc).
genderOf[p] = g -> Person(p), Gender(g).
genderOf[_] = g -> g = "M" ; g = "F".
Person(p) -> genderOf[p] = _ .
```

The following aggregation rule may now be used to derive the maximum IQ for each gender:

```
maxIQof[g] = n -> Gender(g), int(n).
maxIQof[g] = n <- agg<<n = max(iq)>> iqOf[p] = iq,
    genderOf[p] = g.
// maxIQof gender g is maximum IQ of people of
// gender g.
```

TABLE 3.2   Genders and IQs of Famous People

Person	Gender	IQ
Albert Einstein	M	160
Bill Gates	M	160
Dwight Eisenhower	M	122
Marilyn vos Savant	F	228
Hillary Clinton	F	140
Nicole Kidman	F	132

Note: M, male; F, female.

Note that the condition for an aggregation function may be a conjunction, as in the example above. When run with the data in the extended report, a print of the maxIQof predicate returns the following results:

```
/- - start of maxIQof facts- -\
   F, 228
   M, 160
\- - end of maxIQof facts- - /
```

The code for the complete IQ program discussed in this unit is available as IQ3.logic and the data is available as IQ3data.logic.

Argmin and Argmax

Suppose that in the above IQ example maxIQ is not yet defined and we want to compute not only the maximum IQ but also the person who has it. Would it be acceptable to include this computation in the following rule?

```
isBrightest(p) -> Person(p).
isBrightest(p) <- iqOf[p] = n, agg<<n = max(iq)>>
    iqOf[_] = iq.
```

No! The above code generates an error because of the following syntax requirement. If an aggregation function definition is used in the body of a rule, it must comprise the whole body of the rule. The aggregation function definition (of the form agg<<y = f(x)>> Cx) cannot be combined with any other formula in the body. This requirement is violated in the above rule because another conjunct (iqOf[p]=n) is included in the rule body.

When computing a maximum value, it is often desirable to determine not only the value but also the item that has that value. For example, in computing the maximum IQ value, we also wanted to know who has that value. The set of one or more instances of a function argument that returns the maximum value for that function is said to be the *argmax* of the function. For example, the set of person(s) with the highest IQ is the *argmax* of the iqOf function. Similarly, the set of one or more instances of a function argument that returns the minimum value for that function is the *argmin* of the function. Background on the use of argmax and argmin in mathematics may be found in the Wikipedia article on "Arg_max."

Intuitively, for a given function, its argmax or argmin may be computed in two steps, by first computing the maximum or minimum value, respectively, and then determining the set of item(s) associated with that maximum/minimum value. For example, above we used the max function to compute maxIQ, the maximum value returned from iqOf, and then used the isBrightest rule to derive the person(s) with that maximum IQ.

Summary of Aggregation Functions

The aggregation functions considered so far are summarized in Table 3.3.

Tip: When including aggregation function definitions in the body of a rule, ensure that nothing else is included in the rule body.

Exercise 1A: A program and data for the following expense report are shown in Table 3.4. You may also access them as the files expenses. logic and expensesData.logic. Extend the program to derive which item(s) is/are the most expensive, run the program with the data shown, and print the result:

```
// Schema
Item(i), hasItemName(i:n) -> string(n).
expenseOf[i] = e -> Item(i), decimal(e).
Item(i) -> expenseOf[i] = _.
// Each item has an expense.

// Data
+expenseOf["Travel"] = 300.50.
+expenseOf["Accommodation"] = 300.50.
+expenseOf["Meals"] = 100.20.
```

TABLE 3.3   Aggregation Functions

Aggregation Function	Result Returned
count ()	Number of instances satisfying the specified condition
total (x)	Sum of numeric x values satisfying the specified condition
max (x)	Maximum x value satisfying the specified condition
min (x)	Minimum x value satisfying the specified condition

TABLE 3.4   Travel Expenses

Item	Expense (US$)
Travel	300.50
Accommodation	300.50
Meals	100.20

TABLE 3.5   Expense Report Claims

Expense Claim	Item	Expense (US$)
1	Travel	300.50
1	Accommodation	300.50
1	Meals	100.20
2	Travel	55.05
2	Meals	30.10

Exercise 1B: The program and data for the expense claims for the report in Table 3.5 are available as the files `expenses5.logic` and `expenses5Data.logic`. Extend the program to compute, for each claim, the most expensive item(s) for that claim. Then run the program with the data supplied and print the results.

UNIT 3.2: SAFETY CONDITIONS FOR RULES AND QUERIES

As a programmer, you want to write high-quality code. This means not only that the code is correct, efficient, and well documented, but that it is robust (able to deal with a variety of inputs) and that it does not go into infinite loops. LogiQL constraints help you write robust programs, and the LogiQL compiler helps you ensure that your program does not run indefinitely. Roughly speaking, a derivation rule or query is **safe** if and only if it is guaranteed to return a finite result using a procedure that terminates in a finite time. In this unit we discuss a number of restrictions that the LogiQL compiler places on rules and queries to ensure that they are safe. If you try to compile a rule or query that violates any of these restrictions, you will get an error message.

This unit is primarily concerned with helping you avoid situations where a computation might be required to look at an infinite number of possibilities. If we have a simple predicate populated with a finite number of asserted facts, and we try to compute a subset of the facts satisfying a simple condition, then we do not run into any trouble. For example, if we have a list of people along with their IQ data and we ask for the IQ of a particular person, then we cannot get in trouble, even if the person is not in the database. The computation merely checks each of the finite number of asserted facts to produce its answer.

There are some features of LogiQL, however, that could potentially get you into trouble. This unit talks about several of them including negation, disjunction, and built-in datatypes. We begin by reviewing some of LogiQL's syntax.

Recall that an atom is the application of a predicate to a list of terms, such as variables (possibly anonymous) or literals. For example, the following are atoms:

```
Person(p)                      // p is a person.
loves(p, _)                    // p loves something.
loves(p, "Juliet")             // p loves Juliet.
loves("Romeo", "Juliet")  // Romeo loves Juliet.
```

An atom that is not in the scope of a *logical not* operator ('!') is called a *positive atom*. An atom in the scope of a *logical not* operator is called a *negated atom*. Here are some examples of negated atoms:

```
!Person(x)                     // x is not a person.
!likes(p1, p2)                 // p1 does not like p2.
!likes("Leopold Kronecker", "Georg Cantor")
// Leopold Kronecker does not like Georg Cantor.
```

Let us use the term **domain predicate** for a predicate specific to the application domain that can be populated with only a finite set of data. The facts that populate domain predicates are either explicitly asserted by the user (and hence their number is finite), or they are derived from other domain predicates using safe rules. Domain predicates are distinct from the predicates used for built-in datatypes (e.g., int, string) and predefined operations (e.g., '=', '+', '<').

Let's look at a typical rule that takes the form of a head consisting of a positive atom and the body comprising a conjunction of one or more positive or negative atoms. For example, the body of the following rule is a conjunction of two positive atoms involving a domain predicate (isParentOf), and one negative atom involving a built-in equality predicate ('=').

```
isBrotherOf(x, y) -> Person(x), Person(y).
isBrotherOf(x, y) <- isParentOf(z, x),
    isParentOf(z, y), x ! = y.
// x is a brother of y if some z is a parent of x and y
// and x is not equal to y.
```

The following safety condition provides one syntactic check to help determine whether a rule or query of this type is safe.

SC1: *Each variable appearing in the head of a rule must also appear in the rule's body. Moreover, its appearance in the body must be in a positive context, as an argument of either a domain predicate or a domain equality. In the case of a domain equality, the other operand of the equality must be either a constant expression or a domain variable that occurs in a positive context.*

The purpose of this rule is to prevent situations where a variable in the body of a rule can take on an unlimited number of values. For example, the isBrotherOf derivation rule above satisfies this safety condition because each of its head variables (x and y) can only take values that arise from the isParentOf predicate. (Note that in the next chapter we discuss two cases, derived-only predicates and head existentials, where the above condition may be safely broken.)

As a simple example of a rule that violates the above safety condition, consider the following unsafe rule:

```
isFemale(x) <- !isMale(x).      // Unsafe rule!
// x is female if x is not male.
```

This illegal rule declares that everything that is not male is female. This is far too strong a rule, as it includes anything in the application domain that is not male (e.g., houses, names, etc.). Moreover, in an infinite domain, the result could be infinite. To fix the derivation rule, we need to restrict the variable to range over the relevant domain predicate (e.g., Person or Animal). For example, the following rule satisfies SC1 because its sole head variable (x) occurs in the body as the argument of the positive domain atom Person(x):

```
isFemale(x) <- Person(x), !isMale(x).
// x is female if x is a person and not male.
```

Each of the following rules also violates SC1. Can you see why?

```
isText(x) <- string(x). // Unsafe rule!
positiveNumber(x) <- decimal(x), x > 1.0.
// Unsafe rule!
```

Although the head variable x appears in positive context in the body of the above rules, it appears only with built-in predicates, not domain predicates.

Conceptually, there are infinitely many strings and numbers, so the result is potentially infinite. Even though computer systems store strings and numbers using only a finite number of bits, for all practical purposes it would still be undesirable to deal with such a large number of possible strings or numbers.

The following two safe rules illustrate cases where a head variable does not appear in the body in a domain predicate, but it does appear in a simple equality, where the other operand is either a constant expression or a domain variable in a positive context:

```
isEven(n) <- n = 2.
uses(p, c) <- drives(p, b), b = c.
```

In the first rule, n can only take one value, the integer 2. In the second rule, p appears positively inside of the drives predicate. Although c is not inside of drives, it must be equal to b, and b is inside of drives. So c is similarly finitely bounded.

Now consider the following schema and data:

```
// Schema
Person(p), hasPersonName(p:n) -> string(n).
CarModel(cm), hasModelName(cm:n) -> string(n).
drives(p, cm) -> Person(p), CarModel(cm).
NonDriver(p) -> Person(p).
NonDriver(p) <- Person(p), !drives(p, _).
// A nondriver is a person who does not drive any car
// model.
lang:isEntity['NonDriver] = true.

// Data
+Person("Terry"), +Person("Norma"), +Person("Lee").
+drives("Terry", "Mazda").
+drives("Lee", "Ford").
```

If you run the program with the data shown, and then print the NonDriver predicate, you will obtain the correct result: Norma. The rule for NonDriver satisfies SC1 because the sole head variable (p) occurs in the body in the positive domain atom Person(p). Note that an anonymous variable (_) occurs only in a negated atom, but this does not violate the safety condition because it is not a head variable.

Now consider the following two lines from our program. On first look, the use of the anonymous variable in the `NonDriver` rule indicates that a nondriver is a person who does not drive anything (not just car models). However, given the type declaration for the `drives` predicate, the LogiQL compiler can infer that anything driven is a car model, so there is no need to state that explicitly:

```
drives(p, cm) -> Person(p), CarModel(cm).
NonDriver(p) <- Person(p), !drives(p, _).
```

LogiQL is able to handle some variants of the above that involve more complex syntax. For example, it can handle simple negated conjunctions such as the following:

```
isUnsuitable(p) <- Person(p), !(isHardworking(p),
    isIntelligent(p)).
```

> **SC2:** *Each named variable appearing in the scope of a negation within the body of a rule must also appear in a positive context in that rule body.*

In addition to conjunctions and simple negations, LogiQL allows the body of a rule to include logical disjunctions, whose main operator is *inclusive-or*. The language treats a disjunctive rule as shorthand for a set of simpler rules, each containing one of the disjuncts. In order for the original disjunctive rule to be safe, each of the simpler rules must be safe. Since each simple rule in the resulting rule set has the same head, the first safety condition above implies the following safety condition:

> **SC3:** *Each disjunct in the body of a disjunctive derivation rule must include the same selection of head variables; the only other variables allowed are anonymous variables.*

The following safe disjunctive derivation rule satisfies this restriction:

```
isParentOf(p1, p2) <- fatherOf[p2] = p1 ;
    motherOf[p2] = p1.
```

This disjunctive rule is shorthand for the following two rules, both of which are safe:

```
isParentOf(p1, p2) <- fatherOf[p2] = p1.
isParentOf(p1, p2) <- motherOf[p2] = p1.
```

The following disjunctive rule, however, violates the above restriction:

```
p(x, y) <- q(x) ; r(y). // Unsafe!
```

Notice that if you try to rewrite this rule as a pair of simpler, non-disjunctive, rules each of the resulting rules violates our original safety condition:

```
p(x, y) <- q(x). // Unsafe!
p(x, y) <- r(y). // Unsafe!
```

As another variant, consider queries. A query is essentially a derivation rule where we do not care about the name of the head predicate, because we simply want to see the result of the derivation. So the safety restrictions discussed for derivation rules also apply to queries. For example, the following query to return male persons is safe, but the query after it is unsafe:

```
_(x) <- Person(x), !isFemale(x).  // Safe query
_(x) <- !isFemale(x).             // Unsafe query!
```

There is one other, subtler, situation you need to be aware of when constructing safe and robust programs. This situation arises when you have a collection of safe rules, which, when treated as a whole, can lead to a program that never terminates.

To understand this situation, consider a set of rules. A typical rule in the set has a right-hand side that refers to other predicates. If any of these other predicates is also derived, then the computation of the original rule depends on the computation of this derivation rule. This dependency may extend to predicates mentioned in the bodies of the new rules. A problem arises if the rules are mutually recursive, that is, if the overall set of dependencies is cyclic. In particular, if there is a cycle in the dependency structure that includes either a negated atom, or an aggregation, then the LogiQL compiler cannot guarantee termination. Hence, the following safety condition applies.

SC4: *Any cyclic dependencies in a LogiQL program should not contain negated atoms or aggregations.*

Here is a program sketch illustrating a violation of this safety condition:

```
Youth(y), hasYouthName(y:n) -> string(n).
Boy(b) -> Youth(b).
Girl(g) -> Youth(g).
Boy(x) <- Youth(x), !Girl(x).
Girl(x) <- Youth(x), !Boy(x).
```

Note that Boy depends upon Girl, that Girl depends upon Boy, and that negation is involved.

Imagine now the following fact assertions:

```
+Youth("Adam").
+Girl("Eve").
+Boy("Colin").
```

When the execution engine tries to compute a gender for Adam, a problem arises. Adam is a Youth that is not (initially) a Girl, which makes Adam a Boy. However, Adam is also not (initially) a Boy, which makes Adam a Girl, violating the premise of the computation that made Adam a Boy in the first place. To avoid situations like this from causing trouble, the LogiQL compiler issues an error message. Aggregations can lead to similar problems.

Tip: When declaring rules or queries, make sure they satisfy the safety conditions discussed in this unit.

Exercise 2A: Explain what is wrong with the following program, and modify it to fix the error:

```
Light(l), hasLightNr(l:n) -> int(n).
isOn(l) -> Light(l).
isOff(l) <- !isOn(l).
```

Exercise 2B: Identify the safety violations in each of the following rules:

```
p(x, y, z) <- q(x), !r(y), z > 1.
p(x, y, z) <- q(x), r(y), s(z); q(y), r(z).
```

UNIT 3.3: DERIVATION RULE SEMANTICS

This unit provides a simplified account of how the LogiQL engine uses derivation rules to compute new facts. The intent is to give you an idea of how your program is actually executed by the LogiQL execution engine. The example that we will use is a simple ancestry graph. Because the ancestry relationship is recursive, multiple computation steps are required to complete the computation.

In the graph shown in Figure 3.1, each node denotes a person, which we identify by a single given name. An arrow from a node to a node below it

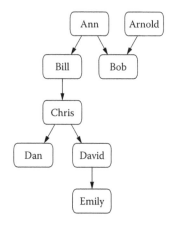

FIGURE 3.1   Parenthood example.

denotes a parenthood relationship (e.g., Ann is a parent of Bill and Bob). As our knowledge of parenthood is incomplete, some parenthood facts are missing (e.g., for most nodes, only one parent is shown).

The following code (available in ancestry.logic and ancestry-Data.logic) may be used to store these parenthood facts and derive who is an ancestor of whom. For simplicity, some ring constraints (e.g., nobody can be an ancestor of himself/herself) are omitted:

```
Person(p), hasPersonName(p:n) -> string(n).
isParentOf(p1, p2) -> Person(p1), Person(p2).
!isParentOf(p, p). // Nobody is his/her own parent.

isAncestorOf(p1, p2) <-
    isParentOf(p1, p2) ;
    isParentOf(p1, p3), isAncestorOf(p3, p2).
// p1 is an ancestor of p2 if p1 is a parent of p2 or
// p1 is a parent of some p3 who is an ancestor of p2.
```

Here are the corresponding fact assertions:

```
+isParentOf("Ann", "Bill").
+isParentOf("Ann", "Bob").
+isParentOf("Arnold", "Bob").
+isParentOf("Bill", "Chris").
+isParentOf("Chris", "Dan").
+isParentOf("Chris", "David").
+isParentOf("David", "Emily").
```

Visually, the descendants of a person node in the graph are the nodes on the path(s) starting at that person and proceeding downward. For example, the descendants of Bill are Chris, Dan, David, and Emily. Here is what you would see upon querying `isParentOf` and `isAncestorOf`.

```
isParentOf:                isAncestorOf:
    Chris, David               Chris, David
    David, Emily               Bill, David
    Bill, Chris                Ann, David
    Chris, Dan                 David, Emily
    Ann, Bill                  Chris, Emily
    Arnold, Bob                Bill, Emily
    Ann, Bob                   Ann, Emily
                               Bill, Chris
                               Ann, Chris
                               Chris, Dan
                               Bill, Dan
                               Ann, Dan
                               Ann, Bill
                               Arnold, Bob
                               Ann, Bob
```

From the seven parenthood facts, 15 ancestry facts were derived using the recursive rule for `isAncestorOf`. But how was this computation performed by the LogiQL execution engine? There are several possibilities, and the actual approach used is quite complex due to optimizations that the engine performs. We will now describe a simple bottom-up approach that approximates what the engine does. The approach iteratively applies the recursive rule to find new facts that are immediate consequences of the currently known facts until we reach a state called the **fixedpoint**, after which reapplication of the rule generates no new facts.

For convenience, the recursive rule is restated below. It can be thought of as two rules, one for each disjunct in the body, with the first rule providing the basis clause, and the second rule providing the recursive clause:

```
isAncestorOf(p1, p2) <-
    isParentOf(p1, p2) ;
    isParentOf(p1, p3), isAncestorOf(p3, p2) .
// p1 is an ancestor of p2 if p1 is a parent of p2
// or p1 is a parent of some p3 who is an ancestor
// of p2.
```

Note that in the above, `isParentOf` is an EDB predicate, and `isAncestorOf` is an IDB predicate. (Its facts are computed by the above rule.)

When the `isAncestorOf` rule is first executed, the `isParentOf` predicate is populated with seven facts, and the `isAncestorOf` predicate is empty, which we picture as shown below:

```
isParentOf:                 isAncestorOf:
    Ann, Bill
    Ann, Bob
    Arnold, Bob
    Bill, Chris
    Chris, Dan
    Chris, David
    David, Emily
```

Applying the basis clause, `isAncestorOf(p1,p2)<-isParentOf(p1,p2)` instantiates `isAncestorOf` with the seven tuples in `isParentOf`. Applying the recursive clause has no effect in this iteration because `isAncestorOf` was empty when the rule began executing. So at the end of this first iteration, the database is as shown below. The new facts added in the iteration are highlighted in *italics*:

```
isParentOf:                 isAncestorOf:
    Ann, Bill                   Ann, Bill
    Ann, Bob                    Ann, Bob
    Arnold, Bob                 Arnold, Bob
    Bill, Chris                 Bill, Chris
    Chris, Dan                  Chris, Dan
    Chris, David                Chris, David
    David, Emily                David, Emily
```

The state of the database at the end of the first iteration is the same as the state at the start of the second iteration of the rule. From here on, the basis clause can add no new facts because we already have all the parenthood tuples in `isAncestorOf`, so we need consider only the recursive clause, that is,

```
isAncestorOf(p1, p2) <- isParentOf(p1, p3),
    isAncestorOf(p3, p2).
```

We can apply this rule to the database by looking for situations where a child in the second role of the `isParentOf` predicate matches an ancestor in the first role of the `isAncestorOf` predicate. For example, Bill, child of Ann, is an ancestor of Chris, which makes Ann also an ancestor of Chris. These matches are depicted with matching numbers in the following display:

```
isParentOf:                    isAncestorOf:
   Ann, Bill  (1)                  Ann, Bill
   Ann, Bob                        Ann, Bob
   Arnold, Bob                     Arnold, Bob
   Bill, Chris  (2)            (1) Bill, Chris
   Chris, Dan                  (2) Chris, Dan
   Chris, David  (3)           (2) Chris, David
   David, Emily                (3) David, Emily
```

As a result, the state of the database immediately after this second iteration is as shown below (just the facts added in this second iteration are highlighted):

```
isParentOf:                    isAncestorOf:
   Ann, Bill                       Ann, Bill
   Ann, Bob                        Ann, Bob
   Arnold, Bob                     Arnold, Bob
   Bill, Chris                     Bill, Chris
   Chris, Dan                      Chris, Dan
   Chris, David                    Chris, David
   David, Emily                    David, Emily
                                   Ann, Chris
                                   Bill, Dan
                                   Bill, David
                                   Chris, Emily
```

In the third iteration, applying the recursive clause to the database results in three new ancestry facts being derived by matching a child in a parenthood fact with an ancestor in one of the new ancestry facts, as shown below by the matching numbers:

```
isParentOf:                    isAncestorOf:
   Ann, Bill  (1)                  Ann, Bill
   Ann, Bob                        Ann, Bob
   Arnold, Bob                     Arnold, Bob
   Bill, Chris  (2)                Bill, Chris
   Chris, Dan                      Chris, Dan
   Chris, David                    Chris, David
   David, Emily                    David, Emily
                                   Ann, Chris
```

```
(1) Bill, Dan
(1) Bill, David
(2) Chris, Emily
```

As a result, the state of the database immediately after this third iteration is as shown below (just the new facts added in this third iteration are highlighted):

isParentOf:
   Ann, Bill
   Ann, Bob
   Arnold, Bob
   Bill, Chris
   Chris, Dan
   Chris, David
   David, Emily

isAncestorOf:
   Ann, Bill
   Ann, Bob
   Arnold, Bob
   Bill, Chris
   Chris, Dan
   Chris, David
   David, Emily
   Ann, Chris
   Bill, Dan
   Bill, David
   Chris, Emily
   Ann, Dan
   Ann, David
   Bill, Emily

In the fourth iteration, applying the recursive clause to this database results in one new ancestry fact being derived by matching a child in a parenthood fact with an ancestor in one of the new ancestry facts, as pictured below by the matching number:

isParentOf:
   Ann, Bill (1)
   Ann, Bob
   Arnold, Bob
   Bill, Chris
   Chris, Dan
   Chris, David
   David, Emily

isAncestorOf:
   Ann, Bill
   Ann, Bob
   Arnold, Bob
   Bill, Chris
   Chris, Dan
   Chris, David
   David, Emily
   Ann, Chris
   Bill, Dan
   Bill, David
   Chris, Emily
   Ann, Dan
   Ann, David
(1) Bill, Emily

The state of the database immediately after this fourth iteration is as shown below:

```
isParentOf:              isAncestorOf:
    Ann, Bill                Ann, Bill
    Ann, Bob                 Ann, Bob
    Arnold, Bob              Arnold, Bob
    Bill, Chris              Bill, Chris
    Chris, Dan               Chris, Dan
    Chris, David             Chris, David
    David, Emily             David, Emily
                             Ann, Chris
                             Bill, Dan
                             Bill, David
                             Chris, Emily
                             Ann, Dan
                             Ann, David
                             Bill, Emily
                             Ann, Emily
```

Looking at these parenthood and ancestry facts, we see that the new fact added will not lead to any more ancestry facts because Ann does not appear as a child in a parenthood fact. Hence, if we applied a fifth iteration of the derivation rule, the database state would remain the same as it was in the previous state. This means that we have reached a fixedpoint of the computation, so the derivation rule has now been fully evaluated. If you look at the final population above, you will see that the 15 ancestry facts are precisely those that were obtained earlier by running the program. (The order in which the facts are displayed is irrelevant.)

Note that in the above description, the numbers in the second column were always adjacent to facts that had been added on the previous iteration. Hence, there was no need to recompute facts that had been already derived. By default, derivation rules without delta modifiers are evaluated incrementally by the LogiQL execution engine. This means that each subsequent execution, rather than recomputing from scratch, is driven by the changes made in the previous execution. This approach can significantly reduce the amount of effort required to complete the execution.

Exercise 3: In the map shown in Figure 3.2, nodes denote airports (BNE = Brisbane, KUL = Kuala Lumpur, BKK = Bangkok, LHR = London Heathrow, HEL = Helsinki), and the arrows denote direct (nonstop) flights.

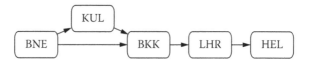

FIGURE 3.2   Direct flights between airports.

The following code is used to store direct flights and derive flight connections (direct or indirect):

```
Airport(a), hasAirportCode(a:c) -> string(c).
hasDirectFlightTo(a1, a2) -> Airport(a1), Airport(a2).
hasFlightTo(a1, a2) <- Airport(a1), Airport(a2).
hasFlightTo(a1, a2) <-
    hasDirectFlightTo(a1, a2) ;
    hasDirectFlightTo(a1, a3), hasFlightTo(a3, a2).
```

Using the iterative algorithm discussed above for evaluating recursive rules, specify the population of the predicate hasFlightTo at the end of each iteration.

UNIT 3.4: DELTA RULES AND PULSE PREDICATES

Previously, we have used delta modifiers to indicate that facts should be added to a database. In this unit we discuss other uses of delta modifiers in derivation rules to express changes to the database. Such uses are called **delta rules** to distinguish them from the **IDB rules** we have seen previously. We also discuss how delta rules can be used to record transitory changes or events using a particular kind of predicate called a **pulse predicate**.

For the examples in this unit, let us assume that persons may be identified simply by their names. Countries may be identified by their two-letter ISO country codes (e.g., "IE" for Ireland, "DE" for Germany, and "US" for the United States). The following program may now be used to record facts about persons and countries, as well as who is president of what country. The final constraint ensures that each person is president of at most one country at any given time:

```
Person(p), hasPersonName(p:pn) -> string(pn).
Country(c), hasCountryCode(c:cc) -> string(cc).
presidentOf[c] = p -> Country(c), Person(p).
presidentOf[c1] = p, presidentOf[c2] = p -> c1 = c2.
```

Delta Modifiers

Suppose the following assertions were made in 2008 to declare who was then president of Germany, Ireland, and the United States:

```
+presidentOf["IE"] = "Mary McAleese".
+presidentOf["DE"] = "Angela Merkel".
+presidentOf["US"] = "George W. Bush".
```

Recall that the delta modifier "+" indicates that the fact is to be added to the database. After adding the facts, the result of querying the presidentOf predicate is as follows:

```
US, George W. Bush
DE, Angela Merkel
IE, Mary McAleese
```

The compiler treats the above fact assertions as shorthand for longer assertions that populate not just the presidentOf predicate but also Person, Country, and their refmode predicates. For example, here is the result of querying Person:

```
George W. Bush
Angela Merkel
Mary McAleese
```

In January 2009, Barack Obama replaced George W. Bush to become the president of the United States, and in June 2010, Christian Wulff became the new president of Germany. As of May 2011, Mary McAleese was still president of Ireland. Suppose we now want to update the database accordingly. One way to do this would be to delete the presidency facts that no longer hold and then add the new presidency facts. To delete a fact, the delete modifier, denoted with a hyphen ('-'), is used. For example, the following code is used to retract two of the previous presidency facts:

```
-presidentOf["DE"] = "Angela Merkel".
-presidentOf["US"] = "George W. Bush".
```

Just as you may think of the "+" modifier as a plus sign for adding a fact, you may think of the "-" modifier as a minus sign for subtracting a fact. Querying presidentOf now displays just one fact:

```
IE, Mary McAleese
```

Note that deleting the presidency facts did not delete the `Person` or `Country` facts. For example, querying `Person` still returns the following:

```
George W. Bush
Angela Merkel
Mary McAleese
```

If you want to delete George W. Bush and Angela Merkel as instances of `Person` from the database, you will need to do that explicitly. For example, you may delete the two former presidents of Germany and the United States using the following fact retractions:

```
-Person("Angela Merkel").
-Person("George W. Bush").
```

A similar comment applies for countries. However, as we intend to add the new presidents for these countries, there is no point in deleting them. The two new president facts may be added as follows:

```
+presidentOf["US"] = "Barack Obama".
+presidentOf["DE"] = "Christian Wulff".
```

Querying `presidentOf` after these upserts displays the following:

```
US, Barack Obama
DE, Christian Wulff
IE, Mary McAleese
```

Note that combining the two deletions and two insertions just discussed in the same workspace update will not work. This is because LogiQL checks the validity of each delta rule individually with respect to the state of the workspace before any changes are made. That is, you cannot count on the order in which your assertions and retractions occur in your update. For example, placing the fact retractions before the assertions does not ensure that the deletions are done first. In the next unit, we will see how you can use LogiQL transactions to control the order in which workspace updates occur.

As a single-step way to replace a current value in a functional predicate with a new value, you may use the **upsert modifier**, depicted as a circumflex ('^'):

```
^presidentOf["US"] = "Barack Obama".
^presidentOf["DE"] = "Christian Wulff".
```

As the name *upsert* suggests, it may be used to either update or insert. If the key of the functional predicate already exists (e.g., "US" or "DE"), an update is performed, as in this example. Otherwise an insertion is made. Executing the above two upserts causes the `presidentOf` predicate to hold the following values:

```
US, Barack Obama
DE, Christian Wulff
IE, Mary McAleese
```

If you had not explicitly deleted George W. Bush and Angela Merkel as instances of `Person` from the database, then querying `Person` would now display:

```
George W. Bush
Angela Merkel
Mary McAleese
Christian Wulff
Barack Obama
```

Delta Logic

In the above, delta modifiers were used to unconditionally assert changes to a database. However, we might wish to make such changes conditionally; that is, we might want to use derivation rules for making such changes. In fact, delta modifiers may be used to qualify atoms in derivation rules, yielding what are called *delta rules*. In a delta rule, all head atoms must have delta modifiers. A delta rule such as `+p(x)<-+q(x)` can be interpreted as follows: If the database experiences an addition to the q predicate with argument x, then add a p fact with the same argument. Delta rules along with the assertions, retractions, and upserts described above together comprise a program's **delta logic**.

Pulse Predicates

One specialized form of delta rule makes use of pulse predicates. A pulse predicate is useful for asserting short-lived facts. Examples of such facts are those computed for the purpose of producing query results. Another use is for expressing one-time events, such as user interactions with the database through a graphical user interface (GUI).

A pulse predicate behaves as follows: For any given execution of the LogiQL engine, the predicate starts empty. A program may assert facts to the predicate, but retractions are not allowed. Moreover, any assertions made during the execution are discarded at the end of the execution.

You have already seen one use of (unnamed) pulse predicates in the heads of queries. For example, consider the following query to list the presidents of countries other than the United States:

```
_(p) <- presidentOf[c] = p, !hasCountryCode(c:"US").
```

For the population given above, the query result is

```
Mary McAleese
Christian Wulff
```

Once this result is computed and displayed to the user, it is thrown away and is unavailable for later queries. That is, this **anonymous predicate**, denoted by the underscore, is a pulse predicate that temporarily holds a set of derived facts. If you want to persist these facts, you should give the predicate a name.

The other common use of pulse predicates is for capturing one-time events such as the pressing of a button on a screen form. As a simplified example, suppose that employee details are entered via instances of a Web form like the one shown in Figure 3.3. Forms like this may be created using GUI frameworks that support the creation and management of user interfaces. In this example, the framework includes a predefined entity type called *form* whose instances in a workspace are in one-to-one correspondence with instances of the form in the Web browser.

Components in the form have associated predicates in the workspace that hold their values. The above sample form includes three textfield components to capture the employee number, family name, and a given name of an employee. The form also includes a button (labeled "OK") that the user presses to submit the details on the form to the LogiQL execution engine. The schema for the form could be declared as follows. (Note the

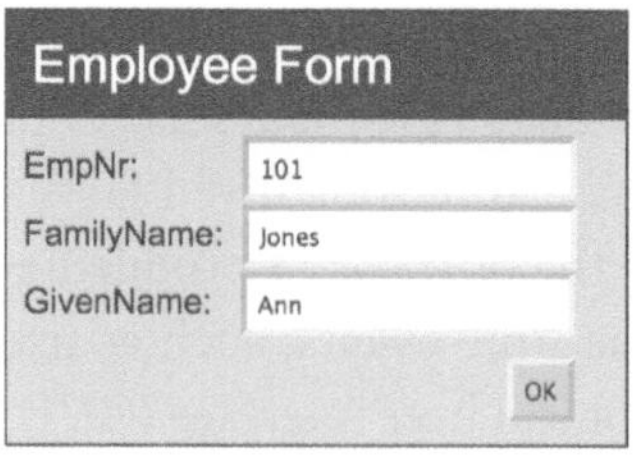

FIGURE 3.3   Screen form with submit button.

use of the colon [':'] after textField in the following code is similar to its earlier use with datetime and string. That is, it provides a name for a group of related predicates.)

```
textField:empNrOn[f] = n -> Form(f), int(n).
textField:familyNameOn[f] = fn -> Form(f), string(fn).
textField:givenNameOn[f] = gn -> Form(f), string(gn).
okButtonIsPressedOn(f) -> Form(f).
lang:isPulse[`okButtonIsPressedOn] = true.
```

Notice the use of the metapredicate lang:isPulse for declaring that okButtonIsPressedOn is a pulse predicate. The name of the pulse predicate is enclosed in brackets and preceded by the grave accent character ('`').

When the user enters the details and submits the form instance by pressing the OK button, we want to store the relevant data in the database. The part of the database schema used to capture the data could be declared as follows:

```
Employee(e), hasEmpNr(e:n) -> int(n).
familyNameOf[e] = fn -> Employee(e), string(fn).
givenNameOf[e] = gn -> Employee(e), string(gn).
```

The following code may now be used to copy the data entered on the form instance to the database in response to the pressing of the OK button:

```
+Employee(e), +hasEmpNr(e:n), +familyNameOf[e] = fn,
    +givenNameOf[e] = gn <-
    +okButtonIsPressedOn(f),
    +textField:empNrOn[f] = n,
    +textField:familyNameOn[f] = fn,
    +textField:givenNameOn[f] = gn.
```

The third line above references okButtonIsPressedOn. When the user enters the data and presses the OK button, the GUI framework asserts this fact, thereby invoking the execution of the rule to insert the relevant facts into the predicates appearing in the head of the rule. Once this is done, the pulse predicate okButtonIsPressedOn is effectively reset to be empty again.

The above example illustrates a common use of pulse predicates to implement event–action rules. In this case, the event is the pressing of a button, and the action is the updating of the database.

Tip: While insert (+) and delete (–) may be performed on any predicate (functional or non-functional), upsert (^) is allowed only on functional predicates.

Tip: Avoid applying retractions and insertions to the same functional predicate during the same update of a workspace. You cannot count on the order in which these actions are applied.

Tip: Indicate your intent to treat a predicate as a pulse predicate with the `lang:isPulse` metapredicate.

Tip: Pulse predicates may only be asserted and not retracted.

Exercise 4A: The following program (accessible as `Ex4a.logic`) is used to record the name and gender of various people, as well as what languages they speak and what languages they are fluent in. The last constraint is a subset constraint to ensure that people are fluent only in languages that they speak:

```
// Declarations
Person(p), hasPersonName(p:pn) -> string(pn).
Gender(g), hasGenderCode(g:gc) -> string(gc).
Language(lang), hasLanguageName(lang:ln) ->
     string(ln).
genderOf[p] = g -> Person(p), Gender(g).
speaks(p, lang) -> Person(p), Language(lang).
isFluentIn(p, lang) -> Person(p), Language(lang).
// Constraints
Person(p) -> genderOf[p] = _.
hasGenderCode(_:gc) -> gc = "M" ; gc = "F".
isFluentIn(p, lang) -> speaks(p, lang).
```

Compile this program and then populate it with the following data (accessible as `Ex4aData.logic`):

```
+genderOf["Norma"] = "F", +genderOf["Terry"] = "F".
+speaks("Norma", "English"), +speaks("Norma",
     "French").
+isFluentIn("Norma", "English").
+speaks("Terry", "English"), +speaks("Terry",
     "Japanese"),
```

```
+speaks("Terry", "Latin").
+isFluentIn("Terry", "English"), +isFluentIn("Terry",
    "Latin").
```

Query the predicate genderOf. It is now discovered that Terry is actually male, not female. Write delta logic to update Terry's gender accordingly, and again query the predicate genderOf to check that your update worked. The answer is in Ex4aAnswer.logic.

Exercise 4B: Now add a delta rule to the above program to ensure that if a fact is added that a person is fluent in a language, another fact will automatically be added indicating that person speaks that language. Test your code by then executing the following update (accessible as Ex4bData. logic), and querying the speaks predicate. *Hint*: Remember, you will need to have delta-modified atoms in both the head and body of the delta rule. The answer is in Ex4bAnswer.logic.

```
+isFluentIn("Norma", "Spanish").
```

Exercise 4C: Would it be possible to use the following IDB rule instead of the delta rule in the answer to the previous question? That is, what happens if a predicate contains both asserted and derived facts? Alter the above declarations and constraints to implement this approach. Edit the fact assertions to remove references to the speaks predicate. Print the speaks predicate and compare it to the previous results. Explain what has happened.

```
speaks(p, lang) <- isFluentIn(p, lang).
```

UNIT 3.5: TRANSACTION PROCESSING

We saw in the previous unit that during the execution of a rule, you could not count on the order in which changes are made to a workspace. Sometimes, of course, you want to control this order, and database designers have invented the idea of a **transaction** to organize such changes. In this unit we introduce transactions and describe at a high level their effect on a workspace. We then briefly look under the covers of transactions, to better understand how they are processed. Finally, we present a syntactic device, called a **stage suffix**, that gives you fine-grained control over how your data are handled during transaction processing.

Transactions

LogiQL workspaces contain both data (the facts we have asserted or derived) and program code (both what we have written and system code). Figure 3.4 provides a simplified, high-level picture of the activities that take place during the lifetime of a given workspace.

First we create the workspace. The newly created workspace contains a standard set of system predicates, but as yet has none of our program code. Once created, we can access and update the workspace through a series of transactions that either succeed or fail. Successful transactions update the workspace, whereas failing transactions leave the workspace in the state it was in before the transaction commenced.

In order to understand more thoroughly how transactions are processed, you need to be aware of two concepts: blocks and stages. A *block* is a unit of LogiQL code, typically originating in a file with a name ending in `.logic`. We have seen how, with the `lb` command, we can **install** code blocks into workspaces. In particular, we used either the `addblock` or the `exec` option to enter code. When the `addblock` option is used, the code becomes an active block, which means that it is automatically evaluated during every transaction. Conversely, the `exec` option can be used to request that a block should be evaluated exactly once. Such a block is a called an *inactive block*. More generally, your program has the ability to control the activated/deactivated status of installed blocks.

The LogiQL execution engine divides evaluation into two stages as illustrated in Figure 3.5.

The **initial stage** is used to process queries and provide on-demand evaluation of inactive blocks, such as you request with the `exec` option to `lb`. The updates requested by these blocks are tentatively accepted into the EDB, ignoring constraints.

In the **final stage**, first installed delta rules residing in active blocks are evaluated and checked against constraints. If no constraints are violated, the IDB rules in active blocks (previously installed or included in the transaction) are evaluated and checked against the constraints. If no constraints are violated during the execution of a transaction, the transaction is **committed**, and the tentative data updates are applied to the workspace. Otherwise, the transaction is **aborted** and the workspace is *rolled back* to its previous state (the state it was in just prior to the beginning of the transaction). In this sense, transactions are *atomic*, since either the whole of a transaction is accepted or none of it is.

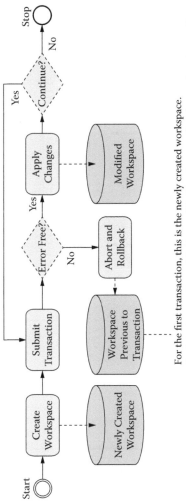

For the first transaction, this is the newly created workspace.
For later transactions, it is the modified workspace after the previous transaction.

FIGURE 3.4 Workspace activity flow.

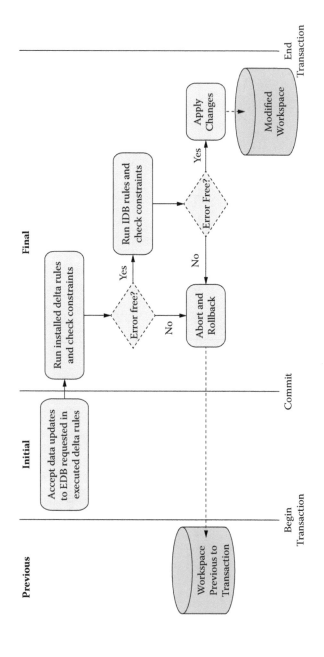

FIGURE 3.5 Transaction evaluation process.

We can continue this process with further transactions that install blocks of code or execute data updates until we are finished. At any moment of time between transactions, we are guaranteed that the state of the workspace represents the cumulative effect of applying all previous transactions, in the order in which they were committed.

Transaction Processing Example

To illustrate how transactions are processed, we will examine an example from the monarchy domain. To understand how the example is handled, an additional concept, **delta predicates,**[*] needs to be introduced. When you declare a new predicate, the LogiQL compiler automatically provides for you two additional predicates, called delta predicates, one each for recording the *requests* for adding and deleting data to the declared predicate. At the start of the initial stage of each transaction, these delta predicates are set to be empty. If the transaction includes a request to execute a data update against the declared predicate, the update is tentatively recorded into the associated delta predicates during the transaction's initial stage. During the final stage, the delta predicates are used to effect the actual changes made to the declared predicate.

For example, consider the code found in the file `transactions.lb`:

```
create --unique
addblock '// First transaction: install schema;
    see below'
exec '// Second transaction: assert data; see below'
echo "Printing Monarch"
print Monarch
echo "Querying isFemale:"
print isFemale
close --destroy
```

The file's first transaction installs the following code to declare the predicates and constraints:

```
Monarch(m), hasMonarchName(m:n) -> string(n).
Gender(g), hasGenderCode(g:gc) -> string(gc).
genderOf[m] = g -> Monarch(m), Gender(g).
Monarch(m) -> genderOf[m] = _.
hasGenderCode(_:gc) -> gc = "M" ; gc = "F".
```

---

[*] Delta predicates should not be confused with delta rules, delta modifiers, or delta logic discussed earlier.

```
isFemale(m) -> Monarch(m).
isMale(m) -> Monarch(m).
isFemale(m) <- genderOf[m] = "F".
isMale(m) <- genderOf[m] = "M".
```

At the end of the first transaction, these predicates and their associated delta predicates are not populated, as shown in Table 3.6 for the genderOf and isFemale predicates. The same is true for the other predicates, but for simplicity let's follow the state of just the predicates shown here, focusing on the second transaction. Note that in this and subsequent tables in this section, the two delta predicates for these predicates are given names with prepended plus and minus signs. For example, the delta predicates for genderOf are labeled +genderOf and −genderOf.

The second transaction in the file includes the following 12 requests to insert data into the genderOf predicate:

```
+genderOf["Anne"] = "F".
+genderOf["George I"] = "M".
+genderOf["George II"] = "M".
+genderOf["George III"] = "M".
+genderOf["George IV"] = "M".
+genderOf["William IV"] = "M".
+genderOf["Victoria"] = "F".
+genderOf["Edward VII"] = "M".
+genderOf["George V"] = "M".
+genderOf["Edward VIII"] = "M".
+genderOf["George VI"] = "M".
+genderOf["Elizabeth II"] = "F".
```

At the beginning of the initial stage of the second transaction, the workspace is the same as at the end of the first transaction, with these predicates all empty. By the end of the initial stage of the second transaction, the data updates for genderOf are tentatively accepted, which we may picture as shown in Table 3.7. Though not shown here, the system also manages the implied updates for Monarch, and so on.

TABLE 3.6   Initial Predicates and Delta Predicates

genderOf	+genderOf	−genderOf	isFemale	+isFemale	−isFemale

TABLE 3.7   Predicates during the Initial Stage of the Second Transaction

genderOf	+genderOf	-genderOf
("Anne", "F")	("Anne", "F")	
("George I", "M")	("George I", "M")	
("George II", "M")	("George II", "M")	
("George III", "M")	("George III", "M")	
("George IV", "M")	("George IV", "M")	
("William IV", "M")	("William IV", "M")	
("Victoria", "F")	("Victoria", "F")	
("Edward VII", "M")	("Edward VII", "M")	
("George V", "M")	("George V", "M")	
("Edward VIII", "M")	("Edward VIII", "M")	
("George VI", "M")	("George VI", "M")	
("Elizabeth II", "F")	("Elizabeth II", "F")	

TABLE 3.8   isFemale Predicates during the Final Stage of the Second Transaction

isFemale	+isFemale	-isFemale
"Anne"	"Anne"	
"Victoria"	"Victoria"	
"Elizabeth II"	"Elizabeth II"	

TABLE 3.9   isMale Predicates during the Final Stage of the Second Transaction

isMale	+isMale	-isMale
"George I"	"George I"	
"George II"	"George II"	
"George III"	"George III"	
"George IV"	"George IV"	
"William IV"	"William IV"	
"Edward VII"	"Edward VII"	
"George V"	"George V"	
"Edward VIII"	"Edward VIII"	
"George VI"	"George VI"	

In the final stage of the second transaction the system evaluates the derivation rules, which in this case are isMale and isFemale. These predicates, which were empty at the start of the final stage, are now populated as in Tables 3.8 and 3.9.

At this point, the constraints are checked, and none are violated, so the transaction succeeds and changes to the program's predicates (not their associated delta predicates) are applied to the workspace.

The third transaction in the file interrogates the workspace about the `Monarch` and `isFemale` predicates:

```
echo "Printing Monarch"
print Monarch
echo "Querying isFemale:"
print isFemale
```

At the start of the third transaction, the `genderOf`, `isFemale`, and `isMale` predicates are populated as shown above, but their associated delta predicates are reset to be empty. The other predicates (`Monarch`, `hasMonarchName`, `Gender`, `hasGenderCode`) are also populated accordingly. The output produced by querying `isFemale` comprises the three `isFemale` facts in the above table.

Suppose that we now try to submit the following, fourth transaction. This would be a mistake, because Anne is already recorded to be a female, but let's see how the system would process this transaction:

```
echo "Adding a contradictory fact"
lb exec '+genderOf["Anne"] = "M".'
```

At the start of the initial phase, `genderOf` is populated as previously and its delta predicates are empty. At the end of the initial stage, the `genderOf` predicate has one more entry, and its delta predicates are populated as shown in Table 3.10.

TABLE 3.10   genderOf Predicates in the Initial Phase of Transaction Four

genderOf	+genderOf	–genderOf
("Anne", "F")	("Anne", "M")	
("George I", "M")		
("George II", "M")		
("George III", "M")		
("George IV", "M")		
("William IV", "M")		
("Victoria", "F")		
("Edward VII", "M")		
("George V", "M")		
("Edward VIII", "M")		
("George VI", "M")		
("Elizabeth II", "F")		
("Anne", "M")		

When execution moves into the final stage and constraints are checked, it is found that the functional nature of the genderOf predicate is violated because Anne is now assigned two genders. Therefore, the fourth transaction is aborted. The information recorded in the program predicates and their delta predicates is sufficient for the system to determine the state of the workspace before the transaction began, simply by reversing the proposed changes. The workspace is now rolled back to that previous state.

Stage Suffixes

LogiQL provides some syntax that enables you to explicitly denote the various transaction stages of a predicate by qualifying its name with a **stage suffix**. For a specific predicate p, p@previous (or p@prev) references the population of the predicate as it was immediately before the start of the transaction, p@initial (or p@init) references the population of the predicate at the end of the initial stage, and p@final references the predicate in the final stage. In the absence of a suffix, the @final suffix is assumed.

A stage suffix can be valuable when you are trying to assess the impact of a new fact. Say, for example, that you wish to detect when someone's net worth has gone down. Here is a simple illustration:

```
Person(p), hasPersonName(p:n) -> string(n).
netWorth[p] = n -> Person(p), int(n).
status[] = s -> string(s).
^status[] = "Trouble City!!" <-
    ^netWorth[p] = _, netWorth[p] < netWorth@prev[p].
```

Each person has a name and a net worth. We also keep track of status with a unary predictate named status. If there is a change to the netWorth predicate such that the new net worth is less than the old, then we want the status to change. Let's assume that the workspace state is initialized as follows:

```
+status[] = "Okay".
+netWorth["Bob"] = 30.
```

Now, if we assert a new netWorth fact for Bob with a reduced value, we should expect the status predicate to change, which it does:

```
^netWorth["Bob"] = 10.
```

This approach for evaluating impact could be applied to audit changes coming into an application through a GUI. Alternatively, the above delta rule could be converted into a constraint such that the negative change in net worth would cause the containing transaction to abort.

Summary

The processing of transactions is complex. Here is a summary of how the LogiQL execution engine handles them:

1. Computation is broken down into a sequence of atomic transactions, each of which is self-contained and leaves the workspace in a consistent state.

2. The processing of a transaction comprises two stages, initial and final. The initial stage begins with the same database state as the final state of the previous transaction.

3. The initial stage is responsible for recording fact assertion and retraction requests in delta predicates and handling queries. At the beginning of this stage, delta predicates are empty. If no delta rules exist, then this stage has no effect, other than producing the results of any queries.

4. The final stage is responsible for processing derivation rules of active blocks.

5. Derivation rule processing is made up of a series of steps, each of which may update the delta predicates. Steps continue until a fixed-point is reached.

6. At the end of the final stage, declared predicates are updated from delta predicates.

Tip: The `@previous` suffix may be used in the body of a rule but not in the rule head.

Exercise 5A: Alter the net worth example above to change the `status` message for any change (positive or negative) to an individual's net worth of more than 100%. Such a change might indicate that a data entry error had been made. *Hint:* You may wish to make use of the absolute value `abs` numeric function.

Exercise 5B: The following code (accessible as `grandparent.lb`) includes transactions to add program code for recording parenthood facts and deriving grandparenthood facts, to execute some sample data, and to issue relevant queries:

```
create --unique
addblock '
  Person(p), hasPersonName(p:pn) -> string(pn).
  isParentOf(p1, p2) -> Person(p1), Person(p2).
  isGrandparentOf(p1, p2) -> Person(p1), Person(p2).
  isGrandparentOf(p1, p2) <- isParentOf(p1, p3),
    isParentOf(p3, p2).
'
exec '
  +isParentOf("Ivor", "Norma").
  +isParentOf("Norma", "Linda").
  +isParentOf("Norma", "David").
  +isParentOf("Terry", "Linda").
  +isParentOf("Terry", "David").
  +isParentOf("David", "Emily").
  +isParentOf("David", "Sam").
'
echo "Querying isParentOf:"
print isParentOf

echo "Querying isGrandparentOf:"
print isGrandparentOf

close --destroy
```

The program code is fine so long as our knowledge of relevant parenthood facts is complete. However, suppose instead that our knowledge is incomplete, and that we want to record a known grandparenthood fact even if we do not know the parenthood facts from which it could be derived. For example, we might know that Ivor is a grandparent of Graham without knowing which of Ivor's children is a parent of Graham. In this case, we need to assert the fact that Ivor is a grandparent of Graham directly, such as by executing the following fact assertion:

```
+isGrandparentOf("Ivor", "Graham").
```

Explain what happens if you make this assertion. How would you fix the problem?

Exercise 5C: One way we might try to deal with this situation is to use delta rules instead of IDB rules to automatically add grandparent facts when relevant parenthood facts are added. Copy the file `grandparent2.lb` and modify its program code to test this new approach. For this question, you may ignore any need to provide delta rules to manage fact retractions.

Exercise 5D: An alternative approach to that of Exercise 5C for dealing with incomplete knowledge of parenthood is to use an EDB predicate `asserted_isGrandparentOf` for asserting grandparenthood facts, an IDB rule `derived_isGrandparentOf` to derive grandparenthood from parenthood, and then use the disjunction of these two rules to derive `isGrandparentOf`, whose population is the union of the facts in the other two predicates. Copy the file `grandparent4.lb` and modify its program code to test this new approach.

UNIT 3.6: ADDITIONAL BUILT-IN OPERATORS AND FUNCTIONS

Previous units have discussed various arithmetic operators (e.g., +, −, *), comparison operators (e.g., <, >, =, < =, > =, ! =), logical operators (e.g., !, comma, ;), scalar functions (e.g., `divide`), and aggregation functions (`count`, `total`, `min`, and `max`). This unit discusses some further built-in operators and functions that you may find useful.

Arithmetic

LogiQL includes a variety of mathematical functions for manipulating numeric data. As a simple example, the following program (`maths.lb`) uses `abs` to compute the absolute value of a number and `sqrt` to compute the square root. Note that while the `absoluteValueOfTemp` predicate contains two facts, the `sqrtOfTemp` has only one. Can you think why this might be?

One of the two temperatures is negative; its square root is undefined:

```
create --unique
addblock ws '
  Temperature(t), hasCelsiusValue(t:cv) -> float(cv).
  absoluteValueOfTemp[t] = at -> Temperature(t),
    float(at).
  absoluteValueOfTemp[t] = at <-
    hasCelsiusValue(t:cv), abs[cv] = at.
```

```
  sqrtOfTemp[t] = st -> Temperature(t), float(st).
  sqrtOfTemp[t] = st <- hasCelsiusValue(t:cv),
    sqrt[cv] = st.
'
exec '
  +Temperature(25f), +Temperature(-20f).
'
echo "Querying absoluteValueOfTemp:"
print absoluteValueOfTemp
echo "Querying sqrtOfTemp:"
print sqrtOfTemp
close --destroy
```

The query output is as follows

```
Querying absoluteValueOfTemp:
25, 25
-20, 20
Querying sqrtOfTemp:
25, 5
```

String Manipulation

LogiQL also includes operators and functions that are handy for string manipulation. For example, you can use the *string concatenation* operator ('+') to paste together two string arguments. The following program (concatNames.lb) uses + to derive the full name of employees by concatenating their given name to a space character and then to their family name:

```
create --unique
addblock '
  Employee(e), hasEmpNr(e:n) -> int(n).
  givenNameOf[e] = gn -> Employee(e), string(gn).
  familyNameOf[e] = fn -> Employee(e), string(fn).
  Employee(e) -> givenNameOf[e] = _,
    familyNameOf[e] = _.
  fullNameOf[e] = pn -> Employee(e), string(pn).
  fullNameOf[e] = pn <- pn = givenNameOf[e] + " " +
    familyNameOf[e].
'
exec '
  +givenNameOf[1] = "John", +familyNameOf[1] =
    "Smith".
```

122 ■ LogiQL: A Query Language for Smart Databases

```
   +givenNameOf[2] = "Eve", +familyNameOf[2] = "Jones".
 '
echo "Querying fullNameOf:"
print fullNameOf
close --destroy
```

When run, the query output is as follows:

```
Querying fullNameOf:
  2, Eve Jones
  1, John Smith
```

The string:like function is handy for string pattern matching. It has the form string:like(str,pattern) where str is a
string expression and pattern is a quoted string that may include the
wildcard characters (' _ '), meaning any single character, and ('%'),
meaning any sequence of zero or more characters. The following program (courses.lb) demonstrates its use for finding the computer science courses (those courses whose course codes begin with "CS") and
the entry-level courses (those courses whose course codes have "1" as
their third character):

```
create --unique
addblock '
  Course(c), hasCourseCode(c:cc) -> string(cc).
  ComputerScienceCourse(c) -> Course(c).
  ComputerScienceCourse(c) <- hasCourseCode(c:cc),
    string:like(cc, "CS%").
  EntryLevelCourse(c) -> Course(c).
  EntryLevelCourse(c) <- hasCourseCode(c:cc),
    string:like(cc, "__1%").
 '
exec '
  +Course("CS100"), +Course("CS200"),
    +Course("MA100").
 '
echo "Querying ComputerScienceCourse:"
print ComputerScienceCourse
echo "Querying EntryLevelCourse:"
print EntryLevelCourse
close --destroy
```

The query results are as shown below:

```
Querying ComputerScienceCourse:
  CS100
  CS200
Querying EntryLevelCourse:
  CS100
  MA100
```

To illustrate some other string manipulation functions, consider the problem of extracting a person's last name when given the person's full name. To make things interesting, the last name may contain several parts, such as "Marilyn vos Savant." Here is how you might accomplish this task, assuming the full names are given to you in the predicate hasPersonName:

```
lastName(s) -> string(s).
// Extract the last name from a Person's full name
lastName(s) <-
    hasPersonName(_:n),
    f = string:length[string:split[n, " ", 0]],
    // Length of first name
    t = string:length[n], // Length of full name
    string:substring[n, f + 1, t - f - 1] = s.
```

Several other string functions are used to perform the extraction. The string:length function is used twice, once to compute the length of the first name and once to compute the total name length. Its argument is the string whose length is desired.

The person's first name is extracted using string:split to break out that part of the full name from its start up until the first space character. Its arguments are the string to be split, the character upon which the split is based, and an index into the resulting segment. The result of string:split is the specified segment of the argument string.

Finally, the last name is extracted using the string:substring function, beginning with the character after the first space and continuing for a number of characters computed by subtracting off the length of the first name.

We will see this code segment again in the next section when used to demonstrate some of the LogiQL functions for ordering data.

TABLE 3.11   IQs of Famous People

Person	IQ
Albert Einstein	160
Bill Gates	160
Dwight Eisenhower	122
Marilyn vos Savant	228
Hillary Clinton	140
Nicole Kidman	132

Aggregation Functions for Ordering

We now discuss two more aggregate functions useful for ordering the facts in a predicate. Recall Table 3.11 of IQs considered in Unit 2.6.

Suppose we want to see these values in ascending order. Such *ranking* queries assign numeric ranks to the objects in an ordered list. For this to be possible, the values must be based on one of LogiQL's primitive types, for which an ordering relation (e.g., less than, <) is ensured.

LogiQL provides two aggregation functions for ranking the facts in a predicate based on the values of one of the predicate's roles: seq generates ranks suitable for indexing into the facts according to the order of the role's values; list enables navigation through the predicate's facts from least to greatest in single steps. As with other aggregation functions, the data that is being ranked can be computed using a condition.

Aggregation rules using the seq function take the following form, where xValueOfRank is replaced by the name of a ranking predicate that associates each rank r with the x value that has that rank. Cx is the condition that provides the data being ranked.

```
xValueOfRank[r] = x <- seq<<r = x>> Cx.
// For each rank r, return the x value of that rank ,
// where Cx is true.
```

Note that since the ranking predicate is populated with a set of facts as a result of this derivation, the seq "function" is not a function in the usual sense (where a single value is returned), unlike the aggregation functions considered previously (count, total, min, and max).

As an example of the use of seq, the following program (taken from IQtop.lb) returns the IQ values from the data in the table in ascending order. First, the Person entity is declared along with a property predicate providing IQs for Persons and corresponding constraints:

```
Person(p), hasPersonName(p:pn) -> string(pn).
iqOf[p] = iq -> Person(p), int(iq).
iqOf[_] = iq -> iq < = 250. // Each IQ is at most 250.
Person(p) -> iqOf[p] = _.   // Each person has an IQ.
```

We can populate these predicates with data as follows:

```
+iqOf["Albert Einstein"] = 160.
+iqOf["Bill Gates"] = 160.
+iqOf["Dwight Eisenhower"] = 122.
+iqOf["Marilyn vos Savant"] = 228.
+iqOf["Hillary Clinton"] = 140.
+iqOf["Nicole Kidman"] = 132.
```

If we query iqOf, the following results are as shown here:

```
Nicole Kidman, 132
Hillary Clinton, 140
Marilyn vos Savant, 228
Dwight Eisenhower, 122
Bill Gates, 160
Albert Einstein, 160
```

Now, we would like to see the IQ scores in ascending order. To do this, we first separate out the IQ scores into a separate predicate, iqScores.:

```
iqScores(iq) -> int(iq).
iqScores(iq) <- iqOf[_] = iq.
```

We will now use seq to compute the rankings and store them into the iqOfRank functional predicate:

```
iqOfRank[i] = iq -> int(i), int(iq).
iqOfRank[i] = iq <- seq<<i = iq>> iqScores(iq).
```

A query of iqOfRank then produces the following results:

```
0, 122
1, 132
```

```
2, 140
3, 160
4, 228
```

There are several ways that we can extend this simple example to deal with more interesting situations. Say we wanted to know not only what the order of scores was, but which people had those scores. This is easily done by adding another predicate, orderedIQof that combines the ordering information with the original iqOf predicate:

```
orderedIQof [p, iq] = i -> Person (p), int (iq), int (i).
orderedIQof [p, iq] = i <- iqOfRank [i] = iq,
    iqOf [p] = iq.
```

The result of printing orderedIQof is the following. Note, in particular, that the actual rankings are specified in the third column and not in the order in which the facts are displayed:

```
"Nicole Kidman" 132 1
"Marilyn vos Savant" 228 4
"Bill Gates"        160 3
"Albert Einstein" 160 3
"Hillary Clinton" 140 2
"Dwight Eisenhower" 122 0
```

Other variants you might find useful are to sort the facts in descending order or to see just a subset of the values. Here are the addition rules you would use to compute just the largest three values of IQ data:

```
numberOfIQs [] = n -> int (n).
numberOfIQs [] = n <- agg<<n = count ()>>
    iqOfRank [i] = _.
// The number of different IQ values.

topThreeIQvalues [i] = iq -> int (i), int (iq).
topThreeIQvalues [i] = iq <- numberOfIQs [] = n ,
    iqOfRank [j] = iq, j > = n - 3, i = n - j.
// The top three IQ values.
```

Another way of accessing ordered data is using a linked list. The list aggregation supports this approach by populating two predicates. The first, unary, predicate holds the head of the list, and the second, binary, predicate holds pairs containing an element of the list as well as the next element.

Here is an example of using `list` to compute a report of IQs in alphabetical order of the person's last name. The example also illustrates use of some of the `string` functions described the earlier in this unit.

The example reuses the same basic schema as the previous example:

```
Person(p), hasPersonName(p:s) -> string(s).
iqOf[p] = iq -> Person(p), int(iq).
iqOf[_] = iq -> iq < = 250. // Each IQ is at most 250.
Person(p) -> iqOf[p] = _.  // Each person has an IQ.
```

It also reuses the rule we developed in the last section for extracting last names:

```
lastName(s) -> string(s).
// Extract the last name from a Person's full name
lastName(s) <- hasPersonName(_:n),
    f = string:length[string:split[n, " ", 0]],
    // Length of first name
    t = string:length[n], // Length of full name
    string:substring[n, f + 1, t - f - 1] = s.
```

Once the last names have been extracted, they can be ordered using the `list` aggregation function:

```
head(n) -> string(n).
// The head node of a linked list.
next(n1, n2) -> string(n1), string(n2).
// The source-target links in a linked list.
head(n1), next(n1, n2) <- list<< >> lastName(n1).
// Store the sorted last names into a linked list.
```

In the above snippet, two predicates (`head` and `next`) are defined. `Head` holds the alphabetically least last name, and `next` holds pairs of last names such that the first element of the pair is immediately succeeded, in alphabetical order, but the second `list<< >>` is used to simultaneously populate these two predicates, taking its source data from the `lastName` predicate.

To produce the output report, the nodes of the linked list are visited in order, each providing the data to produce a segment of the report. The segments are pasted together to produce the final report:

```
visit[n] = s -> string(n), string(s).
// Traverse the linked list
```

```
visit[n1] = s <- next(n1, n2), s = format[n1] +
    visit[n2].
// Format head and recursively concatenate to the
// remainder
visit[n] = s <- next(_, n), !next(n, _), s = "".
// The last element must be in the list and not have a
// successor
```

Traversal is accomplished with the visit function, which, for each node visited, recursively computes the report for the contents of the linked list from that node on, concatenating the results using the string addition function ('+').

Visit makes use of a utility function, format, for retrieving the IQ information associated with a given last name and formatting the results. Note that for this example, format assumes that last names are unique. Also, format makes use of the string:like and string:convert predicates described above:

```
format[n] = s -> string(n), string(s).
// Format one line of the output report
format[n] = s <- lastName(n), hasPersonName(p:fn),
    string:like(fn, "% " + n),
    iqOf[p] = iq,
    int:string:convert[iq] = siq,
    s = fn + ": " + siq + "\n".
```

It remains only to start off the visiting process on the first element of the linked list:

```
report(s) -> string(s).
report(s) <- head(n), s = visit[n].
```

The code for this example can be found in the file IQlist.lb.

Tip: Become familiar with the full set of available built-in functions so you can make use of them when the occasion arises.

Exercise 6A: Table 3.12 (available in USCitiesData.logic) stores name and population data for various major cities in the United States. Population figures are for the year 2010. Although cities are primarily

TABLE 3.12   City Populations

City Number	City Name	State Name	Population
1	Cleveland	Ohio	396,815
2	Columbus	Georgia	189,885
3	Columbus	Ohio	787,033
4	New York	New York	8,175,133
5	Portland	Maine	66,194
6	Portland	Oregon	583,776
7	Los Angeles	California	3,792,621
8	San Diego	California	1,307,402
9	San Jose	California	945,942
...	...	...	...

identified here by a city number, the combination of their city name and state is also unique.

A basic schema for this example is shown below:

```
City(c), hasCityNr(c:n) -> int(n).
State(s), hasStateName(s:sn) -> string(sn).
cityNameOf[c] = cn -> City(c), string(cn).
stateOf[c] = s -> City(c), State(s).
populationOf[c] = n -> City(c), int(n).
City(c) -> cityNameOf[c] = _, stateOf[c] = _,
    populationOf[c] = _.
cityNameOf[c1] = cn, stateOf[c1] = s,
    cityNameOf[c2] = cn, stateOf[c2] = s ->
    c1 = c2.
// Each combination of city name and state refers to
// at most one city.
```

The file USCities.lb includes this schema and extends it with the following declaration and rule stub, as well as the relevant data and query:

```
extendedCitynameOf[c] = ecn -> City(c), string(ecn).
extendedCitynameOf[c] = ecn <-
// *** supply the rule body here
```

The derived predicate extendedCitynameOf is intended to store the extended name of cities, where an extended name consists of the city name and its state name, separated by a comma. Complete the derivation rule for this predicate and run the program. The expected output from querying this predicate is as follows:

```
Querying extendedCitynameOf:
  9, San Jose, California
  8, San Diego, California
  7, Los Angeles, California
  6, Portland, Oregon
  5, Portland, Maine
  4, New York, New York
  3, Columbus, Ohio
  2, Columbus, Georgia
  1, Cleveland, Ohio
```

Exercise 6B: Add a derivation rule to your solution for endsInLand(cn) to determine each city name cn that ends in the characters "land".

Exercise 6C: Add code to your solution to derive the names of the cities having the three highest populations.

UNIT 3.7: CONSOLIDATION EXERCISE 3

This exercise gives you a chance to test how well you have mastered the new topics covered in this chapter. As much of the content of this chapter has been theoretical and wide ranging, the questions are less integrated than in previous chapters.

Q1: Explain what is wrong with the following code, and revise it to fix the problem. The answer can be found in the file Q1Answer.logic.

```
Customer(c), customerNR(c:n) -> int(n).
Vehicle(v), vehicleVIN(v:n) -> string(n).
Accessory(a), accessorySerialNr(a:n) -> string(n).
purchased(c, v) -> Customer(c), Vehicle(v).
purchased(c, a) -> Customer(c), Accessory(a).
```

Q2: Given the following declarations, correctly classify each of the rules below as safe or unsafe. The answers can be found in the file Q2Answer. logic:

```
Person(p), hasPersonName(p:pn) -> string(pn).
Book(b), hasISBN(b:isbn) -> string(isbn).
```

```
smokes(p) -> Person(p).
isPairedWith(p1, p2) -> Person(p1), Person(p2).
isOdd(n) -> int(n).
isLonely(p) -> Person(p).
```

(a) `isNonSmoker(p) <- !smokes(p).`

(b) `isOdd(n) <- n = 1 ; n = 3.`

(c) `isPairedWith(p1, p2) <- smokes(p1) ; smokes(p2).`

(d) `isPairedWith(p1, p2) <- smokes(p1), smokes(p2).`

(e) `isPairedWith(p1, p2) <- !smokes(p1), !smokes(p2).`

(f) `isLonely(p) <- Person(p), !isPairedWith(p, _).`

Q3: The file `ages.lb` includes transactions to add the following schema, execute the data shown, and query the `ageOf` and `isaSenior` predicates:

```
// Schema
Person(p), hasPersonName(p:pn) -> string(pn).
ageOf[p] = n -> Person(p), int(n).
isaSenior(p) -> Person(p).
```

```
// Data
+ageOf["Elvis"] = 42.
+ageOf["Terry"] = 64.
+ageOf["Walter"] = 90.
+ageOf["Xena"] = 90.
+isaSenior("Walter").
+isaSenior("Xena").
+isaSenior("Methuselah").
```

(a) Write a delta rule to insert the fact that a person is a senior if a fact is added or updated that the person has an age of at least 65. Test this by writing other delta rules to insert the fact that Bertie is aged 97 and to update Terry's age to 65.

(b) Starting again from `ages.lb`, write delta rules to retract the fact that a person is a senior if that person's age is changed to a value below 65 or that person's age is deleted. Test this by updating Xena's age to 30 and deleting Walter's age fact.

(c) Starting again from `ages.lb`, write a delta rule that will delete the fact that a person exists if the fact for that person's age is deleted. Test this by writing another delta rule to delete Xena's age fact.

(d) Suppose that instead of the delta rule approach used in (b), the following derivation rule is used: `isaSenior(p)<-ageOf(p)> = 65`. Discuss the advantages and disadvantages of this alternative approach.

The answers can be found in the file `Q3Answer.logic`.

Q4: Devise a rule for computing the number of descendants of a British monarch. You can make use of the schema provided in `foo.lb` and the parenthood information in `bar.lb`. *Hint:* You will need to combine aggregation and recursion. Normally LogiQL does not allow this because of the danger of infinite loops. However, you can instruct the compiler to allow you to do this by adding the following metarule to your code:

```
lang:compiler:disableWarning:AGGREGATE_RECURSION[]
    = true.
```

Of course, you should be careful when doing this that your code is, in fact, guaranteed to terminate. An answer can be found in `Q4Answer.logic`.

Q5: The table presented in Exercise 3.6.5 was used to illustrate aggregation functions for ordering data, stores name and population data for various major cities in the United States. The files `USCities5.logic` and `USCitiesData.logic` contain the schema and city population data describing it that are used in the next several exercises. We wish to produce a report describing the population of each city. Here is an appropriate predicate declaration:

```
populationStatementOf[c] = psc -> City(c), string(psc).
```

Provide an IDB rule to populate this predicate. *Hint:* The built-in type conversion predicate `int:string:convert[n]=s` converts the value of the integer expression n to a character string s. Your output should look like the following:

```
Querying populationStatementOf:
9, The population of San Jose, California = 945942
8, The population of San Diego, California = 1307402
7, The population of Los Angeles, California = 3792621
6, The population of Portland, Oregon = 583776
```

```
5, The population of Portland, Maine = 66194
4, The population of New York, New York = 8175133
3, The population of Columbus, Ohio = 787033
2, The population of Columbus, Georgia = 189885
1, The population of Cleveland, Ohio = 396815
```

The answer can be found in the file Q5Answer.logic.

Q6: Use the max and min aggregation functions to extend the program in USCities5.logic to derive the following: **(a)** the highest population; **(b)** the lowest population; **(c)** the extended name of the city/cities with the highest population; **(d)** for each state, the name of the city with the highest population for that state (based on the data supplied). The answers are provided in the file Q6Answer.logic.

Q7: Extend the file USCities5.lb with code to derive the extended name of the city with the seventh highest population (assuming no ties in the population figures). The answer is provided in the file Q7Answer.logic.

Q8: Consider the following three rules, in which a given baseball player has a batting average expressed in the property predicate hasAverage. Also, players are considered *heavy hitters* if their batting averages are greater than 0.300.

(a) Installed derivation rule:

```
heavyHitter(p) <- playerHasAverage[p] > .300.
```

(b) Installed delta rule:

```
+heavyHitter(b) <- +playerHasAverage[b] > .300.
```

(c) Executed delta rule:

```
+heavyHitter(b) <- playerHasAverage[b] > .300.
```

Provide a comment for each rule describing its behavior. *Hint:* Each of the three has a different behavior. The answer can be found in the file Q8Answer.logic.

ANSWERS TO EXERCISES

Answer to Exercise 1A:

```
Item(i), hasItemName(i:n) -> string(n).
expenseOf[i] = e -> Item(i), decimal(e).
Item(i) -> expenseOf[i] = _.
// Each item has an expense.

maxExpense[] = n -> decimal(n).
maxExpense[] = n <- agg<<n = max(e)>>
    expenseOf[_] = e.
// The maximum expense is the largest expense.

isMostExpensive(i) -> Item(i).
isMostExpensive(i) <- expenseOf[i] = maxExpense[].
// Item is most expensive if it has the greatest
// expense.
```

Result:

```
/- - start of isMostExpensive facts- -\
 Accommodation
 Travel
\- - end of isMostExpensive facts- - /
```

Answer to Exercise 1B:

```
Claim(c), hasClaimNr(c:n) -> int(n).
Item(i), hasItemName(i:n) -> string(n).
claimItemExpense[c, i] = e -> Claim(c), Item(i),
    decimal(e).
Claim(c) -> claimItemExpense[c, _] = _.
// Each claim has an item with an expense.

maxExpenseOf[c] = n -> Claim(c), decimal(n).
maxExpenseOf[c] = n <- agg<<n = max(e)>>
  claimItemExpense[c, _] = e.
// The maximum expense of claim c is the
// the greatest single expense amount on claim c.

hasMostExpensiveItem(c, i) -> Claim(c), Item(i).
hasMostExpensiveItem(c, i) <- claimItemExpense[c, i] =
    maxExpenseOf[c].
// Claim c has most expensive item i if
// the expense of item i is the max expense on
    claim c.
```

Result:

```
/- - start of hasMostExpensiveItem facts- -\
   2, Travel
   1, Travel
   1, Accommodation
\- - end of hasMostExpensiveItem facts- - /
```

Answer to Exercise 2A:

The derivation rule for isOff is unsafe because its head variable does not occur in a positive context in the rule body. To fix the rule, modify it as shown:

```
isOff(l) <- Light(l), !isOn(l).
// A light is off it is a light that is not on.
```

Answer to Exercise 2B:

```
p(x, y, z) <- q(x), !r(y), z > 1.
```

The head variable y does not appear in a positive context in the body. The head variable z does not appear in a positive context of a domain predicate in the body:

```
p(x, y, z) <- q(x), r(y), s(z) ; q(y), r(z).
```

The second disjunct includes only two of the three head variables.

Note that the *and* operator has priority over the *or* operator, so the above disjunctive rule is equivalent to the following:

```
p(x, y, z) <- (q(x), r(y), s(z)) ; (q(y), r(z)).
```

Answer to Exercise 3:

```
hasFlightTo (Iteration 1):
BNE, KUL
BNE, BKK
KUL, BKK
BKK, LHR
LHR, HEL

hasFlightTo (Iteration 2):
BNE, KUL
BNE, BKK
```

```
KUL, BKK
BKK, LHR
LHR, HEL

hasFlightTo (Iteration 3):
BNE, KUL
BNE, BKK
KUL, BKK
BKK, LHR
LHR, HEL
BNE, LHR
KUL, LHR
BKK, HEL
```

Answer to Exercise 4A:

The update may be done in a single step: thus,

```
^genderOf["Terry"] = "M".
```

Consider the alternative of first executing this retraction:

```
-genderOf["Terry"] = "F".
```

and later executing this assertion:

```
+genderOf["Terry"] = "M".
```

What goes wrong if you try this approach? *Answer*: During the period between the retraction and the assertion, "Terry" will not have an associated Gender. This violates the first constraint, that all Persons have Genders.

Answer to Exercise 4B:

```
+speaks(p, lang) <- +isFluentIn(p, lang).
```

After asserting that Norma is fluent in Spanish, a query of speaks displays the following:

```
Terry, English
Norma, English
Terry, Latin
Terry, Japanese
```

```
Norma, French
Norma, Spanish
```

Answer to Exercise 4C:

Results of first query:

```
Terry, English
Norma, English
Terry, Latin
Terry, Japanese
Norma, French
```

Result of second query:

```
Terry, English
Norma, English
Terry, Latin
```

A predicate in LogiQL can either be an IDB predicate or an EDB predicate, but not both. Note that in the IDB version two facts have disappeared.

In the next unit, we discuss how to write a *cascading* delta rule for speaks to deal with retractions, while still preserving the subset constraint from fluency to speaking.

Answer to Exercise 5A:

The additional rule is shown below. A file to test the program with relevant updates is accessible as netWorth.lb:

```
^status[] = "Big Changes Happening!!" <-
^netWorth[p] = _,
  abs[netWorth[p] - netWorth@prev[p] /
      netWorth@prev[p]] >= 2.
```

Answer to Exercise 5B:

isGrandparentOf is an IDB predicate; trying to directly assert a fact into it, which is an EDB operation, raises an exception. That is, a predicate cannot be part of both the IDB and the EDB.

One way to get around this limitation is to break the grandparent relation into two parts, one for the IDB and one for the EDB:

```
isGrandparentOfIDB(p1, p2) -> Person(p1), Person(p2).
isGrandparentOfIDB(p1, p2) <- isParentOf(p1, p3),
    isParentOf(p3, p2).
```

```
isGrandparentOfEDB(p1, p2) -> Person(p1), Person(p2).
isGrandparentOfIDB(p1, p2) <-
    isGrandparentOfEDB(p1, p2).
```

You can then add the new fact into the EDB predicate as follows:

```
+isGrandparentOfEDB("Ivor", "Graham").
```

During the initial stage of the transaction, the isGrandparentOfEDB fact is added. Then, during the final stage, the second isGrandparentOfIDB rule fires, adding the new fact into the IDB predicate.

Answer to Exercise 5C:

The delta rules to deal with assertions are shown below. A file to test the program with relevant updates is accessible as grandparent3.lb:

```
+isGrandparentOf(p1, p2) <- +isParentOf(p1, p3),
    isParentOf(p3, p2).
+isGrandparentOf(p1, p2) <- isParentOf(p1, p3),
    +isParentOf(p3, p2).
```

Note: If you wish grandparenthood facts to be deleted when parenthood facts that imply them are deleted, delta rules to cater for such fact retractions are also needed. As the answer to the next question shows, use of IDB rules is typically preferable to writing sets of delta rules for such a case, since the maintenance of data updates is then managed for you automatically.

Answer to Exercise 5D:

The program including IDB rules is shown below. A file to test the program with relevant updates is accessible as grandparent5.lb:

```
Person(p), hasPersonName(p:pn) -> string(pn).
isParentOf(p1, p2) -> Person(p1), Person(p2).
asserted_isGrandparentOf(p1, p2) -> Person(p1),
    Person(p2).
derived_isGrandparentOf(p1, p2) -> Person(p1),
    Person(p2).
derived_isGrandparentOf(p1, p2) <-
isParentOf(p1, p3), isParentOf(p3, p2).
isGrandparentOf(p1, p2) -> Person(p1), Person(p2).
    isGrandparentOf(p1, p2) <-
```

```
    asserted_isGrandparentOf (p1, p2) ;
    derived_isGrandparentOf (p1, p2).
```

Answer to Exercise 6A:

```
extendedCitynameOf [c] = ecn -> City(c), string(ecn).
extendedCitynameOf [c] = ecn <- stateOf [c] = s,
    hasStateName (s:sn),
    ecn = cityNameOf [c] + ", " + sn.
```

The full program is accessible as USCities2.lb.

Answer to Exercise 6B:

```
endsInLand (cn) <- cityNameOf [_] = cn,
    string:like (cn, "%land").
```

The relevant output is shown below. The full program is accessible as USCities3.lb:

```
Querying citynames ending in 'land':
  Cleveland
  Portland
```

Answer to Exercise 6C:

```
population(i) -> int(i).
population(i) <- populationOf [_] = i.

populationOfRank [i] = pop -> int(i), int(pop).
populationOfRank [i] = pop <- seq<<i = pop>>
    population(pop).

numberOfCities [] = n -> int(n).
numberOfCities [] = n <- agg<<n = count()>> City(_).

threeMostPopulatedCities [i] = s -> int(i), string(s).
threeMostPopulatedCities [i] = s <-
    n = numberOfCities [],
    j > = n - 3,
    i = n - j,
    populationOfRank [j] = pop,
    populationOf [p] = pop,
    cityNameOf [p] = s.
```

The relevant output is shown below. The full program is accessible as USCities4.lb.

```
Querying threeMostPopulatedCities:
   1 "New York"
   2 "Los Angeles"
   3 "San Diego".
```

Advanced Aspects

CONTENTS

IF YOU HAVE COMPLETED the first three chapters of this book, you should feel comfortable programming in LogiQL. In this chapter, you will learn about some other aspects of the language useful for specialized purposes. The first unit illustrates the power and scope of the language by describing how to use LogiQL to implement some features of imperative programming languages. Some additional constraints are presented in the second unit. The third unit introduces an advanced technique, called *derived entities*, useful in situations where your knowledge of a particular entity comes from its properties. Although most of the examples you have seen in this book are relatively small, LogiQL can be used to develop industrial-scale applications. With this in mind, Unit 4 describes some techniques you can use for structuring large programs. The last unit presents three topics (derived-only views, hierarchical syntax, and file predicates) that do not warrant a unit of their own, but that can nevertheless be quite useful in certain circumstances. Finally, the chapter ends with a consolidation exercise giving you an opportunity to practice the skills you have learned in the chapter.

UNIT 4.1: EMULATING IMPERATIVE PROGRAMMING CONSTRUCTS

Imperative programming languages like Java include various control structures for carrying out tasks in a procedural rather than declarative fashion. These include alternation or selection constructs for choosing one action from various alternatives (e.g., **if-then, if-then-else,** and **case/switch** statements) and iteration constructs for looping through some code either a specified number of times or while/until some condition applies (e.g., **for** and **while** statements). In this unit we discuss how to emulate these structures in LogiQL.

To help explain some of the techniques, we use *flowcharts* to provide simple diagrams of their control flows. The non-programming example shown in Figure 4.1 is a flowchart for the following procedure: *if you are tired, then go to sleep.* Here a diamond shape depicts a decision box for some condition, and a rectangular shape depicts a command box for some instructions. The condition indicated in the decision box corresponds to a proposition (e.g., you are tired), so it is either true or false but not both. Flowlines with arrowheads direct the control flow from one step to the next, and the flow-annotations "T" and "F" indicate which way to move when the condition is true or false, respectively. The command box includes one or more sentences, each of which expresses a command, instruction, or action (e.g., go to sleep) to be carried out.

Figure 4.2 generalizes this example, using *c* to denote the condition and *s* to denote the programming statement to be carried out. In an imperative language like Java, this is called an **if** statement. In imperative programming, the term *statement* is used to indicate an instruction rather than a proposition, so is somewhat misleading, since in ordinary usage statements express propositions.

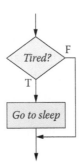

FIGURE 4.1   Nighttime flowchart.

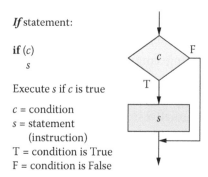

If statement:

if (*c*)

   s

Execute *s* if *c* is true

c = condition
s = statement
   (instruction)
T = condition is True
F = condition is False

FIGURE 4.2   Flowchart for *if* statement.

LogiQL is a declarative language, so its statements or formulas are used to declare propositions rather than instructions. For example, the following derivation rule declares that *if p1 is male and is a sibling of p2 then p1 is a brother of p2*:

```
isBrotherOf(p1, p2) <- isMale(p1), isSiblingOf(p1, p2).
```

The left arrow "<-" denotes the propositional operator **if**. You may take this to be the case even for delta rules. For example, the following delta rule may be read propositionally as follows: *if it is added that p1 is male and it is added that p1 is a sibling of p2, then it is added that p1 is a brother of p2*. If you were instead to read the "+" in the rule head as "add" rather than "it is added that," then the rule head would effectively correspond to a command rather than a proposition:

```
+isBrotherOf(p1, p2) <- +isMale(p1),
    +isSiblingOf(p1, p2).
```

If Statements

In imperative programming languages, the **if-then-else** statement has the semantics shown in the Figure 4.3 flowchart. If the condition *c* is true, execute statement s_1; otherwise, execute statement s_2. As a non-programming example, the following instruction fits this pattern: *if you are tired then go to bed, else go for a walk.*

In everyday life, we often encounter statements of the form *if p then q else r*, where *p*, *q*, and *r* all denote propositions. For example: *if you score at least half the total points on the exam, then you pass, else you fail.*

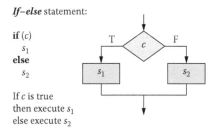

If–else statement:

if (c)
  s_1
else
  s_2

If c is true
then execute s_1
else execute s_2

FIGURE 4.3   Flowchart for *if-else* statement.

TABLE 4.1   Student Names

Student Number	Given Name	Family Name	Full Name
101	John	Smith	John Smith
102	Ann	Jones	Ann Jones
103		Ah	Ah
104	John	Smith	John Smith
...	...	...	...

LogiQL does not support this construct directly, so we instead emulate it using a pair of rules as shown below:

Construct	LogiQL	
if p **then** q	`q <- p.`	`// q if p.`
else r	`r <- !p.`	`// r if not p.`

As a simple example, consider Table 4.1 about students at a university. Students are identified by their student number. All students have a family name. Although most students have a given name, it is possible for some students to have no given name. (Although rare, this can be the case, especially for international students.)

Our task is to write a rule to derive the full names of students from their given name (if any) and family name. In cases like this, it often helps to first write down the syntax of the required term. The notation we use is Extended Backus-Naur Form (EBNF), which is described in Appendix C. For now, we use "::=" to denote "is defined as" and append a question mark "?" to an item that is optional. Here, the parentheses delimit a list composed of a given name followed by a space character:

```
FullName ::= (GivenName " ")? FamilyName.
```

So a full name optionally starts with a given name followed by a space character, and must end with a family name. Using "+" as the string concatenation operator, it is natural to phrase this rule informally in terms of an **if-the-else** statement; thus,

```
if the student has a given name
  then the fullname is the given name + " " + the
    family name
  else the fullname is the family name.
```

Replacing the **if-then-else** pattern by two **if** rules as discussed above, we may now code the task in LogiQL:

```
// Schema
Student(s), hasStudentNr(s:n) -> int(n).
givenNameOf[s] = gn -> Student(s), string(gn).
familyNameOf[s] = fn -> Student(s), string(fn).
fullNameOf[s] = gn -> Student(s), string(gn).
fullNameOf[s] = gn + " " + familyNameOf[s] <-
givenNameOf[s] = gn.
fullNameOf[s] = familyNameOf[s] <- !givenNameOf[s] = _.
// If student s has the givenName gn
// then the fullName of s is gn + " " + the
// familyName of s
// else the fullName of s is the familyName of s.

// Data
+givenNameOf[101] = "John",
    +familyNameOf[101] = "Smith".
+givenNameOf[102] = "Ann", +familyNameOf[102] = "Jones".
+familyNameOf[103] = "Ah".
+givenNameOf[104] = "John",
    +familyNameOf[104] = "Smith".
```

Querying the predicate `fullNameOf` yields the following result. The program and data are available in the files `FullName1.logic` and `FullName1Data.logic`, respectively:

```
104, John Smith
103, Ah
102, Ann Jones
101, John Smith
```

Now let's extend the example to also record a student's second given name, if any. Table 4.2 includes a sample population.

TABLE 4.2   Student Names and Numbers

Student Number	Given Name 1	Given Name 2	Family Name	Full Name
101	John	Thomas	Smith	John Thomas Smith
102	Ann	Linda	Jones	Ann Linda Jones
103			Ah	Ah
104	John		Smith	John Smith
...	...		...	...

The syntax for full names of students may now be set out as follows:

```
FullName ::= (GivenName1 " " (GivenName2 " ")?)?
    FamilyName.
```

The derivation rule for full names could now be stated informally as the following nested **if-then-else** statement:

```
if the student has givenname1
   then if the student has givenname
      then fullname is givenname1 + " " + givenname2 +
      " " + family name
      then fullname is givenname1 + " " + family name
else fullname is the family name.
```

Note that the family name is appended in each of the three alternatives. To avoid such repetition, it is better to split the task into two parts: Derive the list of given names (if any), and then append the full name. One way to code this is as follows:

```
// Schema
Student(s), hasStudentNr(s:n) -> int(n).
givenName1Of[s] = gn -> Student(s), string(gn).
givenName2Of[s] = gn -> Student(s), string(gn).
familyNameOf[s] = fn -> Student(s), string(fn).
givenName2Of[s] = _ -> givenName1Of[s] = _.
// If s has a 2nd given name then s has a first
// givenName.
givenNamesOf[s] = gn1 -> Student(s), string(gn1).
givenNamesOf[s] = gn1 + " " + gn2 + " " <-
    givenName1Of[s] = gn1, givenName2Of[s] = gn2.
givenNamesOf[s] = gn1 + " " <-
```

```
      givenName1Of[s] = gn1, !givenName2Of[s] = _.
fullNameOf[s] = gns -> Student(s), string(gns).
fullNameOf[s] = gns + familyNameOf[s] <-
      givenNamesOf[s] = gns.
fullNameOf[s] = familyNameOf[s] <- !givenNamesOf[s] = _.

// Data
+givenName1Of[101] = "John",
      +givenName2Of[101] = "Thomas",
+familyNameOf[101] = "Smith".
+givenName1Of[102] = "Ann",
      +givenName2Of[102] = "Linda",
+familyNameOf[102] = "Jones".
+familyNameOf[103] = "Ah".
+givenName1Of[104] = "John",
      +familyNameOf[104] = "Smith".
```

Querying the predicate fullNameOf yields the following result. The program and data are available in the files FullName2.logic and FullName2Data.logic:

```
104, John Smith
103, Ah
102, Ann Linda Jones
101, John Thomas Smith
```

Switch Statement

As a generalization of the **if-then-else** statement, most imperative programming languages provide a **switch** statement (or **case** statement) for choosing one of many options based on the value of some expression. A flowchart for this statement is shown in Figure 4.4, along with the basic statement syntax used in Java (typically a **break** statement is included after each case option to exit immediately if that option is executed). In the case where the expression e evaluates to the value v_1, statement s_1 is executed. If e evaluates to v_2, then s_2 is executed, and so on. If e evaluates to none of the values $v_1 \ldots v_n$, then the default statement s_{n+1} is executed.

As a simple example, consider the report shown in Table 4.3 about prices of expensive items for a store chain. Customers may pay an annual membership fee to enroll as members of a discount program at one of three levels (bronze, silver, gold). The base price for an item is the price to non-members.

Switch statement:

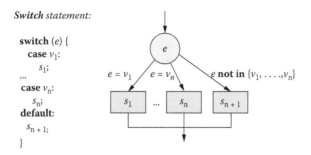

```
switch (e) {
    case v₁:
        s₁;
    ...
    case vₙ:
        sₙ;
    default:
        sₙ₊₁;
}
```

FIGURE 4.4   Flowchart for the *switch* statement.

TABLE 4.3   Discount Program Data

Item Code	Base Price (US$)	Bronze-Level Price (US$)	Silver-Level Price (US$)	Gold-Level Price (US$)
A1	100.00	95.00	90.00	80.00
B2	200.00	195.00	180.00	160.00
C3	100.00	95.00	90.00	80.00
D4	100.90	95.90	90.90	80.90

The rule for determining prices for members at various levels may be specified in pseudocode as follows, using a simpler cases syntax, ":=" for assignment, and assuming prices are in U.S. dollars (US$). The `floor` function truncates a number to remove any digits after the decimal point, for example, `floor(80.72)` `=` `80`:

```
cases for memberLevel
  bronze: price : = basePrice - 5.0
  silver: price : = floor(basePrice * 0.9)
  gold: price : = floor(basePrice * 0.8)
else price : = basePrice
```

Algorithms like this may be easily emulated in LogiQL using multiple rules, one for each case option. The following program and data show one way to compute the report. The function `floor[n]` is a built-in function in LogiQL. Note that the three rules have a head but no body and that argument of the `floor` function is itself a function expression:

```
// Schema
Item(i), hasItemCode(i:c) -> string(c).
Item(i) -> basePriceOf[i] = _.
Level(l), hasLevelName(l:n) -> string(n).
```

```
priceOf_AtLevel_[i, l] = n -> Item(i), Level(l),
    float(n).
basePriceOf[i] = p -> Item(i), float(p).
priceOf_AtLevel_[i, "Bronze"] = basePriceOf[i] - 5.0f.
priceOf_AtLevel_[i, "Silver"] = floor[basePriceOf[i]
    * 0.9f].
priceOf_AtLevel_[i, "Gold"] = floor[basePriceOf[i]
    * 0.8f].

// Data
+Level("Bronze").
+Level("Silver").
+Level("Gold").

+basePriceOf["A1"] = 100.0f.
+basePriceOf["B2"] = 200.0f.
+basePriceOf["C3"] = 100.0f.
+basePriceOf["D4"] = 100.90f.
```

The following query returns the result shown, to reproduce the data in the report:

```
_(i, bp, brp, sp, gp) <-
    basePriceOf[i] = bp,
    priceOf_AtLevel_[i, "Bronze"] = brp,
    priceOf_AtLevel_[i, "Silver"] = sp,
    priceOf_AtLevel_[i, "Gold"] = gp.
```

Result:
```
D4, 100.9, 95.9, 90, 80
C3, 100, 95, 90, 80
B2, 200, 195, 180, 160
A1, 100, 95, 90, 80
```

This solution may be easily extended to include members and their membership levels and to determine item prices for them based on their membership level. The program and data are available in the files Cases.logic and CasesData.logic.

Iteration Statements

While the above approach can be extended to handle students with more than two given names, it would require a lot of code to deal with lengthy

TABLE 4.4 Given Names and Houses of British Monarchs

Monarch	Given Names	House
Anne	Anne	Stuart
George I	George, Louis	Hanover
George II	George, Augustus	Hanover
George III	George, William, Frederick	Hanover
George IV	George, Augustus, Frederick	Hanover
William IV	William, Henry	Hanover
Victoria	Alexandrina, Victoria	Hanover
Edward VII	Albert, Edward	Saxe-Coburg and Gotha
George V	George, Frederick, Ernest, Albert	Windsor
Edward VIII	Edward, Albert, Christian, George, Andrew, Patrick, David	Windsor
George VI	Albert, Frederick, Arthur, George	Windsor
Elizabeth II	Elizabeth, Alexandra, Mary	Windsor

lists of given names. For example, recall the facts shown in Table 4.4 about British monarchs, in which Edward VIII has seven given names.

Suppose we need to derive the full name of a monarch by appending the house name of the monarch to his/her list of given names. The syntax for full names of monarchs may be set out as follows. Here, appending an asterisk ("*") to an item indicates zero or more occurrences of that item. Since each monarch has at least one given name, we do not need to cater to the case of no given name:

```
GivenNames ::= GivenName (" " GivenName)*.
FullName ::= GivenNames " " HouseName.
```

We could set an upper limit (e.g., 10) on the number of given names for a monarch and use different predicates (givenName1Of, given-Name2Of, ..., givenName10Of) for each given name position. However, it is simpler to use a single ternary predicate that includes the position of the given name in the list:

```
givenNameOf_AtPosition_[m, n] = gn -> Monarch(m),
    int(n), string(gn).
```

This functional naming style uses underscores (" _ ") in the predicate name to indicate the placeholders for the function's arguments (in this case m and n). So you can read the function declaration as *given name of m at position n = gn*. Apart from being simpler, using this ternary predicate is more flexible than using multiple binary predicates, because it caters for cases where it is impractical to set an upper limit on the size of the given-name list. The derivation rule for given names could now be stated informally as the following imperative pseudocode, using ":=" for *becomes* or "*is assigned the value of*":

```
for each monarch m
    n : = count of given names of m
    givenNames of m : = givenName1 of m
  for i : = 2 to n do
      givenNames of m : = givenNames of m + " " +
          givenName[i] of m
```

Here, for each monarch we use the count function to determine the number of given names of the monarch. Then we initialize givenNames to the first given name. Finally, we use a **for** loop to iterate over the rest of the names, appending them one at a time until we have appended the last given name.

A flowchart for a general **for** loop is shown in Figure 4.5, using ":=" for the assignment operator. As usual, *s* indicates a programming statement. The statement syntax at the top is from the Pascal language, which was also used in our pseudocode. The lower statement syntax is that used in Java, where "=" is used for assignment, and "++" is used to increment the value of a variable by 1.

Although deriving lists of given names for monarchs is naturally conceived imperatively in terms of the algorithm specified above in pseudocode, LogiQL does not provide iterative control structures like **for** loops.

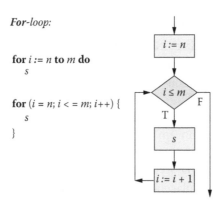

FIGURE 4.5   Flowchart for a *for* loop.

Happily, such iterative procedures can be reformulated declaratively in LogiQL by using recursion.

For any given monarch m, we compute nrOfGivenNamesOf[m], the number of given names of m, using the count aggregation function as shown below. We then recursively derive givenNamesOf_ ToPosition_[m,n], the list of m's first n given names, in multiple steps. First, we use m's first given name as the basis for position n = 1, then we append a space and the given name at position n (where n > 1) to givenNamesOf_ToPosition_[m,n-1], the list of m's first n-1 given names. Doing this recursively calls the function until the value of n-1 decrements to the basis value 1. The functional predicate givenNamesOf[m] may now be computed by setting n in the functional predicate givenNamesOf_ToPosition_[m,n] to equal the number of given names of m. Finally, the full name of m is derived by appending a space and the house name of m to m's given name list:

```
Monarch(m), hasMonarchName(m:mn) -> string(mn).
House(h), hasHouseName(h:hn) -> string(hn).
houseOf[m] = h -> Monarch(m), House(h).
givenNamesOf_ToPosition_[m, n] = gn -> Monarch(m),
    int(n), string(gn).
givenNameOf_AtPosition_[m, n] = gn -> Monarch(m),
    int(n), string(gn).
Monarch(m) -> givenNameOf_AtPosition_[m, _] = _.
// Each Monarch has a given name.
nrOfGivenNamesOf[m] = n -> Monarch(m), int(n).
nrOfGivenNamesOf[m] = n <-
    agg<<n = count()>>
    givenNameOf_AtPosition_[m, _] = _.

givenNamesOf_ToPosition_[m, 1] = gn <-
    givenNameOf_AtPosition_[m, 1] = gn.
// Basis clause: first given name of monarch m.

givenNamesOf_ToPosition_[m, n] = gns + " " + gn <-
    givenNameOf_AtPosition_[m, n] = gn, n > 1,
    givenNamesOf_ToPosition_[m, n-1] = gns.
// Recursive clause: first n names = first n-1 names
// + nth name.
```

```
givenNamesOf[m] = gns -> Monarch(m), string(gns).
givenNamesOf[m] = gns <-
    nrOfGivenNamesOf[m] = n,
    givenNamesOf_ToPosition_[m, n] = gns.

fullNameOf[m] = gns -> Monarch(m), string(gns).
fullNameOf[m] = gns + " " + hn <-
    givenNamesOf[m] = gns,
    houseOf[m] = h, hasHouseName(h:hn).
```

The first few lines of the data file are shown below. To save space, data for only the first two monarchs are shown here:

```
// Data
+givenNameOf_AtPosition_["Anne", 1] = "Anne",
+houseOf["Anne"] = "Stuart".
+givenNameOf_AtPosition_["George I", 1] = "George",
+givenNameOf_AtPosition_["George I", 2] = "Louis",
+houseOf["George I"] = "Hanover".
etc.
```

Querying the predicate `fullNameOf` yields the following result. Note that with the current page width and font size, the full name for Edward VIII spills over onto a second line. The program and data are available in the files `FullName3.logic` and `FullName3Data.logic`:

```
Elizabeth II, Elizabeth Alexandra Mary Windsor
George VI, Albert Frederick Arthur George Windsor
Edward VIII, Edward Albert Christian George Andrew
    Patrick
David Windsor
George V, George Frederick Ernest Albert Windsor
Edward VII, Albert Edward Saxe-Coburg and Gotha
Victoria, Alexandrina Victoria Hanover
William IV, William Henry Hanover
George IV, George Augustus Frederick Hanover
George III, George William Frederick Hanover
George II, George Augustus Hanover
George I, George Louis Hanover
Anne, Anne Stuart
```

Above we used a **for** loop for the imperative procedure, because the number of iterations to be performed was known from counting. Alternatively, the **for** loop could have been replaced by the following pseudocode, which instead makes use of a **while** loop:

```
i : = 2
while i < = n do
givenNames of m : = givenNames of m + " " +
    givenName [i] of m
i : = i + 1
```

A flowchart for a **while** loop is shown in Figure 4.6. If the condition c is false, the loop instruction s is never executed. A **do-until** loop (called **repeat-until** in Pascal) and a **do-until-not** loop (misleadingly called a **do-while** loop in Java) place the condition last, so always execute the loop instruction at least once. Depending on the condition, such loops can be emulated using recursion in a similar way to that discussed above.

Tip: Emulate **if-then-else** and **switch/case** constructs by using multiple rules, and emulate iterative loops via recursion.

Exercise 1A: The report in the Table 4.5 extract identifies famous authors by their author number, and also records the given names and family names that they used as authors. Each author has between one and three given names.

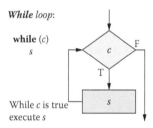

FIGURE 4.6   Flowchart for a *while* loop.

TABLE 4.5   Author Names

Author Number	Given Name 1	Given Name 2	Given Name 3	Family Name
1	John	Ronald	Reuel	Tolkien
2	Isaac			Asimov
3	Joanne	Kathleen		Rowling
...	...		...	...

The stub of a LogiQL program and data for this report are provided below and are accessible in the file `AuthorNames.logic` and `AuthorNamesData.logic`. Extend the program to derive the author full names without using recursion:

```
// Schema
Author(a), hasAuthorNr(a:n) -> int(n).
givenName1Of[a] = gn -> Author(a), string(gn).
givenName2Of[a] = gn -> Author(a), string(gn).
givenName3Of[a] = gn -> Author(a), string(gn).
familyNameOf[a] = fn -> Author(a), string(fn).
Author(a) -> givenName1Of[a] = _, familyNameOf[a] = _.
givenName2Of[a] = _ -> givenName1Of[a] = _.
givenName3Of[a] = _ -> givenName2Of[a] = _.


// Data
+givenName1Of[1] = "John", +givenName2Of[1] = "Ronald",
    +givenName3Of[1] = "Reuel",
    +familyNameOf[1] = "Tolkien".
+givenName1Of[2] = "Isaac", +familyNameOf[2] = "Asimov".
+givenName1Of[3] = "Joanne",
    +givenName2Of[3] = "Kathleen",
    +familyNameOf[3] = "Rowling".
```

Exercise 1B: In mathematics, *factorial n*, written as *n*!, where *n* is a whole number, is defined as follows: if $n = 0$, $n! = 1$; if $n > 0$ then $n! = 1 \times \ldots \times n$ (i.e., the product of all natural numbers up to *n*). For example, Table 4.6 lists the factorials of the first six whole numbers.

TABLE 4.6   Factorial Function

n	*n!*
0	1
1	1 (i.e., 1×1)
2	2 (i.e., 1×2)
3	6 (i.e., $1 \times 2 \times 3$)
4	24 (i.e., $1 \times 2 \times 3 \times 4$)
5	120 (i.e., $1 \times 2 \times 3 \times 4 \times 5$)
..	..

An iterative procedure that uses a **for loop** to derive x = factorial n for any whole number n may be specified as the following pseudocode, using ":=" for assignment:

```
x : = 1
for i : = 2 to n do
  x : = x * i
return x
```

Write a LogiQL program that uses recursion to derive the function `factorial[n]=x`. Test your program for values of n in the range 0 .. 20. A program stub that includes the following code is accessible as `Factorial.logic`. Complete the program by adding your rules to compute `factorial[n]`. *Hint:* To ensure that your recursive clause is safe, you need to restrict the values of n to just the values in the range. You can use the `int:range` function to do this. Its arguments are, respectively, the first element in the range, the last element, the increment between elements, and the variable into which the generated values should be placed:

```
factorial[n] = x -> int(n), int(x).
SmallInteger(n) -> int(n).
SmallInteger(n) <- int:range(0, 20, 1, n).
```

Exercise 1C: A test with possible scores of 0 through 10 is given to students. An extract of a report containing the test results is shown in Table 4.7. Students are identified by their student numbers.

Letter grades for the test are determined by the following procedure specified in pseudocode:

```
cases for testScore
  10: grade : = 'A'
  7, 8, 9: grade : = 'B'
```

TABLE 4.7   Student Grades

Student Number	Score	Letter Grade
101	7	B
102	9	B
103	5	C
104	10	A
105	4	F
106	7	B

```
5, 6: grade : = 'C'
else grade : = 'F'
```

The stub of a program and data for this report, available as `Grades.logic` and `GradesData.logic`, include the following code:

```
// Schema
Student(s), hasStudentNr(s:n) -> int(n).
scoreOf[s] = n -> Student(s), int(n).
scoreOf[_] = n -> n > = 0, n < = 10.

// Data
+scoreOf[101] = 7, +scoreOf[102] = 9, +scoreOf[103] = 5.
+scoreOf[104] = 10, +scoreOf[105] = 4, +scoreOf[106] = 7.
```

Extend the program to assign letter grades to the students.

UNIT 4.2: FURTHER CONSTRAINTS

To help ensure that data entered in the workspace agree with the application domain being modeled, it is important to include code to enforce various constraints that apply in that domain. Previously we discussed how to code various kinds of constraints in LogiQL, such as uniqueness constraints, mandatory role constraints, subset constraints, simple exclusion constraints, and ring constraints. This unit discusses how to encode several other kinds of constraints, including equality constraints, further value constraints, frequency constraints, and subset and exclusion constraints

Equality Constraints

Consider Table 4.8 containing blood pressure (BP) readings for hospital patients. Patients are identified by patient numbers. Blood pressure readings involve two measurements: the systolic BP is the maximum pressure during a heartbeat, and the diastolic BP is the minimum pressure.

TABLE 4.8   Patient Blood Pressure (BP) Readings

Patient Number	Systolic BP (mm Hg)	Diastolic BP (mm Hg)
1001	120	80
1002	135	95
1003	120	80
1004		

A basic schema to capture the data is shown below. For simplicity, the code assumes that the pressure unit (millimeters of mercury) is understood:

```
Patient(p), hasPatientNr(p:n) -> int(n).
systolicBPof[p] = n -> Patient(p), int(n).
diastolicBPof[p] = n -> Patient(p), int(n).
```

If instead you wish to explicitly declare pressure and its unit, replace the last two lines of code above by the following:

```
Pressure(pr), has_mmHgValue(pr:n) -> int(n).
systolicBPof[p] = pr -> Patient(p), Pressure(pr).
diastolicBPof[p] = pr -> Patient(p), Pressure(pr).
```

Either way, the data for the table may be entered as follows:

```
+systolicBPof[1001] = 120, +diastolicBPof[1001] = 80.
+systolicBPof[1002] = 135, +diastolicBPof[1002] = 95.
+systolicBPof[1003] = 120, +diastolicBPof[1003] = 80.
+Patient(1004).
```

Not all patients might have their BP taken (e.g., patient 1004 has not been tested yet), but if the BP is taken, both the diastolic and systolic readings are needed. Hence, the population of patients who have their systolic BP taken must *equal* the population of patients who have their diastolic BP taken. This is a simple example of an **equality constraint**.

An equality constraint between two roles is equivalent to two subset constraints between the roles, one constraint in each direction. So the equality constraint above may be coded as follows:

```
systolicBPof[p] = _ -> diastolicBPof[p] = _.
diastolicBPof[p] = _ -> systolicBPof[p] = _.
// If patient p has systolic BP then p has diastolic
// BP.
// If patient p has diastolic BP then p has systolic
// BP.
```

To check that the constraint is enforced properly, you can try either of the following updates. Each should generate a constraint violation error message, because if the update were accepted, the relevant patient would have only one of the two pressure readings:

```
+diastolicBPof[1004] = 90. // Error (no systolic BP)!
-diastolicBPof[1001] = 80. // Error (no diastolic BP)!
```

As an example of an equality constraint between pairs of roles, suppose that we wish to record the history of patient blood pressures, where a patient may have at most one BP reading per day. The functional, ternary predicates to record the relevant pressure n for patient p on date d may be declared as follows:

```
systolicBPfor[p, d] = n -> Patient(p), datetime(d),
    int(n).
diastolicBPfor[p, d] = n -> Patient(p), datetime(d),
    int(n).
```

The equality constraint between the populations of (p, d) pairs may now be coded as follows:

```
systolicBPfor[p, d] = _ -> diastolicBPfor[p, d] = _.
diastolicBPfor[p, d] = _ -> systolicBPfor[p, d] = _.
// If patient p has a systolic BP on date d
// then p has a diastolic BP on date d.
// If patient p has a diastolic BP on date d
// then p has a systolic BP on date d.
```

An equality constraint between two or more compatible roles requires the populations of those roles to be equal. More generally, equality constraints can apply between sequences of compatible roles. In either case, an equality constraint may always be enforced by multiple subset constraints.

Value Constraints

Recall that a value constraint restricts the values that may be assigned to an argument of a predicate. Previously, we met some simple value constraints that restrict an argument to an enumerated list of values. For example, we may constrain color codes to be "R", "G", or "B", and thus,

```
Color(c), hasColorCode(c:cc) -> string(cc).
hasColorCode(_:cc) -> cc = "R" ; cc = "G" ; cc = "B".
```

In addition to an enumerated list of values, a value constraint may constrain an argument's value to lie within one or more value ranges. A range with a single bound may be expressed as a simple comparison. For example, if we assume that ages are measured in years, the following constraint confines a person's age to be at most 140 years:

```
ageOf[_] = n -> n <= 140.
```

A range bounded at both ends may be expressed as a conjunction of simple comparisons. For example, the following code constrains product ratings to integers in the range 1..5:

```
productRatingOf[_] = n -> n >= 1, n <= 5.
```

To constrain a value to lie within one of multiple ranges, use a disjunction of expressions, one for each range. For example, the following code constrains the extreme score of an item to be either at least 95 or a nonnegative number less than 20. Since conjunction has priority over disjunction, parentheses are not needed around the conjunction that is the second disjunct, although you may include them if you wish:

```
extremeScoreOf[_] = n -> n > 95 ; n >= 0, n < 20.
```

Frequency Constraints

Recall that an internal uniqueness constraint on a single role of a predicate ensures that each instance in the population of that role is unique. Internal uniqueness constraints can also be applied to a list of roles in a predicate. An external uniqueness constraint is a restriction on roles from two or more predicates. In general, a uniqueness constraint on a list of one or more roles ensures that, at any given time, each instance of that role list appears there at most once. A **frequency constraint** generalizes the notion of uniqueness constraint, allowing the number of times the constrained role list appears in any given population to be set to any positive integer, or even to a range of positive integers.

Consider, for example, Tables 4.9 and 4.10 contain reports from a paper-review system. Reviewers are identified by name and papers by number.

TABLE 4.9   Paper Reviewers

Reviewer	Papers Assigned
Ann Jones	1, 2
Bill Smith	1
Cate Wong	1, 2
Dan Green	
Eve Noon	1, 2
Fred Jones	

TABLE 4.10   Unassigned Papers

Unassigned Papers
3

The first report lists the reviewers and the papers they have so far been assigned to review. The latter indicates papers not yet assigned for review. A basic schema for these reports is as follows:

```
Reviewer(r), hasReviewerName(r:rn) -> string(rn).
Paper(p), hasPaperNr(p:n) -> int(n).
isAssigned(r, p) -> Reviewer(r), Paper(p).
```

The schema may be populated with the data shown by executing these updates:

```
+isAssigned("Ann Jones", 1), +isAssigned("Ann Jones", 2).
+isAssigned("Bill Smith", 1).
+isAssigned("Cate Wong", 1), +isAssigned("Cate Wong", 2).
+Reviewer("Dan Green").
+isAssigned("Eve Noon", 1), +isAssigned("Eve Noon", 2).
+Reviewer("Fred Jones").
+Paper(3).
```

Now suppose we wish to ensure that each reviewer is assigned at most two papers to review. The current data satisfy this frequency constraint, but there is nothing to stop us updating the database to violate the constraint (e.g., assert that Ann Jones is assigned paper 3). To code the frequency constraint that each reviewer is assigned at most two papers, we use the count function to count the positive number of papers assigned to reviewers, and then constrain that number to be at most 2:

```
positiveNrPapersAssignedTo[r] = n -> Reviewer(r), int(n).
positiveNrPapersAssignedTo[r] = n <-
    agg<<n = count()>> isAssigned(r, _).
// If r is assigned a paper to review, then the number
// of papers assigned to r is the count of its
// assignments.
positiveNrPapersAssignedTo[_] = n -> n <= 2.
// Each reviewer is assigned at most 2 papers to
// review.
```

The use of "positive" in the name of the derived function clarifies that we are interested only in reviewers who have been assigned at least one paper to review. Here, the count function returns nothing (rather than 0) for reviewers with no paper assignments. For example, querying the `positiveNrPapersAssignedTo` predicate returns the following result:

```
Eve Noon, 2
Cate Wong, 2
Bill Smith, 1
Ann Jones, 2
```

Now suppose that we wish to ensure that each paper that is assigned for review is assigned to at least three reviewers. The current data satisfy this constraint but would be violated if we retracted the fact that Ann Jones is assigned paper 2. We may code this constraint using a `count` function to count the positive number of reviewers for each paper:

```
positiveNrReviewersOf[p] = n -> Paper(p), int(n).
positiveNrReviewersOf[p] = n <-
    agg<<n = count()>> isAssigned(_, p).
// If paper p is assigned a reviewer, then the number
// of reviewers assigned to p is the count of its
// assignments.
positiveNrReviewersOf[_] = n -> n >= 3.
// Each assigned paper is assigned at least 3
// reviewers.
```

Querying the `positiveNrReviewersOf` predicate returns the following result:

```
1, 4
2, 3
```

The code for the above program (including both frequency constraints) and data, as well as a counterexample test are available in the files `PaperReview*.logic`.

If the number specified in the frequency constraint is small (e.g., 2 or 3), the frequency constraint may often be coded explicitly, without using the `count` function. However, if the number is higher, using the `count` function is more convenient and requires far less code.

The frequency constraints just considered are *internal frequency constraints*, because each applies to a single predicate. An *external frequency constraint* applies to roles from different predicates and is a generalization of an external uniqueness constraint. As an example, consider the following extract from a report shown in Table 4.11 about enrollments of

TABLE 4.11   Student Course Enrollment

Enrollment Number	Student Number	Course Code
1001	120	CS100
1002	120	CS135
1003	501	CS135
3001	120	CS100

students in courses. Enrollments are identified by enrollment numbers, students by student numbers, and courses by codes.

A basic schema for this report may be coded as follows:

```
Enrollment(e), hasEnrollmentNr(e:n) -> int(n).
Student(s), hasStudentNr(s:n) -> int(n).
Course(c), hasCourseCode(c:cc) -> string(cc).
studentInvolvedIn[e] = s -> Enrollment(e), Student(s).
courseInvolvedIn[e] = c -> Enrollment(e), Course(c).
// Each Enrollment involves both a student and a
// course.
Enrollment(e) ->
    studentInvolvedIn[e] = _, courseInvolvedIn[e] = _.
```

The data for this report may be entered as follows:

```
+studentInvolvedIn[1001] = 120,
    +courseInvolvedIn[1001] = "CS100".
+studentInvolvedIn[1002] = 120,
    +courseInvolvedIn[1002] = "CS135".
+studentInvolvedIn[1003] = 501,
    +courseInvolvedIn[1003] = "CS135".
+studentInvolvedIn[3001] = 120,
    +courseInvolvedIn[3001] = "CS100".
```

Now suppose that no student may enroll more than twice in the same course. (This is common practice at many universities, where one is excluded from a course if one fails it twice.) This frequency constraint involves roles from two predicates (studentInvolvedI n and courseInvolvedIn), so this is an external frequency constraint. To enforce this constraint, we first derive a function to compute the number of enrollments of any given student in any given course in which that student has enrolled:

```
nrEnrollmentsFor[s, c] = n -> Student(s), Course(c),
    int(n).
nrEnrollmentsFor[s, c] = n <-
```

```
    agg<<n = count()>> studentInvolvedIn[e] = s,
    courseInvolvedIn[e] = c.
// For each student s who enrolled in course c,
// n is the number of cases where there exists an
// enrollment e involving that s and that c.
```

You may wish to prepend the function name by "positive" to emphasize that function returns nothing (instead of 0) if s is not enrolled in c. For the data shown, querying the function nrEnrollmentsFor returns the following result:

```
120, CS100, 2
120, CS135, 1
501, CS135, 1
```

Now that this function is defined, we enforce the frequency constraint:

```
nrEnrollmentsFor[_, _] = n -> n <= 2.
// Each student enrolls at most twice in the same
// course.
```

If you attempt to violate this constraint (e.g., by adding a third enrollment of student 120 in CS100), an error is generated. The code for the above program and data, including a counterexample test, is available in the files Enrollment*.logic.

Subset and Exclusion Constraints Involving Join Paths

The conjunctive condition for the above nrEnrollmentsFor predicate uses the same enrollment variable e to equate the enrollment in both the studentInvolvedIn predicate and the courseInvolvedIn predicate. Such a matching of an argument in one atom with an argument in another atom is said to perform a **join** between the predicate roles involved.

A **join path** is a sequence of connected atoms, with each subsequent atom joined to the previous atom by matching an argument variable. For the purposes of this definition, we use the term *atom* liberally, to include functional applications such as fatherOf[p1]=p2.

Recall the following example of a subset constraint presented in Unit 2.4. This code expresses the constraint that stores with garden centers are a subset of stores that sell lawn mowers:

```
Store(s), hasStoreNr(s:n) -> int(n).
hasGardenCenter(s) -> Store(s).
sellsLawnMowers(s) -> Store(s).
```

```
hasGardenCenter(s) -> sellsLawnMowers(s).
// If store s has a garden center, then s sells
// lawn mowers.
```

Exclusion constraints also compare sets but require the constrained sets to be mutually exclusive. Here is an example from Unit 1.7. In this case, the exclusion constraint indicates that male monarchs and female monarchs form disjoint sets:

```
Monarch(m) ->. // Monarch is an entity type
// isMale(m) -> Monarch(m).
// If m is male then m is a monarch.
isFemale(m) -> Monarch(m).
// If m is female then m is a monarch.
isMale(m) -> !isFemale(m).
// If m is male then m is not female.
```

For a single role, the arguments of subset and exclusion constraints must be compatible with each other, and the relevant set-comparison operation (subset or exclusion) should be applied between them. Note that both kinds of constraints may also apply to compatible sequences of roles.

For any predicate, a subset of its arguments can be selected for comparison with other predicates. Such a subset is called a **projection**. Projections can also be performed on the set of predicates involved in a join path. If an argument of a subset or exclusion constraints is projected from a join path, it is called a *join-subset constraint* or *join-exclusion constraint*, respectively.

As an example of a join-subset constraint, recall the following constraint from the Consolidation Exercise in Chapter 2: If person p has a title pt that applies to only one gender g, then person p must be of gender g. Here the set of (p, g) pairs projected from the join path personTitleOf[p]=pt, applicableGenderOf[pt]=g is required to be a subset of the set of (p, g) pairs populating genderOf[p]=g:

```
personTitleOf[p] = pt, applicableGenderOf[pt] = g ->
    genderOf[p] = g.
// If person p has a person title pt that applies only
// to a specific gender g, then person p must be of
// gender g.
```

As an example of a join-exclusion constraint, consider the report shown in Table 4.12 from a paper-review system. Each person is affiliated with

TABLE 4.12   Reviewer Participation Data

Person	Institute	Papers Assigned	Papers Authored
Ann Jones	UCLA	20	10
Bill Smith	MIT		15
Cate Wong	UCLA	20	
Dan Green	MIT	10	15, 20
Eve Noon	UCLA	15	

exactly one institute, and each person authored a paper or is assigned to review a paper (or both).

A basic schema for this report is as follows:

```
Person(p), hasPersonName(p:n) -> string(n).
Institute(i), hasInstituteName(i:n) -> string(n).
Paper(p), hasPaperNr(p:n) -> int(n).
instituteOf[p] = i -> Person(p), Institute(i).
authored(p, ppr) -> Person(p), Paper(ppr).
isAssigned(p, ppr) -> Person(p), Paper(ppr).
Person(p) -> instituteOf[p] = _.
Person(p) -> isAssigned(p, _) ; authored(p, _).
```

To avoid potential bias in reviews, it is common practice to ensure that no person may review a paper authored by a person from the reviewer's institute. The current data satisfy this constraint but could easily be violated by another update (e.g., assign paper 10 to be reviewed also by Cate Wong).

Conceptually, this constraint involves projecting person-and-paper pairs from one join path (from institute to author to paper) and excluding these from the person-and-paper pairs projected from another join path (from institute to reviewer to paper). To facilitate the coding of this join-exclusion constraint, it helps to first derive predicates that project the person-and-paper pairs from the relevant join paths and then assert exclusion between these derived predicates:

```
hasAnAuthorOf(i, ppr) -> Institute(i), Paper(ppr).
hasAnAuthorOf(i, ppr) <- instituteOf[p] = i,
    authored(p, ppr).
hasAReviewerOf(i, ppr) -> Institute(i), Paper(ppr).
hasAReviewerOf(i, ppr) <- instituteOf[p] = i,
    isAssigned(p, ppr).
```

```
hasAnAuthorOf(i, ppr) -> !hasAReviewerOf(i, ppr).
// Nobody may review a paper authored by someone from
// the same institute.
```

If you attempt to violate this constraint (e.g., by assigning paper 10 to be reviewed also by Cate Wong), an error is generated. The code for the above program and data, as well as a counterexample test, is available in the files JoinExclusion*.

Tip: To join two predicates with a common argument type, use a conjunction with a common variable for the matching argument.

Exercise 2A: The report extract shown in Table 4.13 is from a weather bureau that records the minimum and maximum temperatures of some cities for the current day. Temperatures are measured in degrees Celsius. A basic program and data are given below and are also accessible as CityTemp.logic. Extend the program with code to enforce: (i) the equality constraint that for any given city, either both the temperatures are recorded or none are; and (ii) the value constraints that each minimum temperature is above −50°C, and each maximum temperature is in the range −10°C through 50°C (inclusive):

```
// Schema
City(c), hasCityName(c:n) -> string(n).
minCelsiusTempOf[c] = t -> City(c), int(t).
maxCelsiusTempOf[c] = t -> City(c), int(t).

// Data
+minCelsiusTempOf["Brisbane"] = 14.
+maxCelsiusTempOf["Brisbane"] = 27.
+minCelsiusTempOf["Sydney"] = 14.
+maxCelsiusTempOf["Sydney"] = 19.
+City("Melbourne").
```

TABLE 4.13   City Temperature Extremes

City	Minimum Temperature (°C)	Maximum Temperature (°C)
Brisbane	14	27
Melbourne		
Sydney	14	19

Exercise 2B: The report extract shown in Table 4.14 is from a weather bureau that records the minimum and maximum temperatures of some cities for some months of the current year. Temperatures are measured in degrees Celsius. A basic program and data are given below and are also accessible as `CityTemp2.logic`. Extend the program with code to enforce the equality constraint that for any given city and month, either both the temperatures are recorded or none are:

```
// Schema
City(c), hasCityName(c:n) -> string(n).
Month(m), hasMonthCode(m:c) -> string(c).
minCelsiusFor[c, m] = t -> City(c), Month(m), int(t).
maxCelsiusFor[c, m] = t -> City(c), Month(m), int(t).

// Data
+minCelsiusFor["Brisbane", "Jan"] = 20.
+maxCelsiusFor["Brisbane", "Jan"] = 36.
+minCelsiusFor["Brisbane", "Feb"] = 20.
+maxCelsiusFor["Brisbane", "Feb"] = 33.
+City("Melbourne").
```

Exercise 2C: In the report in Table 4.15, the second column records the languages in which the person on that row is fluent. Todd Ler is not yet fluent in any language (perhaps because he is just a baby!). The third and

TABLE 4.14   City Temperature Extremes per Month

City	Month	Minimum Temperature (°C)	Maximum Temperature (°C)
Brisbane	January	20	36
Brisbane	February	20	33
Melbourne			

TABLE 4.15   Languages Mastered

Person	Languages Mastered	Is Bilingual?	Is Translator?
Ann Jones	English	No	No
Bill Smith	English, Spanish	Yes	Yes
Cate Banderas	French, Spanish	Yes	No
Fumie Kano	English, Japanese, Mandarin	Yes	Yes
Todd Ler		No	No

fourth columns indicate whether or not that person is bilingual (i.e., fluent in at least two languages) or employed as a translator, respectively.

A basic program and data are given below and are also accessible as Languages.lb. (i) Extend the program using the count function to derive the positive number of languages in which a person is fluent. Then use that function to derive whether a person is bilingual and enforce the constraint that each translator is bilingual. (ii) Without using the count function, write a derivation rule to determine whether a person is bilingual. Would it be convenient to use this approach for larger frequencies (e.g., to find those people who speak at least five languages)?

```
Person(p), hasPersonName(p:pn) -> string(pn).
Language(la), hasLanguageName(la:ln) -> string(ln).
isFluentIn(p, la) -> Person(p), Language(la).
Translator(t) -> Person(t).
lang:isEntity[`Translator] = true.
```

The schema may be populated with the data shown by executing these updates:

```
+isFluentIn("Ann Jones", "English").
+isFluentIn("Bill Smith", "English"),
    +isFluentIn("Bill Smith", "Spanish"),
    +Translator("Bill Smith").
+isFluentIn("Cate Banderas", "French"),
    +isFluentIn("Cate Banderas", "Spanish").
+isFluentIn("Fumie Kano", "English"),
    +isFluentIn("Fumie Kano", "Japanese"),
    +isFluentIn("Fumie Kano", "Mandarin"),
    +Translator("Fumie Kano").
+Person("Todd Ler").
```

Exercise 2D: The report extracts in Tables 4.16 and 4.17 indicate official languages of some countries (BE, Belgium; CA, Canada; FI, Finland), as well as the languages mastered by ambassadors to those countries.

TABLE 4.16 Official Languages for Countries

Country	Official Languages
Belgium (BE)	Dutch, French, German
Canada (CA)	English, French
Finland (FI)	Finnish, Swedish

TABLE 4.17   Ambassadors and Their Languages

Person	Languages Mastered	Ambassador to Country
Ann Jones	English	Canada (CA)
Bob Adams	English, Finnish	Finland (FI)
Cate Brown	Dutch, French, Swedish	Belgium (BE)

A basic program and data are provided below and are accessible as `Ambassador.lb`. We now wish to ensure that if a person is an ambassador to a country then that person must be fluent in at least one official language of that country. Add code to enforce this join-subset constraint. *Hint*: First derive a predicate to project p and c from the join path:

```
// Schema
Person(p), hasPersonName(p:n) -> string(n).
Language(la), hasLanguageName(la:n) -> string(n).
Country(c), hasCountryCode(c:cc) -> string(cc).
isFluentIn(p, la) -> Person(p), Language(la).
hasOfficialLanguage(c, la) -> Country(c), Language(la).
countryAmbassadoredBy[p] = c -> Person(p), Country(c).

// Data
+hasOfficialLanguage("BE", "Dutch"),
    +hasOfficialLanguage("BE", "French"),
    +hasOfficialLanguage("BE", "German").
+hasOfficialLanguage("CA", "English"),
    +hasOfficialLanguage("CA", "French").
+hasOfficialLanguage("FI", "Finnish"),
    +hasOfficialLanguage("FI", "Swedish").
+isFluentIn("Ann Jones", "English").
+isFluentIn("Bob Adams", "English"),
    +isFluentIn("Bob Adams", "Finnish").
+isFluentIn("Cate Brown", "Dutch"),
    +isFluentIn("Cate Brown", "French"),
    +isFluentIn("Cate Brown", "Swedish").
+countryAmbassadoredBy["Ann Jones"] = "CA".
+countryAmbassadoredBy["Bob Adams"] = "FI".
+countryAmbassadoredBy["Cate Brown"] = "BE".
```

Exercise 2E: In the report extract shown in Table 4.18, products are identified by name, employees by employee numbers (e1, e2, etc.), and reviews by review numbers. A product may have many developers and

TABLE 4.18   Product Review Data

Product Name	Product Developers	Review Number	Reviewer
WordLight	e1, e2	1	e3
		2	e4
FunBlox	e1	3	e2

many reviews, but each review is for exactly one product and is authored by exactly one employee.

A basic program and data for this report are shown below and are also accessible in `ProductReview.lb`. Extend the code by adding a join-exclusion constraint to ensure that no employee may review a product for which he/she was a developer:

```
// Schema
Employee(e), hasEmployeeNr(e:n) -> string(n).
Product(p), hasProductName(p:n) -> string(n).
Review(r), hasReviewNr(r:n) -> int(n).
developed(e, p) -> Employee(e), Product(p).
authorOf[r] = e -> Review(r), Employee(e).
productReviewedIn[r] = p -> Review(r), Product(p).
Review(r) -> authorOf[r] = _, productReviewedIn[r] = _.

// Data
+developed("e1", "Wordlight"), +developed("e1",
    "FunBlox").
+developed("e2", "Wordlight").
+authorOf[1] = "e3", +productReviewedIn[1] =
    "Wordlight".
+authorOf[2] = "e4", +productReviewedIn[2] =
    "Wordlight".
+authorOf[3] = "e2", +productReviewedIn[3] = "FunBlox".
```

UNIT 4.3: DERIVED ENTITIES AND CONSTRUCTORS

This unit discusses a way to add information to the extensional database (EDB) that complements the use of delta logic that we have seen previously. In particular, it allows us to specify predicates that entail the existence of new entities and have the LogiQL execution engine add those entities to the database. These added entities are called **derived entities**, and the predicates used to define them are called **constructor** predicates.

Recall that a derivation rule is used to derive new facts from facts that have already been asserted or derived. For example, the following rule may be used to derive the fact that person p1 is an uncle of person p2, given that we already know that p1 is a brother of some person p3 who is a parent of p2:

```
isUncleOf1(p1, p2) -> Person(p1), Person(p2).
isUncleOf1(p1, p2) <- isBrotherOf(p1, p3),
    isParentOf(p3, p2).
```

Recall also that a delta rule with delta modifiers in its head is used to update the extensional database when triggered by an update to a predicate in the body of the rule. For example, the following delta rule could be used to add relevant unclehood facts into the EDB when the relevant brotherhood and parenthood facts are added to the EDB:

```
isUncleOf2(p1, p2) -> Person(p1), Person(p2).
+isUncleOf2(p1, p2) <- +isBrotherOf(p1, p3),
    +isParentOf(p3, p2).
```

Except for the delta modifiers, this delta rule looks similar to the derivation rule above it. However, it behaves quite differently. Delta rules are triggered by update events noted in their bodies and are fully evaluated in the initial stage of the transaction. In contrast, derivation rules without delta modifiers are evaluated incrementally and are executed in the final stage of the transaction. Moreover, if some facts involved in a rule body are updated in a later transaction, the LogiQL execution engine automatically takes appropriate action.

For example, if a brotherhood or parenthood fact used by the derivation rule to derive an isUncleOf1 fact is subsequently retracted and there are no other brotherhood and parenthood facts that satisfy the condition in the rule body for that unclehood fact, then the derived isUncleOf1 fact is automatically deleted. If instead you use the above delta rule, then you would have to manually write the code to perform compensating updates in response to future updates. Since the maintenance of data updates for derivation rules is automatically managed by the LogiQL execution engine, such rules may often provide a better coding alternative than delta rules that include updates in their heads.

One case where delta rules are useful is when dealing with pulse predicates. Recall the following example from the previous chapter, where a delta rule is used to add an employee to the EDB with the relevant details entered on a screen form:

```
+Employee(e), +hasEmpNr(e:n), +familyNameOf[e] = fn,
    +givenNameOf[e] = gn <-
    +okButtonIsPressedOn(f), +textField:empNrOn[f] = n,
    +textField:familyNameOn[f] = fn,
    +textField:givenNameOn[f] = gn.
```

Note that the updates in the head of this delta rule include a variable e that does not occur in the body of the rule. This is allowed because the Employee predicate is preceded by a delta modifier. If no delta modifier is included, we earlier forbade this situation, because our first safety condition for derivation rules requires each head variable (in a non-delta predicate) to occur in a positive context in the rule body. However, as an extension beyond classical Datalog, LogiQL allows this safety condition to be overridden under the special circumstances described in this unit, thereby enabling a rule to derive the existence of a new entity.

As a simple example to introduce the basic concepts and syntax, consider the report shown in Table 4.19 about countries and their presidents (as of 2011). Here, countries are identified by their country code (DE, Germany; FI, Finland; FR, France; IE, Ireland; US, United States). Note that for this application domain, the names of the presidents are not of interest.

One way of expressing this example in LogiQL is shown below. For simplicity, years are represented simply as integers:

```
// Schema
Country(c), hasCountryCode(c:cc) -> string(cc).
Gender(g), hasGenderCode(g:gc) -> string(gc).
genderOfPresidentOf[c] = g -> Country(c), Gender(g).
birthyearOfPresidentOf[c] = y -> Country(c), int(y).
hasGenderCode(_:gc) -> gc = "M" ; gc = "F".

// Data
+genderOfPresidentOf["DE"] = "M",
    +birthyearOfPresidentOf["DE"] = 1959.
+genderOfPresidentOf["FI"] = "F",
    +birthyearOfPresidentOf["FI"] = 1943.
+genderOfPresidentOf["FR"] = "M",
    +birthyearOfPresidentOf["FR"] = 1955.
```

TABLE 4.19   Gender and Birth Years of Presidents

Country	President's Gender	President's Birth Year
DE	M	1959
FI	F	1943
FR	M	1955
IE	F	1951
US	M	1961

Note: DE, Germany; FI, Finland; FR, France; IE, Ireland; US, United States.

```
+genderOfPresidentOf["IE"] = "F",
    +birthyearOfPresidentOf["IE"] = 1951.
+genderOfPresidentOf["US"] = "M",
    +birthyearOfPresidentOf["US"] = 1961.
```

The data in the report can be retrieved by running the following query, which returns the result shown:

```
_(c, g, y) <-
   genderOfPresidentOf[c] = g,
       birthyearOfPresidentOf[c] = y.
```

Result:
```
US, M, 1961
IE, F, 1951
FR, M, 1955
FI, F, 1943
DE, M, 1959
```

The code is available as `President1.lb`.

Although this approach works, it seems somewhat unnatural to treat the gender and birth details directly as facts about countries, using the `genderOfPresidentOf` and `birthyearOfPresidentOf` predicates. It seems cleaner to think of the gender and birth year details directly as facts about the presidents of those countries (and hence only indirectly as facts about countries). For example, we might informally verbalize the last row of the report thus: "The president of Germany is male and was born in 1959." In so doing, we are explicitly mentioning presidents as an entity type of interest. Moreover, we are using a definite description, "the president of Germany," to identity one entity (the German president) by its presidential relationship to another entity (the country Germany). This is an example of an *entity-to-entity* reference scheme.

In contrast, refmode predicates identify an entity by relating it to a data value, and hence provide an *entity-to-value* reference scheme. For example, the refmode declaration for `Country` enables us to use "`Country("DE")`" as shorthand for the definite description "the country that has the country code 'DE.'" In LogiQL, if an entity type has no associated refmode predicate (is *refmodeless*), you can provide a reference scheme for it by declaring at least one constructor to determine instances of it.

The following lines of code show how to provide such a reference scheme for the entity type `President` in our current example:

```
President(p) ->.
// President is a refmodeless entity type
presidentOf[c] = p -> Country(c), President(p).
lang:constructor(`presidentOf).
// presidentOf is a constructor that maps countries to
// their presidents.
```

The first line declares `President` as an entity type without a refmode. The next two lines of code declare the functional predicate `presidentOf`, using the metapredicate `lang:constructor` to indicate that `presidentOf` is a constructor. This means that the function application `presidentOf[c]` provides a primary way to reference the president of country c and that the `presidentOf` predicate is 1:1.

If a rule containing a constructor in its head executes, one of two things happens, depending on the value of the constructor's key. If the constructor predicate does not already contain a fact with that key, then a new entity is created as the constructor's value, and the constructor predicate is updated to contain a new fact with the given key and new entity. If the constructor does contain a fact with the given key then the already associated value is reused. Hence, there is no need to explicitly code a uniqueness constraint to ensure that a constructor is inverse functional.

In our president example, the following derivation rule may now be used to derive the existence of a president and the presidential relationship to his or her country from the mere fact that its country exists. Note also that the head of the rule in this example is a conjunction:

```
President(p), presidentOf[c] = p <- Country(c).
// For each country there exists a president
// who is the president of that country only.
```

Understanding constructor predicates depends on the concept of *logical quantification*, which is more fully described in Appendix G to this book. Thus far, the variables we have seen in the heads of derivation rules have been *universally quantified*. What this means is that the rules should hold true for all possible values of those variables. In contrast, variables that occur only in the body of a rule are *existentially quantified*. This means that the rule body is satisfied if it holds for at least one value of the variable. For example, the unclehood derivation rule considered above means: *for each* person p1 and *for each* person p2, p1 is an uncle of p2 if *there exists* some person p3 such that p1 is a brother of p3 and p3 is a parent of p2.

However, because President is a refmodeless entity type and has a constructor-based reference scheme, the presidential derivation rule above is interpreted differently from a normal derivation rule. The President variable p is allowed to appear only in the head of the rule and is assumed to be existentially quantified. Hence, the derivation rule may be read as follows: *For each country c, there exists a president p who is the president of c.* Because the individual variable p is existentially quantified in the head of the derivation rule, it is known as a **head existential**. An entity whose existence is inferred from such a derivation rule is called a *derived entity*.

Now that President is explicitly included as an entity type, we may introduce predicates to express gender and birth year details directly as facts about presidents. For example, the following rules may be used to derive these predicates from the predicates used in the original data entry:

```
genderOf[p] = g -> President(p), Gender(g).
genderOf[p] = g <- presidentOf[c] = p,
    genderOfPresidentOf[c] = g.
birthyearOf[p] = y -> President(p), int(y).
birthyearOf[p] = y <-
    presidentOf[c] = p, birthyearOfPresidentOf[c] = y.
```

One advantage of doing this is to enable rules or queries about presidents to be conceptualized and expressed in a more natural fashion that explicitly references presidents. For example, the above query to display the countries and the gender and birth year of their presidents may now be reformulated as follows:

```
_(c, g, y) <- presidentOf[c] = p, genderOf[p] = g,
    birthyearOf[p] = y.
```

The code for the above program, data, and query is available as
`President2.lb`.

Note that its derived entities and derived predicates were not used to
actually enter the data. In practice, this is often the best approach. However,
it is possible to use derived entities and derived predicates to effectively
enter data, as shown by the following code, available in `President3.lb`:

```
// Schema
Country(c), hasCountryCode(c:cc) -> string(cc).
Gender(g), hasGenderCode(g:gc) -> string(gc).
President(p) ->.
presidentOf[c] = p -> Country(c), President(p).
lang:constructor(`presidentOf).
President(p), presidentOf[c] = p <- Country(c).
genderOf[p] = g -> President(p), Gender(g).
birthyearOf[p] = y -> President(p), int(y).
hasGenderCode(_:gc) -> gc = "M" ; gc = "F".

genderOf[p] = "M", birthyearOf[p] = 1959 <-
    presidentOf["DE"] = p.
genderOf[p] = "F", birthyearOf[p] = 1943 <-
    presidentOf["FI"] = p.
genderOf[p] = "M", birthyearOf[p] = 1955 <-
    presidentOf["FR"] = p.
genderOf[p] = "F", birthyearOf[p] = 1951 <-
    presidentOf["IE"] = p.
genderOf[p] = "M", birthyearOf[p] = 1961 <-
    presidentOf["US"] = p.
// Derive the gender and birthyear facts.

// Data
+Country("DE"), +Country("FI"), +Country("FR").
+Country("IE"), +Country("US").
+Gender("M"), +Gender("F"). // Needed for
    genderOf rule.
```

The predicates `genderOfPresidentOf` and `birthyearOfPresi-
dentOf` are absent, and the only asserted facts are for the country and
gender entities. The facts about the gender and birth years of presidents
are now derived from the derivation rules shown. In declaring the genderOf function, we specified `Gender` (an entity type) as the type of
its value parameter. Because of this, the derivation rule for genderOf

relies on the existence of the gender entities, so they must be explicitly added as shown in the final line of the data entry code. In contrast, the `birthyearOf` function returns a primitive value rather than an entity, so its derivation rule needs no prior declaration of the year numbers.

Because constructors provide a way to deal with unnamed, derived entities, they are useful for transforming one structure to a corresponding structure in a different notation. As an example, let's consider a simplified fragment of a program to generate English verbalizations of constraints that are captured in an information model or a LogiQL program. For instance, the functional nature of `genderOf[p]=g` involves a uniqueness constraint to ensure that each person has at most one gender. This hard constraint could be verbalized as follows: *It is necessary that each person has at most one gender.* Similarly, the soft uniqueness constraint that each person ought to have at most one wife could be verbalized as follows: *It is obligatory that each person is husband of at most one person.* In LogiQL, a soft constraint may be implemented by a rule to produce an error message when the constraint is violated. Let us name these hard and soft uniqueness constraints UC1 and UC2, respectively.

The hard or soft nature of a constraint is called its *modality*, and each verbalization starts with some modal text (e.g., "It is necessary that") to express the modality. The rest of the verbalization includes the names of the object types as well as phrases to capture relevant quantifiers and predicates. For simplicity, we consider here just the task of automatically generating the modal text for the constraint verbalization.

A verbalization itself has a textual form but does not have a name; hence, it is refmodeless and may be identified by a definite description such as "the verbalization of constraint UC1." Since we wish to generate the text of the verbalizations from the constraints, this task is an obvious candidate for the derived entity approach, as used in the following program:

```
// Schema
Constraint(c), hasConstraintName(c:cn) -> string(cn).
Modality(m), hasModalityName(m:mn) -> string(mn).
hasModalityName(_:mn) -> mn = "Hard" ; mn = "Soft".
modalityOf[c] = m -> Constraint(c), Modality(m).

ConstraintVerbalization(cv) ->.
verbalizationOf[c] = cv -> Constraint(c),
    ConstraintVerbalization(cv).
lang:constructor(`verbalizationOf).
```

```
modalTextOf [cv] = s -> ConstraintVerbalization(cv),
    string(s).
ConstraintVerbalization(cv), verbalizationOf[c] = cv,
    modalTextOf[cv] = "It is necessary that " <-
    modalityOf[c] = "Hard".
// If a constraint is of hard modality
// then there exists a verbalization of the constraint
// whose modal text reads "It is necessary that ".

ConstraintVerbalization(cv), verbalizationOf[c] = cv,
    modalTextOf[cv] = "It is obligatory that " <-
    modalityOf[c] = "Soft".
// If a constraint is of soft modality
// then there exists a verbalization of the constraint
// whose modal text reads "It is obligatory that ".

// Data
+modalityOf["UC1"] = "Hard".
+modalityOf["UC2"] = "Soft".
```

The following query may now be used to output the modal text parts of the constraint verbalizations, giving the results shown. The code for the program, data, and query is available as Verbalize1.lb:

```
_(c, mt) <-
    Constraint(c), verbalizationOf[c] = cv,
    modalTextOf[cv] = mt.
```

Result:
```
UC2, It is obligatory that
UC1, It is necessary that
```

Thus, head existentials provide a very powerful way to code data transformations, such as that in the previous example. They have also proven useful in other kinds of applications such as those involving data integration or view updates.

N-ary Constructors

The constructors considered so far have all been 1:1 binary predicates. It is also possible to have n-ary constructors ($n > 2$), where their first $n - 1$ roles provide the keyspace, and the value space also functionally determines the keyspace. To illustrate this, consider the report shown in Table 4.20

TABLE 4.20   Names and Birth Years of Presidents

President's Given Name, etc.	President's Family Name	Birth Year
Barack	Obama	1961
George W.	Bush	1946
Bill	Clinton	1946
George H. W.	Bush	1924
..	..	..

about presidents of the United States. Here, "President's Given Name, etc." includes a given name and optionally one or more initials to ensure that the combination of given name and family name suffices to identify a president.

A program schema describing the contents of this report, available as `President5.lb`, is as follows:

```
// Schema - Note: Incomplete without constructor
President(p) ->.
givenNameEtcOf[p] = gn -> President(p), string(gn).
familyNameOf[p] = fn -> President(p), string(fn).
birthyearOf[p] = y -> President(p), int(y).
President(p) -> givenNameEtcOf[p] = _,
    familyNameOf[p] = _.
// Each president has a given name and a family name.
givenNameEtcOf[p1] = gn, familyNameOf[p1] = fn,
givenNameEtcOf[p2] = gn, familyNameOf[p2] = fn ->
    p1 = p2.
// Each combination of GivenNameEtc and FamilyName
// applies to only one president.
```

In this example, the combination of the two names (given and family) provides a *composite reference scheme* for it. This reference scheme is enforced by the mandatory role and external uniqueness constraints shown above. Without these in place, it would be possible to add presidents with no names or with the same name combination as already added presidents. Note, however, that the above schema is not sufficient to describe the data because it does not offer a way to explicitly assert the data. That is, it provides neither a refmode nor a constructor.

It is possible to address the above concern by providing a refmode, but if none is naturally available, the developer must manufacture one.

It may be preferable, instead, to support such a reference scheme by using a ternary constructor to map each name combination to a `President` entity. For example, the following code uses the predicate `pairsWith` to enter the name pairs, and then uses the constructor function `presidentNamed[gn,fn]=p` to derive a president from that name pair. The constructor mapping is 1:1 between name pairs and presidents, so each president is assigned only one name pair:

```
// Schema
pairsWith(gn, fn) -> string(gn), string(fn).
birthyearOf[p] = y -> President(p), int(y).

President(p) ->.

presidentNamed[gn, fn] = p -> string(gn), string(fn),
    President(p).
lang:constructor(`presidentNamed).
// presidentNamed is a constructor
// that maps givenname, familyname pairs to presidents.

President(p), presidentNamed[gn, fn] = p <-
    pairsWith(gn, fn).
// For each paired combination of extended given name
// and family name, there exists a president
// who may be identified by that name combination.

// Data
+pairsWith("Barack", "Obama"),
    +pairsWith("George W.", "Bush"),
    +pairsWith("Bill", "Clinton"),
    +pairsWith("George H. W.", "Bush").
```

The birth year facts for the presidents may be derived as follows:

```
birthyearOf[p] = 1961 <-
    presidentNamed["Barack", "Obama"] = p.
birthyearOf[p] = 1946 <-
    presidentNamed["George W.", "Bush"] = p.
birthyearOf[p] = 1946 <-
    presidentNamed["Bill", "Clinton"] = p.
birthyearOf[p] = 1924 <-
    presidentNamed["George H. W.", "Bush"] = p.
```

The following query may now be used to display the presidential data:

```
_(p, gn, fn, by) <-
    presidentNamed[gn, fn] = p, birthyearOf[p] = by.
```

The program, data, and query are accessible in `President6.lb`.

Constructors may also be used to support *disjunctive reference schemes*, in which entities of a given type may be derived using any one of multiple constructors. In such cases, only one constructor may be used to derive any given instance of that type. For example, we might derive a person from either a Social Security Number or a passport number, but not both. The first question in the following exercise includes a further example of this kind.

Tip: Use constructors for deriving entities in order to provide a more natural way to conceive of some existing data or to transform an existing structure into another form.

Exercise 3A: The constraint verbalizations generated in `Verbalize1.lb` are examples of *positive* verbalizations. A constraint may also have a *negative* verbalization, indicating how to violate the constraint. For example, the hard constraint UC1 with the positive verbalization, *It is necessary that each person has at most one gender,* also has the negative verbalization, *It is impossible that some person has more than one gender.* Similarly, the soft uniqueness constraint UC2 that each person ought to have at most one wife is verbalized in positive form as *It is obligatory that each person is husband of at most one person*, and in negative form as *It is forbidden that some person is husband of more than one person.* For negative verbalizations, hard constraints have the modal text, *It is impossible that,* and soft constraints have the modal text, *It is forbidden that.* Modify the code in `Verbalize1.lb` to generate both positive and negative verbalizations. *Hint*: Replace the `verbalizationOf` constructor by two constructor predicates.

Exercise 3B: Consider the report shown in Table 4.21 about sports played by countries in international competitions. The third column includes the current rank of that country in that sport, if known. We could code this in LogiQL using a binary predicate to record which countries play which sports, and a ternary predicate to record their rank in that sport if known.

TABLE 4.21   Sports Rankings for
Countries

Country	Sport	Rank
AU	Baseball	
AU	Basketball	3
AU	Cricket	4
US	Baseball	1
US	Basketball	1
US	Soccer	

Note: AU, Australia; US, United States.

A schema and data for this approach are shown below and are available in the file Playing.lb. The subset constraint ensures that countries are ranked only in sports that they have been asserted to play:

```
// Schema
Country(c), hasCountryCode(c:cc) -> string(cc).
Sport(s), hasSportName(s:sn) -> string(sn).
plays(c, s) -> Country(c), Sport(s).
sportRankFor[c, s] = r -> Country(c), Sport(s), int(r).
sportRankFor[c, s] = _ -> plays(c, s).
// If a country is ranked in a sport then it plays
// that sport.

// Data
+plays("AU", "baseball"), +plays("AU", "basketball"),
    +plays("AU", "cricket").
+sportRankFor["AU", "basketball"] = 3,
    +sportRankFor["AU", "cricket"] = 4.
+plays("US", "baseball"), +plays("US", "basketball"),
    +plays("US", "soccer").
+sportRankFor["US", "baseball"] = 1,
    +sportRankFor["US", "basketball"] = 1.
```

The second row of the report could be verbalized in two steps, starting with *Australia plays basketball*, and then saying *that playing is at rank 3*. Here the second sentence refers back to the previous sentence, using a noun phrase *that playing* to make an object out of the situation or state of affairs underlying the proposition captured by the first sentence. This linguistic nominalization process is common in data modeling, where it is known as *objectification* or *reification*.

Objectification may be coded in LogiQL by deriving the entity resulting from the nominalization and also deriving link predicates to relate it back to the original entities involved in its derivation.

Write code to extend the above program to derive `Playing(p)` from `plays` facts using the constructor `playingDerivedFrom[c,s]=p`. Then derive the link predicates `sportLinkedTo[p]=s` and `countryLinkedTo[p]=c` and the predicate `rankOf[p]=r` for `Playing(p)`.

UNIT 4.4: PROGRAM ORGANIZATION

The programs you have seen so far in this book have been intentionally quite modest in size so that they could focus on specific language features. Real programs, however, can include thousands of lines of code. Consequently, it is imperative to organize your programs in a way that makes them easy to understand, maintain, and reuse. Fortunately, LogiQL provides a rich array of mechanisms to support this need.

The general concept that you need to understand in order to properly structure your programs is *modularity*. A program is modular to the extent that dependencies among the various units of code that comprise the whole program are weak. If this is the case, the units are said to be *loosely coupled*. Conversely, if two units are *tightly coupled* then a change to one likely means that the other has to be changed, thereby increasing the effort required to make the change.

Another important aspect of modularity is *cohesion*. A unit of code is cohesive to the extent that it has a single purpose. If a unit of code is not cohesive, then it is likely difficult to understand and to reuse. With coupling and cohesion in mind, your goal in structuring your program code should be to break it up into modular units, which, individually, have a single purpose and, collectively, have as few interdependencies as possible.

Legacy Code

Most of the modularity features of LogiQL have recently been added to the language. Consequently, there is a lot of older, *legacy*, code in existence that does not make use of them. Instead, such code uses two informal mechanisms, which we describe here in case you have to maintain or reuse such code.

The first modularity mechanism that programmers used was to organize their code into files. LogiQL code loaded into a workspace from a `.logic` file is called a *block*. A block is nothing more than the internal version of a file containing LogiQL code, and the only operations available on blocks are that they can be loaded into the current workspace and that they can be activated and deactivated.

The second means that programmers used to organize their legacy code was to employ naming conventions to group related predicates. In particular, members of a group of related predicates were given a common prefix, separated from the predicates' individual names with colons. Such a prefix provides an informal **namespace** useful when reading programs. You have already seen this technique used with, for example, the date-time predicates introduced in Chapter 1. In some legacy code, multiple prefixes are used to denote higher-level groupings.

These two mechanisms, while still available in LogiQL, have been superseded by more powerful features including *modules* and *separate compilation*. Besides direct support for modularity, the new features also improve compilation efficiency and provide you with more meaningful error messages.

Program Organization

If you are going to build a large LogiQL program, there are three related constructs you should understand: *projects, modules,* and *concrete blocks.* The highest-level construct is the **project**, which manifests as a directory containing a project description file and a collection of resources, such as legacy code files or modules. A project can correspond to a complete application or to a self-contained library resource that might be of use to other projects. For example, you might build your application by combining a project implementing the application's functionality with a pre-existing statistical-processing library project.

A **module** is also a structuring mechanism, but at a somewhat lower level of abstraction than a project. A module also manifests as a directory containing logic files or subdirectories or both. The directory structure of a module provides a possibly compound namespace for your predicates so that they can be referenced from other modules.

The code files in a module take the form of interdependent **concrete blocks**. In addition to LogiQL code, a concrete block employs special syntax that enables you to provide aliases for predicate names and to specify how the module's predicates can be accessed from other modules.

Projects

You define a project in LogiQL by giving it a name and creating a directory to hold its source code. That directory contains logic files, subdirectories, and a project description file. Two kinds of logic files are allowed, both having the `.logic` suffix. Files of the first kind are the legacy source files mentioned above. Files of the second kind contain concrete blocks, as described below. Likewise, subdirectories (and their sub-subdirectories) are of two sorts—traditional directories containing legacy `.logic` files and modules, also described below.

In the *project description file* (sometimes called a *project manifest*), you describe how these pieces fit together. Each line (other than comment lines beginning with //) specifies a name and a descriptor, separated by a comma.

A name field can be simple, in which case it designates a `.logic` file in the top-level directory, or it can comprise a directory path ending in a `.logic` file.

Table 4.22 lists important descriptors and their intended uses.

Here is an example of a simple project description file. It, along with the other files used in the body of this unit, can be found in the subdirectory `example`:

```
example, projectname

// A legacy code block.
D.logic, active

// A legacy code block in a subdirectory.
subdir/F.logic, active

// Directory containing a module.
mod, module

// Legacy stored query.
G.logic, inactive
```

TABLE 4.22   Project Descriptors

Descriptor	Use
projectname	Name of the project
active	Named file contains legacy code to be installed in a workspace as an active block
inactive	Named file contains a stored query
module	Named directory contains a LogiQL module
library	Named library that has been constructed from a previously compiled project
execute	Named file contains code to be executed when the project is installed in the workspace; normally contains data assertions for initializing the workspace

If this project file is named `example.project`, then the directory for the project could contain the following contents:

```
example.project        project  description file
subdir                 subdirectory  for  legacy code
subdir/F.logic         legacy .logic  program  file
D.logic                legacy .logic  program file
mod                    module  subdirectory
mod/A                  namespace
mod/A/A.logic          concrete  block
mod/B                  namespace
mod/B/B.logic          concrete block
mod/C.logic            concrete  block
mod/E.logic            concrete  block
G.logic                legacy .logic  stored query  file
```

Note that you did not have to list the non-legacy `.logic` files in your project manifest. The LogiQL compiler is smart enough to figure this out for you. Also, subdirectories within a module now constitute namespaces.

The information in the project description file is used by the LogiQL compiler to control the compilation process and to provide access to project resources from other projects. In particular, the resources described in the file are processed in the order listed. If one of your legacy `.logic` files references another (legacy or non-legacy), the latter should appear above the former in the project description file.

If you create the above `example.project` file, the listed subdirectories and corresponding `.logic` files (which, for purposes of illustration, could be empty), you can build the project by running the following command from within the top-level directory:

```
lb compile project - out-dir out example.project
```

In the above command, `out` is a subdirectory that will contain the compiled binary files.

Once compilation is complete, you can install the resulting project into an existing workspace by invoking `lb` as follows:

```
lb addproject workspaceName directoryName
```

where *workspaceName* is the name of an existing workspace and *directoryName* is the name of directory containing your project file.

Alternatively, you can create the workspace during the same lb execution by adding the create option to the command line.

Modules and Concrete Blocks

LogiQL modules provide a disciplined way to manage names and to provide access to resources. This should be contrasted to the informal way in which names are managed in legacy programs.

Using modules, access to predicates defined in one module by predicates defined inside other modules can be controlled by the programmer. For example, if you know that a particular predicate is of use only in supporting a computation internal to a module, then you can prevent its alteration from within rules in other modules by *sealing* it. In this way, if you later wish to change its implementation, you reduce the work required to update the other modules.

Conversely, if you wish to treat a predicate as a resource for use by other modules, you can explicitly *export* it. Similarly, another module can access a predicate defined in your module, possibly giving it an alternative name (an *alias*) to avoid naming conflicts or to better express its responsibility in the importing module.

A module takes the form of a directory containing special (non-legacy) logic files (concrete blocks) and subdirectories (namespaces). The reason that the logic files are special is that they contain instructions to the compiler concerning the way in which the predicates in that file can be accessed. Here is an example of one such file, named B.logic, found in the mod subdirectory:

```
block(`B) {
    export(`{
        r[x] = y -> mod:A:A:p(x), int(y).
        M(x), hasMid(x:i) -> int(i).
    }),
sealed(`{
        q(x, y) -> M(x), M(y).
    }),
alias(`mod:C:p, `otherp),
    clauses(`{
        p(x) -> int(x).
p(x) <- otherp(x).
        q(x, y) <- hasMid(x), hasMid(y), x < y.
    })
} <- .
```

The `block` predicate is a built-in predicate used to indicate that its argument predicate (B) is a concrete block. Note that the name of the predicate must match the name of the file containing this code (ignoring the `.logic` suffix). Within the braces are several kinds of instructions. The first instruction (`export`) indicates that any predicates declared in this section of the block, such as the functional predicate r, the entity type M, and its refmode `hasMid`, should be made available to other modules. Note also that r refers to predicate p defined in concrete block A. The `sealed` instruction is a variant of `export`, the difference being that although the named predicate q is visible outside of module B, its contents cannot be added to or changed externally.

The next instruction, `alias`, indicates that predicate p from concrete block C can be referred to using the name `otherp`. This is useful to avoid confusion with the separate predicate, also named p, referred to in the `export` instruction.

The final instruction, `clauses`, defines yet another predicate named p. This one can be altered only within the current concrete block. It also contains a rule defining how the values of q are derived.

In summary, the LogiQL concrete block described above refers to three predicates named p. The first belongs to concrete block A and is referred to using its full name `mod:A:A:p`. The second p comes from a different concrete block C and is accessed through the alias `otherp`. The third predicate p can only be accessed from within this source file and is referred to by the unadorned name p.

Any logic files wishing to take advantage of the power of modules need to use these instructions. Non-module legacy logic files can still be included in a project by listing them in the project description file.

Namespaces Revisited

In the above example, the name "`mod:A:A:p`" was used to refer to predicate p defined in concrete block A. As the syntax suggests, there is a hierarchy of names, where each level corresponds to a directory or file within the module. Because modules are organized using directories, you can easily manage predicate names by building an appropriate directory hierarchy. In abstract terms, the syntax of names used in concrete blocks is the following, where square brackets ('[]') are used to surround optional constructs, and the asterisk ('*') is used to indicate any number of occurrences:

[[*moduleName*[:*directoryName*]*:]*fileName*:]*predicateName*

That is, a predicate name may be preceded by the name of the non-legacy .logic file containing it (without the .logic suffix) and by a sequence of directory names beginning with the name of the module. All names are separated by colons (':'). The beginning point of the sequence is the directory containing the module. Note that legacy predicates can be named directly, without any prefixes.

Each module describes a scheme for naming resources (predicates, concrete blocks, and namespaces). This is similar to the naming scheme described above for legacy code. However, the difference is that, here, the naming scheme is enforced by the compiler.

Separate Compilation and Libraries

Using modules has another benefit in addition to those described above—they make use of LogiQL's *separate compilation* facility. Previously, logic files were compiled when they were added to a workspace. A disadvantage of doing this is that unchanged code has to be recompiled if the workspace is reconstructed. With separate compilation, the redundant recompilation can be avoided by saving the results of the compilation in an intermediate file.

The result of compiling the file a.logic is the file a.lbb, containing a condensed form of the program that can be efficiently added to a workspace. A file named LB_SUMMARY.lbp is also produced to summarize the results of compiling the entire project. On subsequent executions, the LogiQL compiler uses these files to determine exactly what needs to be recompiled.

The result of compiling a project is called a **library**, and libraries can be used much as they can in other languages to hold pre-compiled collections of related resources. For example, the locations of library resources can be encoded in the LB_LIBRARY_PATH environment variable for use by the compiler.

The code for the above example (project file, directory hierarchy, and example logic files) can be found in the example subdirectory.

Summary

Table 4.23 summarizes the structuring features introduced in this unit.

Tip: Organize your code into modules that exhibit high internal cohesion and low coupling with other modules.

TABLE 4.23   LogiQL Structuring Features

Concept	Realization	Contents	Features
project	Directory and project description file	Legacy and non-legacy code files	Legacy code inclusion, executed assertions, references to external libraries
module	Directory	Submodules and concrete blocks	Naming scheme
concrete block	.logic file	Exports, seals, aliases, level-0 code	Controlled recompilation, aliasing, sealing
library	.lbp file	Rules, declarations, constraints, facts	Resource for use by other projects without recompilation
export	Metapredicate assertion	Set of declarations	Access to predicates
alias	Metapredicate assertion	Pairs of predicate names	More appropriate names and avoidance of name collision
seal	Metapredicate assertion	Set of declarations	Protection from change

Tip: Use an alias when an imported predicate uses the same name as one in your module.

Tip: Export only those predicates which you explicitly wish other modules to make use of.

Exercise 4A: You are hosting a dinner party to be attended by nine of your friends. You wish to arrange seating for the invitees among the three, three-person tables available so that people who already know each other are seated together as much as possible. Here are a schema and data describing the situation:

```
// Schema
Person(p), hasPersonName(p:s) -> string(s).
isFriendsWith(p1, p2) -> Person(p1), Person(p2).
Table(t), hasTableNbr(t:n) -> int(n).
sitsAtTable[p] = t -> Person(p), Table(t).

// Data
+Table(1).
+Table(2).
+Table(3).
```

```
+isFriendsWith("Snoopy", "Spike").
+isFriendsWith("Snoopy", "Marbles").
+isFriendsWith("Snoopy", "Olaf").
+isFriendsWith("Snoopy", "Belle").
+isFriendsWith("Spike", "Belle").
+isFriendsWith("Marbles", "Andy").
+isFriendsWith("Marbles", "Olaf").
+isFriendsWith("World War I Flying Ace", "Olaf").
+isFriendsWith("World War I Flying Ace", "Andy").
+isFriendsWith("Andy", "Missy").
+isFriendsWith("Belle", "Missy").
+isFriendsWith("Missy", "Joe Cool").
```

How would you arrange the tables for your party? *Notes:* There may be more than one best answer; you do not have to worry about seating yourself; you do not have to write any code, just list the seating arrangement.

Exercise 4B: In the Consolidation Exercise in Chapter 1, you built a comprehensive solution to computing various statistics about monarchs, such as their ages and the lengths of their reigns. The solution provided comprised a set of unstructured .logic files. You are now asked to organize your solution and the accompanying schema and data files using the program-structuring mechanisms introduced in this unit.

You can find the .logic files to use for this exercise in the directory exercise/original. Also present is a script file useful for querying the defined predicates (queryTest.lb) and one for loading in the data (dataLoad.lb). Here is a list of the .logic file names, in alphabetical order (ignoring case):

```
base.logic
baseData.logic
birthCountryData.logic
birthDeath.logic
birthDeathData.logic
Q1Query.logic
Q7Query.logic
Q8Query.logic
Q9Query.logic
```

(i) For the first part of this exercise, you should treat these files as legacy LogiQL files and construct a project description file suitable for use in compiling them. *Hint 1:* You need to reorder these entries to ensure that predicates are compiled before they are referenced. *Hint 2*: You can ignore the data files; you will have to add them manually using the `lb` command. *Hint 3*: Use the `inactive` descriptor to describe the files containing queries. Test your solution by installing the project, asserting the facts in the data files, and running the four queries to see that you get the same results you did in Chapter 1.

(ii) The solution presented in part (i) has several problems: Some files provide predicates not closely related to each other (i.e., the files are not cohesive), some files are too tightly coupled with each other, there is no use of the features provided by concrete blocks, and, of course, the filenames are not clear indicators of the resources the named files provide. As a first step to addressing these problems, you are asked to construct a new module (in your project directory) called `chapter1CE` (for "Chapter 1 Consolidation Exercise") containing only a single file, called `Country.logic`. Remember that you will need to list the new module in your project description file.

`Country.logic` should be a concrete block that contains those parts of the other legacy files that pertain to countries. *Hint:* You will need to change legacy files that reference the predicates in `Country.logic` so that they now include a `Country:` prefix.

Make sure that your test queries still produce the same results.

(iii) A more ambitious task is to extract the code having to do with the dates of births, deaths, and reigns. Create a new concrete block in the `chapter1CE` module and call it `Date`. Place into it all of the code in the legacy files associated with these dates. Update the remaining legacy logic files by adding the appropriate prefix. Then compile, install, populate, and test your solution.

(iv) The solution for part (iii), while correct, still exhibits some problems that need to be fixed. One example occurs in the legacy file `Q9Query.logic`, which contains the following stored query:

```
_(m) <- Date:isFirst(m).
```

If you look in `Date.logic`, you will notice that `isFirst` is not exported. This limits its access from other non-legacy files, but not from legacy files. In anticipation of incorporating `Q9Query.logic` into the `chapter1CE` module, examine `Date.logic` and place a declaration for `isFirst` into the `export` section. Also, determine which of the other predicates in the `clauses` section might be useful externally and place declarations for them into the `export` section as well. *Hint:* Only declarations may appear within the `export` section. Hence, you may have to add in some explicit declarations for the predicates you wish to export.

(v) Of the remaining legacy files, four correspond to queries and three to data. The other one—`base.logic`—resulted from collecting the LogiQL files used in Chapter 1. That is, it was not designed to be modular. In particular, it is not cohesive. For this exercise, you should refactor the resources provided by this file into at least three pieces and include them in the `chapter1CE` module.

(vi) Although there is no way in the current version of LogiQL to include data files within modules, query files can be included. To do this, you need to make several changes to the existing files: (1) Move the file containing the query into the module; (2) convert it into a concrete block, placing the query itself in the `clauses` section; and (3) change the query name so it is no longer anonymous. You can also use this opportunity to give the query file/block a more appropriate name. To try this out, take the query found in `Q9Query.logic` and convert it into a query named `FirstMonarchQuery.logic`.

UNIT 4.5: MISCELLANEOUS TOPICS

This unit contains a discussion of three topics that are too small to warrant units of their own. The first has to do with whether predicates are actually stored (*materialized*) in a workspace or are merely computed on demand. Depending on the circumstances, this choice can improve program efficiency. The second topic is LogiQL's hierarchical syntax, which is a shorthand for expressing the contents of a set of related predicates. The final topic concerns file predicates, which are one of LogiQL's ways of performing input from and output to your computer's file system.

Materialized and Derived-Only Views

The LogiQL execution engine normally processes rules that compute updates to a workspace. These derived predicates, whose fact instances are stored in this way for later use, are known as **materialized views**.

For many applications, materialized views provide the best option for realizing derivation rules, because the execution engine's incremental evaluation is often much more efficient than full re-evaluation. For example, consider a derivation rule to compute the current balance of a bank account. By storing the previous balance, when an account transaction (e.g., a deposit or withdrawal) occurs, we need to compute only the effect of that transaction on the account. Alternatively, if we do not materialize the balance, we would need to process all the past transactions on the account every time the account is updated, which could be quite an expensive operation.

However, it is sometimes useful to fully evaluate a derived predicate on the fly, making its result available for other rules within the transaction but not installing its result in the database when the transaction is committed. Such predicates are known as **derived-only predicates**, and using them requires that the compiler must be informed using the lang:derivationType metapredicate. The syntax is as follows, where *predicate* is the name of the derived-only predicate. The default setting for a predicate's derivation type is DerivedAndStored, which is the materialized-view case discussed above:

```
lang:derivationType[`predicate] = "Derived".
```

One reason for using derived-only predicates is to define a complex computation, which could potentially result in an infinite set of facts. Such a predicate can prove useful if we intend to use the result of the computation in a context that finitely constrains its arguments. That is, the full predicate need never be computed and stored. For example, the following program (available in the file energy.lb) uses the derived-only predicate cSquared to compute the energy equivalent (in Joules) of a given mass (in kilograms), by using Einstein's famous equation $E = mc^2$:

```
Mass(m), hasKgValue(m:kg) -> float(kg).
cSquared[kg] = j -> float(kg), float(j).
cSquared[kg] = j <- kg * pow[300000000f, 2f] = j.
lang:derivationType[`cSquared] = "Derived".

isHighEnergySource(m) -> Mass(m).
isHighEnergySource(m) <-
    Mass(m), hasKgValue(m:kg),
    cSquared[kg] = j, j > pow[10f, 18f].
```

```
isVeryHighEnergySource(m) -> Mass(m).
isVeryHighEnergySource(m) <-
    Mass(m), hasKgValue(m:kg),
    cSquared[kg] = j, j > pow[10f, 19f].
```

Here, c (the speed of light) is 3×10^8 meters/second, which we represent as 300000000f. To square c, we raise c to the power of 2 using the built-in predicate pow[base,power]=result.

Two derivation rules are included to classify a mass as a *high-energy source* if its energy equivalent exceeds 10^{18} Joules, or as a *very high-energy source* if its energy equivalent exceeds 10^{19} Joules. Note that in the above code cSquared is designated as Derived. If, instead, it was treated as a derived-and-stored predicate, its rule would be unsafe. Can you see why?

First, of course, is the realization that storing this predicate is impractical. If fully computed, it would contain all pairs of floating-point numbers related by Einstein's formula. Moreover, recall from Chapter 3 that in order for a rule to be safe, each variable in the head of a rule (m in this case) must appear in a positive context as an argument to a domain predicate or a domain equality in the body of the rule, neither of which is the case here. Derived-only predicates, however, are treated specially by the execution engine. Their values are computed only in the context of the other rules that use them. In our example, cSquared is used inside of isHighEnergySource and isVeryHighEnergySource, both of which contain the atom Mass(m), which uses a domain predicate. It is as if the text of the body of cSquared were literally copied into these two rules, thereby overcoming the safety objection.

We can assert the following facts to test our computation:

```
+Mass(10f).
+Mass(100f).
+Mass(1000f).
```

If we now query the computed predicates, the output is as shown below. Note that if you tried to print the population of the cSquared predicate, however, no facts would be displayed, because derived-only predicates do not have their results stored in the workspace:

```
Querying isHighEnergySource:
    1000
    100

Querying isVeryHighEnergySource:
    1000
```

Derived-only predicates can be useful in special circumstances, such as those mentioned above. However, there are several limitations in the rules used to compute them. In particular, the rules may not use negation and may not be disjunctive. The latter restriction means that they may not use the *or* operator and may not be split into several separate rules.

Hierarchical Syntax

A common practice in implementing an application is to begin with entities, and for each, define a set of property predicates expressing the data to be associated with those entities. For example, we might wish to include people in our application, and for each person, provide information about that person's name and address. Such a schema might look like the following:

```
Person(p), hasPersonNr(p:n) -> int(n).
firstNameOf[p] = s -> Person(p), string(s).
lastNameOf[p] = s -> Person(p), string(s).
streetAddressOf[p] = s -> Person(p), string(s).
cityOf[p] = s -> Person(p), string(s).
```

If we then wish to populate these predicates for a particular person, we could enter the data using delta predicates, as follows:

```
+Person(p),
    +hasPersonNr(p:13),
    +firstNameOf[p] = "John",
    +lastNameOf[p] = "Doe",
    +streetAddressOf[p] = "1384 West Peachtree Street",
    +cityOf[p] = "Atlanta".
```

Note that there is some duplication in the above, with p being referred to six times. This repetition would be even more irksome if we were entering data for many people. Fortunately, LogiQL has a shortcut that can reduce some of this burden. It is called **hierarchical syntax**. Here is how the above delta logic would be expressed with it:

```
+Person(p) {
    +hasPersonNr(13),
    +firstNameOf[] = "John",
    +lastNameOf[] = "Doe",
    +streetAddressOf[] = "1384 West Peachtree Street",
    +cityOf[] = "Atlanta"
}.
```

In the above, the curly braces ('{}') serve to enclose a set of atoms or function assignments, each of which is qualified by the particular entity that they describe. Note that the refmode predicate `hasPersonNr` did not have to include a colon. Moreover, because p was used only once, we did not actually have to include it. Instead, we could have replaced it with an underscore.

A hierarchical rule is similar to a normal logic rule, containing both a head and a body. However, instead of separating the two parts with an arrow, the body is enclosed in curly braces.

It gets even better—hierarchical rules can be nested. If we have a schema that warrants it, we can avoid even more repetition by including one set of fact assertions inside of another, as the following example illustrates:

```
// Schema
Person(p), hasPersonNr(p:n) -> int(n).
firstNameOf[p] = s -> Person(p), string(s).
lastNameOf[p] = s -> Person(p), string(s).
Address(a), hasStreetLocation(a:s) -> string(s).
addressOf[p] = a -> Person(p), Address(a).
cityIn[a] = s -> Address(a), string(s).

// Data
+Person(p),
    +hasPersonNr(p:13),
    +firstNameOf[p] = "John",
    +lastNameOf[p] = "Doe",
    +Address(a),
    +hasStreetLocation(a:"1384 West Peachtree
        Street"),
    +addressOf[p] = a,
    +cityIn[a] = "Atlanta".

// Hierarchically expressed data
+Person(_) {
    +hasPersonNr(14),
    +firstNameOf[] = "Jane",
    +lastNameOf[] = "Doe",
    +addressOf[] = +Address(_) {
        +hasStreetLocation("1384 West Peachtree Street"),
        +cityIn[] = "Atlanta"
    }
}.
```

There is one other feature of hierarchical syntax that you should be aware of—multiple entity types can be represented in the head. For example, have a look at the following schema:

```
Person(p), hasPersonName(p:s) -> string(s).
Car(c), hasBrand(c:s) -> string(s).
drives(p, c) -> Person(p), Car(c).
```

Without hierarchical syntax, we might assert facts to these predicates as follows:

```
+Person(p),
    +hasPersonName(p:"McCambridge"),
    +Car(c),
    +hasBrand(c:"Mercedes"),
    +drives(p, c).
```

Using hierarchical syntax, however, we can elide the arguments in the body and somewhat shorten the rule as follows:

```
(+Person(p), +Car(c)) {
    +hasPersonName[] = "McCambridge",
    +hasBrand[] = "Mercedes",
    +drives()
}.
```

Note that the head of the rule now contains two atoms, enclosed within parentheses. Despite the potential for ambiguity, the LogiQL compiler is able to determine which entity types belong with which predicates within the body.

Hierarchical syntax provides no additional power to the LogiQL language. Anything that can be expressed with it can be expressed without it. That being said, using hierarchical syntax can reduce the size of programs, thereby improving their readability.

File Predicates

Nearly every computer program takes data as input and produces data as output. Programs written in LogiQL are no exception. However, thus far, the only means we have seen for input are delta predicates, and the only ways to produce output are with queries or lb print commands.

With real-world programs and their demands for processing *big data*, these devices are clearly inconvenient. This subunit presents a more robust means for dealing with input–output called **file predicates**.

From the point of view of a program, a file predicate is like any other. It contains a sequence of facts. If the file predicate is used for input, then the facts represent exactly the data contained in some existing external file. Conversely, if the predicate corresponds to an output file, then any facts computed by the program and saved into the predicate are also written into the output file.

As a simple example, imagine that we wished to take computed data describing the British monarchs and place it into a *csv* file. *Csv* stands for *comma separated values,* and files in *csv* format are commonly used as a way to import data into spreadsheets.

Table 4.24, copied from the table of birth and death dates given in the consolidation exercise of Chapter 1, is the data we wish to save in the *csv* file, which indicates the dates of birth and death of each of the British monarchs.

The schema for this data is the following:

```
// Schema
Monarch(m), hasMonarchName(m:n) -> string(n).
birthdateOf[m] = d -> Monarch(m), datetime(d).
deathdateOf[m] = d -> Monarch(m), datetime(d).
Monarch(m) -> birthdateOf[m] = _.
birthdateOf[m] = d1, deathdateOf[m] = d2 -> d1 <= d2.
```

TABLE 4.24   Birth and Death Dates for British Monarchs

Monarch	Born	Died
Anne	February 6, 1665	August 1, 1714
George I	May 28, 1660	June 11, 1727
George II	October 30, 1683	October 25, 1760
George III	June 4, 1738	January 29, 1820
George IV	August 12, 1762	June 26, 1830
William IV	August 1, 1765	June 20, 1837
Victoria	May 24, 1819	January 22, 1901
Edward VII	November 9, 1841	May 6, 1910
George V	June 3, 1865	January 20, 1936
Edward VIII	June 23, 1894	May 28, 1972
George VI	December 14, 1895	February 6, 1952
Elizabeth II	April 21, 1926	—

Here are the LogiQL fact assertions for this data:

```
// Data
lang:compiler:disableWarning:DATETIME _ TIMEZONE[] = true.
+birthdateOf ["Anne"] = #02/06/1665#,
    +deathdateOf ["Anne"] = #08/01/1714#.
+birthdateOf ["George I"] = #05/28/1660#,
    +deathdateOf ["George I"] = #06/11/1727#.
+birthdateOf ["George II"] = #10/30/1683#,
    +deathdateOf ["George II"] = #10/25/1760#.
+birthdateOf ["George III"] = #06/03/1738#,
    +deathdateOf ["George III"] = #01/29/1820#.
+birthdateOf ["George IV"] = #08/12/1762#,
    +deathdateOf ["George IV"] = #06/26/1830#.
+birthdateOf ["William IV"] = #08/01/1765#,
    +deathdateOf ["William IV"] = #06/20/1837#.
+birthdateOf ["Victoria"] = #05/24/1819#,
    +deathdateOf ["Victoria"] = #01/22/1901#.
+birthdateOf ["Edward VII"] = #11/09/1841#,
    +deathdateOf ["Edward VII"] = #05/06/1910#.
+birthdateOf ["George V"] = #06/03/1865#,
    +deathdateOf ["George V"] = #01/20/1936#.
+birthdateOf ["Edward VIII"] = #06/23/1894#,
    +deathdateOf ["Edward VIII"] = #05/28/1972#.
+birthdateOf ["George VI"] = #12/14/1895#,
    +deathdateOf ["George VI"] = #02/06/1952#.
+birthdateOf ["Elizabeth II"] = #04/21/1926#.
```

Our first example use of file predicates is to produce as output a *csv* file containing this data. Like any other predicate, a file predicate has a name, and for this example, we will conventionally use the name _out for the file predicate providing data to our output file. Also, like other predicates, each file predicate has a sequence of roles, and in this case, each role corresponds to one of the columns of data in the table. In particular, we have roles for the monarchs' names and their dates of birth and death. Moreover, the roles each have a type corresponding to one of LogiQL's primitive types. Hence, for our example the actual declaration for _out is

```
_out(s, d1, d2) -> string(s), datetime(d1),
    datetime(d2).
```

From the point of view of the computer system in which the program is running, a file predicate is a file, and it therefore has certain properties, such as its name and the type of data it contains. These properties are expressed in the LogiQL program using functional metapredicates similar to the way we assigned properties (like `Derived`) to predicates. For our example, this code has the following form:

```
lang:physical:filePath[`_out] = "dates.csv".
lang:physical:delimiter[`_out] = ",".
```

The first line in the above code indicates that the name of the file is `dates.csv` and that it resides in the directory in which the program runs. In general, a full path name could be used to designate the file. Note that this filename must be a literal string rather than a computed value. The second line indicates that for this example a comma will be used as the delimiter.

What remains to specify in our program for producing the *csv* file is how the file predicate is actually populated. This can be simply expressed with the following rule:

```
_out(n, d1, d2) <-
    Monarch(m), hasMonarchName(m:n),
    birthdateOf[m] = d1, deathdateOf[m] = d2.
```

That is, the three values comprising each line in the output are the monarch's name (n), the monarch's date of birth (d1), and the monarch's date of death (d2).

The collected program fragments can be found in the file `datesOutput.lb`, and the resulting *csv* file found in `dates.csv`. The screenshot in Figure 4.7 shows the spreadsheet after the `dates.csv` file contents are imported.

You should note two things about the resulting file. First, not only do the dates of birth and death appear, but also values for the times appear. Of course, we did not provide those in our fact assertions, so the LogiQL engine supplied defaults. The second thing to note is that Queen Elizabeth does not appear in the table. Can you think why she is not there?

She is not there because she is still alive. In particular, the rule computing `_out` requires a death date, and none exists for her.

As another illustration of the use of file predicates, let's now read in data from a file that contains the names of monarchs and their ages at

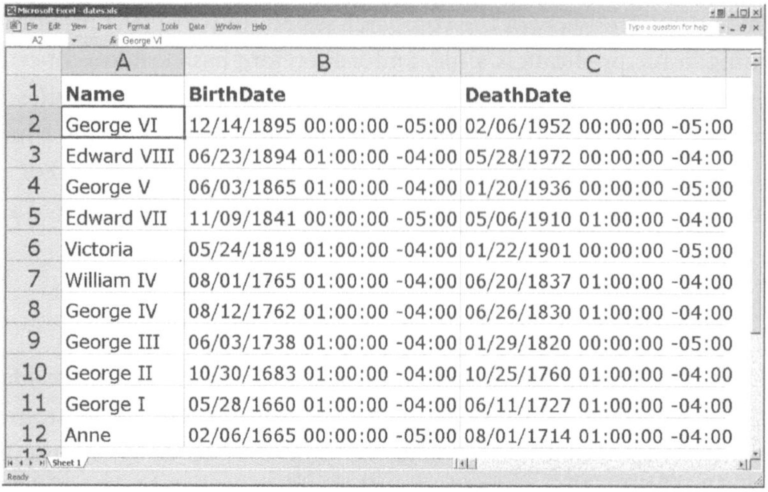

	A	B	C
1	**Name**	**BirthDate**	**DeathDate**
2	George VI	12/14/1895 00:00:00 -05:00	02/06/1952 00:00:00 -05:00
3	Edward VIII	06/23/1894 01:00:00 -04:00	05/28/1972 00:00:00 -04:00
4	George V	06/03/1865 01:00:00 -04:00	01/20/1936 00:00:00 -05:00
5	Edward VII	11/09/1841 00:00:00 -05:00	05/06/1910 01:00:00 -04:00
6	Victoria	05/24/1819 01:00:00 -04:00	01/22/1901 00:00:00 -05:00
7	William IV	08/01/1765 01:00:00 -04:00	06/20/1837 01:00:00 -04:00
8	George IV	08/12/1762 01:00:00 -04:00	06/26/1830 01:00:00 -04:00
9	George III	06/03/1738 01:00:00 -04:00	01/29/1820 00:00:00 -05:00
10	George II	10/30/1683 01:00:00 -04:00	10/25/1760 01:00:00 -04:00
11	George I	05/28/1660 01:00:00 -04:00	06/11/1727 01:00:00 -04:00
12	Anne	02/06/1665 00:00:00 -05:00	08/01/1714 01:00:00 -04:00

FIGURE 4.7 Spreadsheet with imported monarchy data.

death. In this example, rather than using a *csv* file, we will illustrate how to read from a text file. The file is named `monarchDeathAges.txt`, and it contains the following contents:

```
George VI, 56
Edward VIII, 77
George V, 70
Edward VII, 68
Victoria, 81
William IV, 71
George IV, 67
George III, 81
George II, 76
George I, 67
Anne, 49
```

First, here is the schema that we will use. In particular, we include one property predicate to record the monarchs' ages at death (`deathAgeOf`):

```
// Schema
Monarch(m), hasMonarchName(m:n) -> string(n).
deathAgeOf[m] = a -> Monarch(m), int(a).
Monarch(m) -> deathAgeOf[m] = _.
```

We can describe the input file with the following code:

```
_in[] = s -> string(s).
lang:physical:filePath[`_in] = "monarchDeathAges.txt".
lang:physical:delimiter[`_in] = "\n".
```

The name of the file providing the data is monarchDeathAges.txt, and the file predicate that contains its contents is named _in. Instead of using a comma to separate the data values into fields, we treat each line as a single fact, with lines delimited by newline characters ('\n'). This means that there is no automatic processing of the data, such as looking for commas, as was the case with the *csv* file we populated above. We do the work ourselves to illustrate what you may need to do if an input file's data format does not make use of a delimiter character.

The actual line to read the file contents is similar to what we saw with the *csv* file except that there is only one field, a string predicate to hold the contents of each line:

```
+inputString(s) <- _in(s).
```

Once the line is read in, we need to split it into two pieces, and we must make sure that the pieces remain related to each other in the workspace. That is, we want to make sure that Anne's age at death does not somehow become associated with Victoria. To do the former, we make use of the string:split function, and the latter can be accomplished using the seq<< >> aggregation function. We saw both of these functions in Unit 3.6:

```
line[i] = s -> int(i), string(s).
line[i] = s <- seq<<i = s>> inputString(s).
// The name of each of monarch as a string.
nameString[i] = s -> int(i), string(s).
nameString[i] = n <- string:split[line[i], ",", 0] = n.
// The age of each monarch as a string.
ageString[i] = s -> int(i), string(s).
ageString[i] = d <- string:split[line[i], ",", 1] = d.
// The age of each monarch as an integer.
ageInt[i] = d -> int(i), int(d).
ageInt[i] = d <- ageString[i] = s,
    string:int:convert[s] = d.
```

Here are the rules that actually do the parsing:

```
line[i] = s <- seq<<i = s>> inputString(s).
nameString[i] = n <- string:split[line[i], ",", 0] = n.
ageString[i] = d <- string:split[line[i], ",", 1] = d.
ageInt[i] = d <- ageString[i] = s,
    string:int:convert[s] = d.
```

The seq aggregation function associates an index number with each fact in inputString. That number is then used with both the name (nameString) and the age (ageInt). The next two rules use string:split. Recall that the three arguments in string:split's keyspace comprise the string to be parsed (line[i]), a delimiter character (',') used to separate the string's pieces, and an integer literal to identify the parsed pieces. The computed result of string:split is the text segment identified by the literal. (Recall the convention that the indices into the results of parsing start counting at zero rather than one.)

The fourth rule in the above code converts ageString into an int, which we name ageInt. It makes use of LogiQL's conversion function string:int:convert. In general the names of conversion functions are formed by concatenating the names of the two primitive data types involved (string and int in this case) and appending "convert". The upshot is that ageInt is populated with the monarchs' ages at death.

Finally, we can complete our computation by populating the Monarch and deathAgeOf predicates from our utility predicates:

```
+Monarch(n), +deathAgeOf[n] = d <- nameString[i] = n,
    ageInt[i] = d.
```

After executing this program, we issue the query:

```
_(n, a) <- hasMonarchName(m:n), deathAgeOf[m] = a.
```

we see the expected results:

```
"Anne" 49
"Edward VII" 68
"Edward VIII" 77
"George I" 67
"George II" 76
```

```
"George III" 81
"George IV" 67
"George V" 71
"George VI" 56
"Victoria" 81
"William IV" 71
```

The program code for this example can be found in the file datesInput.lb.

File predicates are a powerful means for dealing with external data. Note, however, that unless the file data are delimited, you are responsible for processing the data to populate your domain predicates. Moreover, the processing of file predicates does little if any error checking. For a robust program, you need to take care of this yourself, either during parsing or via constraints.

Tip: Use derived-only predicates in situations where a rule might generate an infinite amount of data but is only used in other rules that eliminate this possibility.

Tip: Materialize predicates when previously saved results can be reused in computing new results.

Tip: Use hierarchical syntax in situations where a set of related property predicates are being updated.

Tip: Use file predicates to save computed data to files or to assert a large set of facts.

Exercise 5A: Imagine that product prices are stored in predicates using the following schema and rule:

```
Product(p), hasSKU(p:s) -> int(s).
basePriceOf[p] = d -> Product(p), decimal(d). // USD.
taxRate[] = d -> decimal(d).
totalPriceOf[p] = d -> Product(p), decimal(d).
totalPriceOf[p] = d <-
    Product(p),
    (basePriceOf[p] * (1.0 + taxRate[])) = d.
```

Which of these five predicates should be materialized and which should be derived only?

Exercise 5B: Continuing with the example in **Exercise 5A**, imagine further that you wish to sell products in countries that used different currencies, each of which has an exchange rate against the U.S. dollar:

```
Country(c), hasCountryCode(c:n) -> int(n).
currencyOf[c] = s -> Country(c), string(s).
exchangeRateOf[s] = d -> string(s), decimal(d).
localBasePriceOf_In_[p, c] = f -> Product(p),
    Country(c), float(f).
localBasePriceOf_In_[p, c] = f <-
    Product(p),
    Country(c),
    currencyOf[c] = s,
    (basePriceOf[p] * exchangeRateOf[s]) = f.
```

Which of these five predicates should be materialized and which derived only?

Exercise 5C: This exercise makes use of the following schema about wines, which can be found in the file wineSchema.logic:

```
// Schema
Wine(w), hasWineId(w:id) -> int(id).
descriptionOf[w] = s -> Wine(w), string(s).
yearOf[w] = y -> Wine(w), int(y).
tasteOf[w] = t -> Wine(w), Taste(t).
colorOf[w] = c -> Wine(w), string(c).
// Red, White, Rose.
quantityOf[w] = n -> Wine(w), int(n).
priceOf[w] = d -> Wine(w), decimal(d).
exclusiveUseOf[w] = b -> Wine(w), boolean(b).

Taste(t), hasTasteId(t:id) -> int(id).
sugarOf[t] = s -> Taste(t), string(s).
// Dry, OffDry, Sweet.
flavorOf[t] = f -> Taste(t), string(f).
// Strong, Moderate, Delicate.
bodyOf[t] = b -> Taste(t), string(b).
// Full, Medium, Light.
```

```
// Constraints
Wine(w) -> colorOf[w] = "Red" ; colorOf[w] = "White" ;
           colorOf[w] = "Rose".
Taste(t) -> sugarOf[t] = "Dry" ; sugarOf[t] = "OffDry" ;
           sugarOf[t] = "Sweet".
Taste(t) -> flavorOf[t] = "Strong" ;
           flavorOf[t] = "Moderate" ;
           flavorOf[t] = "Delicate".
Taste(t) -> bodyOf[t] = "Full" ; bodyOf[t] = "Medium" ;
           bodyOf[t] = "Light".
```

Use hierarchical syntax to assert facts about the two wines described in the file wineData.txt.

Exercise 5D: (i) Write a LogiQL program that makes a copy of an input *csv* file comprising lines each of which contains a single string value. Try it on the file input7di.csv. **(ii)** Write a LogiQL program that makes a copy of an input file treating it as a text file. Test your program on the file input7dii.txt.

UNIT 4.6: CONSOLIDATION EXERCISE 4

This exercise gives you a chance to test how well you have mastered the topics covered in this chapter.

Q1: Table 4.25 is an extract of a report that lists kinds of plants. For ease of reference, plant kinds are primarily identified by a plant kind number. However, plant kinds may also be identified by their scientific names. For some plant kinds this is simply their genus names (e.g., *Agrostis*). Some other plant kinds may be identified by their genus and species (e.g., *Acacia interior*). Still other plant kinds may be identified by their genus, species, and infraspecies, which involve both a rank and an infraname (e.g., *Eucalyptus fibrosa* ssp. *nubila*, where ssp. abbreviates *subspecies*).

TABLE 4.25   Plant Species Identifiers

Number	Genus	Species Name	Infraspecies Rank	Infraspecies Infraname
1	Agrostis			
2	Acacia	interior		
3	Eucalyptus	fibrosa	ssp.	nubila

LogiQL code for this report is shown below. The program and data are accessible in the files `Plants.logic` and `PlantsData.logic`. Extend this with derivation rules to derive a printable form of the full scientific name of each plant kind. The answer can be found in the file `Plants2.logic`:

```
// Schema
PlantKind(p), hasPlantKindNr(p:n) -> int(n).
Genus(g), hasGenusName(g:gn) -> string(gn).
Infraspecies(i) -> .
genusOf[p] = g -> PlantKind(p), Genus(g).
speciesNameOf[p] = s -> PlantKind(p), string(s).
infraspeciesOf[p] = i -> PlantKind(p), Infraspecies(i).
rankOf[i] = r -> Infraspecies(i), string(r).
infranameOf[i] = n -> Infraspecies(i), string(n).
PlantKind(p) -> genusOf[p] = _ .
// plantkinds have a genus.
// Each infraspecies has a rank and infraname.
Infraspecies(i) -> rankOf[i] = _, infranameOf[i] = _ .
/* Each combination of rank and infraname
   refers to at most one infraspecies */
rankOf[i1] = r, infranameOf[i1] = n ,
    rankOf[i2] = r, infranameOf[i2] = n -> i1 = i2.
// Each plantkind with an infraspecies also has a
// species.
infraspeciesOf[p] = _ -> speciesNameOf[p] = _.

// Data
+genusOf[1] = "Agrostis".
+genusOf[2] = "Acacia", +speciesNameOf[2] = "interior".
+genusOf[3] = "Eucalyptus",
    +speciesNameOf[3] = "fibrosa",
+Infraspecies(i), +infraspeciesOf[3] = i,
+rankOf[i] = "ssp.", +infranameOf[i] = "nubila".
```

Q2: The report in Table 4.26 shows inflation rates in the United States for the years 1991 through 2011. The inflation rate figures show the percentage inflation relative to the previous year. For example, $100 at the end of 1990 is equivalent in purchasing power to $104.23 at the end of 1991, and is equivalent to $107.388 (= $104.23 times 103.03) at the end of 1992.

TABLE 4.26   Inflation Rates by Year

Year	Inflation Rate
1991	4.23
1992	3.03
1993	2.95
1994	2.61
1995	2.81
1996	2.93
1997	2.34
1998	1.55
1999	2.19
2000	3.38
2001	2.83
2002	1.59
2003	2.27
2004	2.68
2005	3.39
2006	3.23
2007	2.85
2008	3.84
2009	−0.36
2010	1.65
2011	3.10

A schema and the associated data for this table are available in the files `Inflation.logic` and `InflationData.logic`, respectively. Using these files, answer the following questions:

(a) Using imperative pseudocode, specify an algorithm that uses a **for-loop** to compute the cumulative inflation since 1990 at the end of 2011. Express this inflation figure as a ratio relative to 1990. For example, the figures for the cumulative inflation since 1990 at the end of the years 1990, 1991, and 1992 are, respectively, 1, 1.0423, and 1.07388.

(b) Using recursion instead of a **for-loop**, write LogiQL code to compute the cumulative inflation ratio at the end of each of the years in the range 1990 through 2011.

(c) Using your program, write a LogiQL query to determine the salary at the end of 2011 that is equivalent in purchasing power, when adjusted for inflation, to a salary of $100,000 at the end of 1990. The answers can be found in `InflationAnswer.logic`.

TABLE 4.27   Employee Parking Data

Employee	Cars	Parking Bay
101	ABC123,BND007	
102		
103	LNX911	5
104	1ABC123	4

Q3: Table 4.27 is extracted from a company report that records which employees drive which cars to work, as well as the parking bay allocated to them (if any). For this application, cars are identified by their license plate numbers.

The following code and data (accessible in Car.logic and CarData. logic) are the stub of a program and data to model this report:

```
// Schema
Employee(e), hasEmployeeNr(e:n) -> int(n).
Car(c), hasLicensePlateNr(c:n) -> string(n).
ParkingBay(pb), hasParkingBayNr(pb:n) -> int(n).
drives(e, c) -> Employee(e), Car(c).
parkingBayOf[e] = pb -> Employee(e), ParkingBay(pb).

// Data
+drives(101, "ABC123"), +drives(101, "BND007"),
    +parkingBayOf[101] = 3.
+Employee(102).
+drives(103, "LNX911"), +parkingBayOf[103] = 5.
+drives(104, "ABC123"), +parkingBayOf[104] = 4.
```

Although the program works, it lacks the *uniqueness constraint* that each parking bay is allocated to at most one driver and the *equality constraint* that a parking bay is allocated to an employee if and only if that employee drives a car. **(a)** Add code for these missing constraints. The answer can be found in the file Car2.logic. **(b)** Modify the program to replace the equality constraint by a *mandatory role constraint* on a role played by drivers. *Hint:* Introduce a subtype for Driver. The answer can be found in the file Car3.logic.

Q4: (a) Add code to your answer to **(Q3a)**, to enforce the *frequency constraint* that each employee may drive at most two cars to work. Test your constraint by trying to add a third car for employee 101. **(b)** If the *m:n* predicate drives(e,c) is replaced by two functional predicates, car1Of[e]=c, and car2Of[e]=c, is the frequency constraint from part **(a)** now automatically enforced? The answers can be found in the file Car4.logic.

Q5: The report extract shown in Table 4.28 records the membership of mixed doubles teams in tennis. Teams are numbered sequentially based on the week (from week 1 onward) in which a team is to play. In this sense, sometimes the same pair of people may form more than one team. The following code (accessible in Team.logic and TeamData.logic) is the stub of a program and data to model this report:

```
// Schema
Person(p), hasPersonName(p:pn) -> string(pn).
Man(p) -> Person(p).
lang:isEntity[`Man] = true.
Woman(p) -> Person(p).
lang:isEntity[`Woman] = true.
Team(t), hasTeamNr(t:n) -> int(n).
manInTeam[t] = m -> Team(t), Man(m).
womanInTeam[t] = w -> Team(t), Woman(w).

// Data
+manInTeam[1] = "Alan", +womanInTeam[1] = "Betty".
+manInTeam[2] = "Alan", +womanInTeam[2] = "Cathy".
+manInTeam[3] = "Bob", +womanInTeam[3] = "Cathy".
+manInTeam[4] = "Alan", +womanInTeam[4] = "Betty".
```

Extend the program with code to enforce the *external frequency constraint* that the same pair of people may play together in at most two teams. Test your code with a counterexample. The answers can be found in the file Team2.logic and Team2CounterExample.logic.

TABLE 4.28 Tennis Team Pairings

Team Number	Man	Woman
1	Alan	Betty
2	Alan	Cathy
3	Bob	Cathy
4	Alan	Betty
...	...	...

TABLE 4.29   Seminar Facility Needs

Seminar	Special Needs	Room
S1	WiFi	10
S2		15
S3	Public address (PA), WiFi	20
S4	PA	20
S5	WiFi	

TABLE 4.30   Room Facilities

Room	Facilities
5	
10	WiFi
15	
20	Public address (PA), WiFi
...	...

Q6: The report extracts shown in Tables 4.29 and 4.30 are maintained by a company that holds seminars. The first report lists each seminar, the room it uses (if decided), and any special facilities needed for the seminar (e.g., wireless Internet access or a public address system). The second report lists each room and its special facilities, if any.

The following code (accessible in `Seminar.logic` and `Seminar-Data.logic`) is the stub of a program and data to model these reports:

```
// Schema
Seminar(s), hasSeminarCode(s:c) -> string(c).
Facility(f), hasFacilityCode(f:c) -> string(c).
Room(r), hasRoomNr(r:n) -> int(n).
needsFacility(s, f) -> Seminar(s), Facility(f).
roomUsedBy[s] = r -> Seminar(s), Room(r).
providesFacility(r, f) -> Room(r), Facility(f).

// Data
+needsFacility("S1", "WiFi"), +roomUsedBy["S1"] = 10.
+roomUsedBy["S2"] = 15.
+needsFacility("S3", "PA"), +needsFacility("S3", "WiFi"),
    +roomUsedBy["S3"] = 20.
+needsFacility("S4", "PA"), +roomUsedBy["S4"] = 20.
+needsFacility("S5", "WiFi").
+Room(5).
```

```
+providesFacility(10, "WiFi").
+Room(15).
+providesFacility(20, "PA"), +providesFacility(20, "WiFi").
```

Add code to enforce the following constraint: If a room is used by a seminar that needs a facility then that room must provide that facility. Include a counterexample to test your code. The answers can be found in the files Seminar2.logic and Seminar2CounterExample.logic.

Q7: The report extract shown in Table 4.31 concerns bids made by teams for funded projects. Each bid is for a single project and is by a single team. The decision on which bid succeeds for a given project is made by the selection committee for that project.

The following code (accessible in Bid.logic and BidData.logic) is the stub of a program and data to model these reports:

```
// Schema
Project(p), hasProjectName(p:n) -> string(n).
SelectionCtee(c), hasSelectionCteeNr(c:n) -> string(n).
Person(p), hasPersonName(p:n) -> string(n).
Bid(b), hasBidNr(b:n) -> string(n).
Team(t), hasTeamName(t:n) -> string(n).
isOnCommittee(p, c) -> Person(p), SelectionCtee(c).
isOnTeam(p, t) -> Person(p), Team(t).
projectOfBid[b] = p -> Bid(b), Project(p).
teamOfBid[b] = t -> Bid(b), Team(t).
selectionCteeForProject[p] = c -> Project(p),
     SelectionCtee(c).
```

TABLE 4.31   Funding Team Data

Project	Selection Committee Number	Selection Committee Members	Bids	Bidding Team Name	Bidding Team Members
Mars1	C1	C. Sagan	B1	Trekkers	C. Kirk
		A. Clarke			M. Spock
		I. Asimov	B2	Oldies	F. Gordon
					H. Seldon
					M. Yoda
Jupiter2	C2	A. Clarke	B3	Trekkers	C. Kirk
		H. Solo			M. Spock
		H. Wells	B4	Jedi	L. Skywalker
					M. Yoda

```
// Data
+selectionCteeForProject ["Mars1"] = "C1".
+selectionCteeForProject ["Jupiter2"] = "C2".
+isOnCommittee ("C. Sagan", "C1"),
    +isOnCommittee ("A. Clarke", "C1"),
    +isOnCommittee ("I. Asimov", "C1").
+isOnCommittee ("A. Clarke", "C2"),
    +isOnCommittee ("H. Solo", "C2"),
    +isOnCommittee ("H. Wells", "C2").
+projectOfBid["B1"] = "Mars1",
    +projectOfBid["B2"] = "Mars1".
+projectOfBid ["B3"] = "Jupiter2",
    +projectOfBid ["B4"] = "Jupiter2".
+teamOfBid ["B1"] = "Trekkers",
    +teamOfBid ["B2"] = "Oldies".
+teamOfBid["B3"] = "Trekkers", +teamOfBid["B4"] = "Jedi".
+isOnTeam("C. Kirk", "Trekkers"),
    +isOnTeam("M. Spock", "Trekkers").
+isOnTeam("F. Gordon", "Oldies"), +isOnTeam("H. Seldon",
    "Oldies").
+isOnTeam("M. Yoda", "Oldies"),
    +isOnTeam("L. Skywalker", "Jedi").
+isOnTeam ("M. Yoda", "Jedi").
```

Extend the program with code to enforce the *external uniqueness constraint* that for any given project a person may be a member of only one bidding team. Also add code to enforce a *join exclusion constraint* to ensure that a person on a bidding team for a project cannot be on the selection committee for that project. Test your code with counterexamples. The answers can be found in the files Bid2.logic, Bid2CounterExample1.logic, and Bid2CounterExample2.logic.

Q8: The game of tic-tac-toe involves a grid of nine cells formed from three rows and three columns. One player may enter an "O" mark in a cell, and the other player may enter an "X" mark in a cell. Players take turns entering their marks. If a player lines up three of his/her entries in a line (horizontal, vertical, or diagonal) that player wins the game. The diagram in Figure 4.8 shows the grid of a game won by the "X" player. The rows and columns are numbered to allow easy reference. For example, the cell on row 2 and column 3 has the entry "O."

FIGURE 4.8 Tic-tac-toe game board.

The following code (available in `TicTacToe.logic` and `TicTacToeData.logic`) shows a basic program to record the state of play of one game, as well as the data for the example shown:

```
// Schema
entryAt[rowNr, colNr] = e -> int(rowNr), int(colNr),
    string(e).
entryAt[_, _] = e -> e = "O" ; e = "X".

// Data
+entryAt[1, 1] = "O", +entryAt[1, 3] = "X",
+entryAt[2, 2] = "O", +entryAt[2, 3] = "O",
+entryAt[3, 1] = "X", +entryAt[3, 2] = "X",
+entryAt[3, 3] = "X".
```

To better conceptualize the domain, extend the code file available as `TicTacToe.logic` by deriving the entity type `Cell(c)` whose instances are cells in the grid, using the constructor `cellAt[rowNr,colNr]=c` to derive the cells, and `valueOf[c]=v` to return the value entered at cell c. *Hint*: Make use of `int:range()` to populate the cell row numbers and column numbers with data. The program, data, and test query are accessible as `TicTacToe2.logic`.

Q9: This exercise question concerns retail sales data from the U.S. Census Bureau. The data are contained in a file named `retailSales.csv`. This file and the other files used in this exercise are found in the `q11` directory and its subdirectories.

(a) Examine the spreadsheet data and prepare a LogiQL schema to describe it. The schema should include an entity predicate (`RawSalesRecord`) whose instances correspond to the rows of the spreadsheet. Place the schema in the file `Schema.logic` and create a project description file listing it as an `active` block. Check that your schema is correctly described by compiling the project and creating a workspace for it.

(b) Use a file predicate to read the data into a workspace. Place the code to read the spreadsheet data into a file named `readFile.logic`, and use the `lb` command to load the data from the spreadsheet into the workspace.

(c) Note that most of the rows in the spreadsheet contain North American Industry Classification System (NAICS) code numbers. Note also that these code numbers suggest hierarchical groupings. That is, the code 441 describes a class of businesses that is further broken down into subcategories (4411, 4412, and 4413). Define a binary predicate (`childOf`) relating the `RawSalesRecords` of parent categories to those of their children. Use this predicate to define a ternary functional predicate (`totalChildSalesOf`) computing for each parent `RawSalesRecord` and for each year the total sales of all of that business category's children. Define a complementary functional ternary predicate (`parentSalesOf`) that for each category that has subcategories and for each year records that parent's sales. Note that within some groups, such as 441, the sales associated with the subcategories do not add up the sales associated with the category itself. To capture these situations, define a unary predicate (`incompleteParent`) containing `RawSalesRecords` where the total sales of those business categories' children do not completely add up to that of the category itself. Place all of these predicates in a separate logic file named `Children.logic` and include that file in the project description file.

(d) To account for the missing sales, some new sales records must be created. Use a constructor to add a new subcategory code whose last character is an asterisk (e.g., "4481*"), whose "Kind of business" field is "`Other`" and whose sales fields equals the residual amounts not accounted for by the subcategories explicitly listed. Note that your constructor will not work with the `RawSalesRecord` entity because it has a refmode. You can deal with this situation by declaring a new entity type, `ConstructedSalesRecord`, and a constructor for it. You can then combine the two entities (`RawSalesRecord` and `ConstructedSalesRecord`) into a composite entity (`SalesRecord`) containing both types of sales records, leaving out the refmode values, which are no longer needed. *Hint:* You will need two constructors for `SalesRecord`, one that is keyed by `RawSalesRecord`'s refmode and one that is keyed by `ConstructedSalesRecord`'s NAICS code. You will also need to define auxiliary predicates to hold the sales data and descriptions. Include the declarations for these predicates in a file named `Constructor.logic` and the delta logic that adds the actual data in a separate file named `addRecords.logic`. Be sure to add the former to your project description file.

(e) The retail sales data contained in `retailSales.csv` have not been adjusted for inflation. Using the hierarchical syntax, create a new `SalesRecord` whose NAICS Code and description predicates contain the value "inflation" and with inflation values associated with each of the years. Inflation data can be found in the file `inflation.txt`.

Place this code into a separate file named `inflation.logic`, which, because it is delta logic, should not be included in the project description file.

(f) Use the inflation data to adjust the retail sales data. That is, define a ternary functional predicate (`correctedSalesFor`) that for each `SalesRecord` and for each year computes the sales for that year as adjusted for inflation. Because this predicate will be used only in part (g), you should indicate that its values should not be saved (i.e., it should be a `Derived` predicate). Save your code in a file named `Adjust.logic`, and include a reference to the new file in your project description file.

(g) Using the adjusted sales data, compute the compound annual growth rate (CAGR) for each business category. (The CAGR can be computed by the following formula: $CAGR = (V_f/V_i)^{1/t} - 1$ where V_f is the final value, V_i is the initial value, and t is the number of time periods.) That is, define a functional binary predicate (`CAGR`) that, for each `SalesRecord` computes the CAGR for that record, where the CAGR is based on inflation-adjusted sales figures. Save your results in a file named `CAGR.logic`, and add it to your project description file.

(h) Using the growth rates computed in part (g), apply the max aggregation function to determine the largest growth rate and the corresponding business category. Save the resulting code in a file named MaxCAGR.logic and add its name to your project description file. Note that for the purposes of this exercise, you can assume that there is no more than one store with the maximum growth rate.

(i) Prepare a report using the predicates you have defined. Your report should contain one record with three values: the NAICS code for the category with the greatest growth, its "Kind of business" description, and its growth rate. Save your query in a file named query.logic, and add its name to the project description file. *Hint:* Remember to label the block as inactive.

(j) Now that you have a project working with legacy.logic files, convert it to use modules and concrete blocks. In particular, create a module named retail, move the active blocks and query into it, converting them into concrete blocks, and update the project file accordingly. Make sure that the resulting application still runs as you expect.

Solutions containing the described files for all of the parts of this exercise are available in directory q11 and its retail subdirectory.

Q10: In the first exercise of Unit 4.4 you were asked to informally arrange the seating at Snoopy's dinner party. This question asks you to write a LogiQL program for the same task. In particular, for the data given above, your program should produce a report that lists for each table, which three beagles are sitting at that table. That is, the resulting seating arrangement should be such that the total number of friends sitting together is maximized over all possible arrangements. *Hint:* In its general formulation, this problem is called the *uniform graph partition problem (UGPP)*, which can be expensive to compute. However, for nine guests, you should have no problem finding the answer. More information about the UGPP can be found in Wikipedia. *Hint:* You may assume that there is only one best arrangement, which happens to be true for the given data. A solution to this problem can be found in the q10 directory.

ANSWERS TO EXERCISES

Answer to Exercise 1A:

Additional code:

```
upTo2givenNamesOf[a] = t -> Author(a), string(t).
upTo2givenNamesOf[a] = givenName1Of[a] + " " + gn2 <-
    givenName2Of[a] = gn2.
upTo2givenNamesOf[a] = givenName1Of[a] <-
    !givenName2Of[a] = _.
givenNamesOf[a] = t -> Author(a), string(t).
givenNamesOf[a] = upTo2givenNamesOf[a] + " " + gn3 <-
    givenName3Of[a] = gn3.
givenNamesOf[a] = upTo2givenNamesOf[a] <-
    !givenName3Of[a] = _.
fullNameOf[a] = t -> Author(a), string(t).
fullNameOf[a] = givenNamesOf[a] + " " + familyNameOf[a].
```

The program, data, and test query are accessible as AuthorNames-Answer.logic. A query of the results produces the following report:

```
author and full names:
3, Joanne Kathleen Rowling
2, Isaac Asimov
1, John Ronald Reuel Tolkien
```

Answer to Exercise 1B:

Additional code:

```
SmallInteger(n) -> int(n).
SmallInteger(n) <- int:range(0, 20, 1, n).
factorial[n] = x -> int(n), int(x).
factorial[0] = 1.
factorial[n] = n * factorial[n-1] <- n > 0,
    SmallInteger(n).
```

Note the restriction to the specified small integers in the body of the recursive rule. Without this restriction, the rule would be unsafe.

The answer is accessible as `FactorialAnswer.logic`. A query returns the following result:

```
n and n!:
0,    1
1,    1
2,    2
3,    6
4,    24
5,    120
6,    720
7,    5040
8,    40320
9,    362880
10,   3628800
11,   39916800
12,   479001600
13,   6227020800
14,   87178291200
15,   1307674368000
16,   20922789888000
17,   355687428096000
18,   6402373705728000
19,   121645100408832000
20,   2432902008176640000
```

Answer to Exercise 1C:

Additional code:

```
gradeOf[s] = l -> Student(s), string(l).
gradeOf[s] = "A" <- scoreOf[s] = 10.
gradeOf[s] = "B" <- scoreOf[s] > 6, scoreOf[s] < 10.
gradeOf[s] = "C" <- scoreOf[s] = 5 ; scoreOf[s] = 6.
gradeOf[s] = "F" <- scoreOf[s] < 5.
```

The answer is accessible as `GradesAnswer.logic`. A query returns the following result:

```
Students, scores, and grades:
   104, 10, A
   105, 4, F
   106, 7, B
```

```
101, 7, B
102, 9, B
103, 5, C
```

Answer to Exercise 2A:

```
minCelsiusTempOf[c] = _ -> maxCelsiusTempOf[c] = _.
maxCelsiusTempOf[c] = _ -> minCelsiusTempOf[c] = _.
// If city c has a minimum Celsius temperature then it
// has a maximum Celsius temperature, and vice versa.

minCelsiusTempOf[_] = n -> n > -50.
// Each minimum temperature is above -50 degrees
// Celsius.
maxCelsiusTempOf[_] = n -> n > = -10, n < = 50.
// Each maximum temp is in the range -10...50 degrees
// Celsius.
```

The full program is accessible as CityTempAnswer.lb.

Answer to Exercise 2B:

```
minCelsiusFor[c, m] = _ -> maxCelsiusFor[c, m] = _.
maxCelsiusFor[c, m] = _ -> minCelsiusFor[c, m] = _.
// If a city in a month has a minimum temperature
// recorded then it has a maximum temperature, and
// vice versa.
```

The full program is accessible as CityTemp2Answer.lb.

Answers to Exercise 2C:

(i)

```
positiveNrLanguagesMasteredBy[p] = n <-
    agg<<n = count()>> isFluentIn(p, _).
// If person p is fluent in any language then
// n is the number of languages in which he/she is
// fluent.

isBilingual(p) <- positiveNrLanguagesMasteredBy[p] > 1.
// Each bilingual person has mastered more than
// 1 language.
```

```
!(Translator(p), !isBilingual(p)).
// Nothing can be a translator and not bilingual,
// i.e. each translator is bilingual.
```

Note that it is an error to replace the above constraint by the following code, as the compiler treats that as an attempt to assign two supertypes to `Translator`:

```
Translator(p) -> isBilingual(p). // Error!
```

However, you can avoid this error by adding the following metadeclaration that `isBilingual` is not an entity:

```
lang:isEntity[`isBilingual] = false.
```

The full program is accessible as `LanguagesAnswer.lb`.

(ii)

```
isBilingual(p) <-
    isFluentIn(p, la1), isFluentIn(p, la2),
    la1 ! = la2.
```

For large frequencies, this approach requires far more code than use of the `count` function. For example, to ensure that a person is fluent in at least five languages la1, la2, la3, la4, la5, we must assert that the person is fluent in each of these languages, and that no two pairs of these languages are equal—that is, la1 != la2, la1 != la3, la1 != la4, la1 != la5, la2 != la3, la2 != la4, la2 != la5, la3 != la4, la3 != la5, la4 != la5.

Answer to Exercise 2D:

```
isFluentInAnOfficialLanguageOf(p, c) -> Person(p),
    Country(c).
isFluentInAnOfficialLanguageOf(p, c) <-
    isFluentIn(p, la), hasOfficialLanguage(c, la).
// Person p is fluent in an official language of
// country c if p is fluent in some language la
// that is an official language of c.

countryAmbassadoredBy[p] = c -> isFluentInAnOfficial
    LanguageOf(p, c).
```

```
// If person p is an ambassador to country c
// then p is fluent in some official language of c.
```

Would it be acceptable to replace the above constraint on country-AmbassadoredBy by the following constraint?

```
countryAmbassadoredBy[p] = c ->
    isFluentIn(p, la), hasOfficialLanguage(c, la).
```

No. This constraint means something much different. It says that *everything* is an official language of c and is mastered by p, if p is an ambassador to c. Moreover, the LogiQL compiler will complain about the construct because it violates the *SC1* safety condition. Can you see why this is so?

SC1 states that all variables in the head of a rule must appear in the body. For constraints, the head is on the right, and la does not appear in the body. Another way of looking at this problem is to note that in order for the runtime engine to guarantee that the constraint is met, it has to look at all values of la, not just those that correspond to languages. That is, la is unbound, thereby violating the intent of *SC1*.

The full program is accessible as AmbassadorAnswer.lb.

Answer to Exercise 2E:

```
authoredSomeReviewOf(e, p) -> Employee(e), Product(p).
authoredSomeReviewOf(e, p) <-
    authorOf[r] = e, productReviewedIn[r] = p.
// Employee e authored a review of product r
// if e is the author of r, and the product
// reviewed in r is p.
developed(e, p) -> !authoredSomeReviewOf(e, p).
// If employee e is a developer of product p
// then e did not author a review of p.
```

The full program is accessible as ProductReviewAnswer.lb.

Answer to Exercise 3A:

```
Constraint(c), hasConstraintName(c:cn) -> string(cn).
Modality(m), hasModalityName(m:mn) -> string(mn).
hasModalityName(_:mn) -> mn = "Hard" ; mn = "Soft".
modalityOf[c] = m -> Constraint(c), Modality(m).
```

```
ConstraintVerbalization(cv) ->.
positiveVerbalizationOf[c] = pv ->
    Constraint(c), ConstraintVerbalization(pv).
lang:constructor(`positiveVerbalizationOf).

negativeVerbalizationOf[c] = nv ->
    Constraint(c), ConstraintVerbalization(nv).
lang:constructor(`negativeVerbalizationOf).

modalTextOf[cv] = s -> ConstraintVerbalization(cv),
    string(s).
ConstraintVerbalization(pv),
    positiveVerbalizationOf[c] = pv,
    modalTextOf[pv] = "It is necessary that ",
ConstraintVerbalization(nv),
    negativeVerbalizationOf[c] = nv,
    modalTextOf[nv] = "It is impossible that " <-
    modalityOf[c] = "Hard".
// If a constraint is of hard modality
// then there exists a positive verbalization of c
// whose modal text reads "It is necessary that "
// and there exists a negative verbalization of c
// whose modal text reads "It is impossible that ".

ConstraintVerbalization(pv),
    positiveVerbalizationOf[c] = pv,
    modalTextOf[pv] = "It is obligatory that ",
ConstraintVerbalization(nv),
    negativeVerbalizationOf[c] = nv,
    modalTextOf[nv] = "It is forbidden that " <-
    modalityOf[c] = "Soft".
// If a constraint is of soft modality
// then there exists a positive verbalization of c
// whose modal text reads "It is obligatory that "
// and there exists a negative verbalization of c
// whose modal text reads "It is forbidden that ".
```

The program, data, and test query are accessible as Verbalize2.lb.

Answer to Exercise 3B:

```
Playing(p) ->.
playingDerivedFrom[c, s] = p ->
```

```
Country(c), Sport(s), Playing(p).
lang:['playingDerivedFrom].

sportLinkedTo[p] = s -> Playing(p), Sport(s).
countryLinkedTo[p] = c -> Playing(p), Country(c).
Playing(p), sportLinkedTo[p] = s, countryLinkedTo[p] = c ,
    playingDerivedFrom[c, s] = p <- plays(c, s).
// If country c plays sport s , there exists an object p
// that objectifies this playing and is linked to c
// and s.

rankOf[p] = r -> Playing(p), int(r).
rankOf[p] = r <- playingDerivedFrom[c, s] = p ,
    sportRankFor[c, s] = r.
```

The program, data, and test queries are accessible as Playing2.lb.

Answer to Exercise 4A:

```
// Data
+sitsAtTable["Andy"] = 1.
+sitsAtTable["Belle"] = 1.
+sitsAtTable["Missy"] = 1.
+sitsAtTable["Joe Cool"] = 2.
+sitsAtTable["Snoopy"] = 2.
+sitsAtTable["Spike"] = 2.
+sitsAtTable["Marbles"] = 3.
+sitsAtTable["Olaf"] = 3.
+sitsAtTable["World War I Flying Ace"] = 3.
```

Answers to Exercise 4B:

(i) Here is one project description file that works for compiling and installing these files:

```
exercise, projectname
base.logic, active
birthDeath.logic, active
Q1Query.logic, inactive
Q7Query.logic, inactive
Q8Query.logic, inactive
Q9Query.logic, inactive
```

The results can be found in exercise/i.

(ii) `Country.logic` looks like the following:

```
block(`Country) {
  export(`{
    Country(c), hasCountryCode(c:cc) -> string(cc).
    birthCountryOf[m] = c -> Monarch(m), Country(c).
  }),
  clauses(`{
    Monarch(m) -> birthCountryOf[m] = _.
  })
} <- .
```

The project description file should now contain the following line to describe the new module:

```
chapter1CE, module
```

and you need to alter the files `Q1Query.logic` and `birthCoun-tryData.logic` so that references to `birthCountry` now look like `chapter1CE:Country:birthCountry`.

`exercise/ii` is a directory reflecting these changes.

(iii) A solution to this problem involves creating a new concrete block named `Date` contained in the file `Date.logic`. In addition, the project description file can be shrunk by eliminating the files whose contents have been incorporated into `Date.logic`. It now looks like the following:

```
base.logic, active
chapter1CE, module
Q1Query.logic, inactive
Q7Query.logic, inactive
Q8Query.logic, inactive
Q9Query.logic, inactive
```

The resulting files can be found in the directory `exercise/iii`.

(iv) The resulting `Date.logic` file is in `exercise/iv/chapter1CE/Date.logic`.

(v) There are several groups of predicates around which to build concrete blocks. One such group concerns genders and relationships

(Relations.logic). Another concerns houses (House.logic). The remaining predicates have to do with monarchs and their names (Monarch.logic). When you are done constructing these files, the only remaining legacy files should be those concerned with loading data and those containing queries. The modularized project can be found in the directory exercise/v.

(vi) Here is a concrete block to replace Q9Query.logic.

```
block(`ForeignbornMonarchQuery) {
    inactive(),
    clauses(`{
        q(m) <- chapter1CE:Country:birthCountry0
        f(m, c), c ! = "GB".
    })
} <- .
```

A complete solution for this exercise, converting all of the queries, can be found in the directory exercise/vi.

Answer to Exercise 5A:

Product, hasSku, basePriceOf, and taxRate should all be materialized. These are predicates holding stored data that will be referred to repeatedly by applications. totalPriceOf may be either materialized or derived only. The decision comes down to whether the results will be referred to more than once. If so, it makes sense to materialize the result. If not, then treating this predicate as derived only will save some space and time. The code for this example can be found in price1.logic.

Answer to Exercise 5B:

The situation here is similar to that of **Exercise 5A**. Country, has-CountryCode, currencyOf, and exchangeRate all concern data that are often used by the application and should therefore be materialized. localBasePriceOf is more rarely used. Hence, it is a candidate for being derived only. The code for this example can be found in price2.logic.

Answer to Exercise 5C:

```
+Wine(_) {
    +hasWineId(1000),
    +descriptionOf("San Martin Reserve"),
    +yearOf(2007),
    +tasteOf[] = +Taste(_) {
    +hasTasteId(100),
        +sugarOf[] = "Dry",
        +flavorOf[] = "Moderate",
        +bodyOf[] = "Full"
    },
    +colorOf[] = "White",
    +quantityOf[] = 156,
    +priceOf[] = 6.99,
    +exclusiveUseOf[] = false
}.
+Wine(_) {
    +hasWineId(1001),
    +descriptionOf("Saint Ana Chardonnay"),
    +yearOf(2010),
    +tasteOf[] = +Taste(_) {
        +hasTasteId(103),
        +sugarOf[] = "Dry",
        +flavorOf[] = "Strong",
        +bodyOf[] = "Full"
    },
    +colorOf[] = "White",
    +quantityOf[] = 4,
    +priceOf[] = 6.99,
    +exclusiveUseOf[] = false
}.
```

This answer can also be found in the file wineAnswer.logic.

Answer to Exercise 5D:

(i) This program can be found in fileCopy7di.lb:

```
_in(s) -> string(s).
lang:physical:filePath[`_in] = "input7di.txt".
```

```
_out(s) -> string(s).
lang:physical:filePath[`_out] = "output.txt".

_out(s) <- _in(s).
```

(ii) This program can be found in `fileCopy7dii.lb`:

```
_in[] = s -> string(s).
lang:physical:filePath[`_in] = "input7dii.txt".
lang:physical:delimiter[`_in] = "\n".

_out[] = s -> string(s).
lang:physical:filePath[`_out] = "output.txt".

_out[] = s <- _in[] = s.
```

Glossary

abort: An action by the execution engine to reject a set of changes requested by a transaction because a constraint has been violated.

acyclic: A ring predicate R is acyclic if and only if its transitive closure is irreflexive. That is, no object may cycle back to itself by one or more applications of the R predicate. Example: ancestorhood.

aggregation function: A built-in LogiQL function that operates on a collection of facts to produce a value summarizing something about the whole collection. Example: count.

aggregation rule: A rule making use of an aggregate function.

anonymous predicate: A temporary predicate whose name is not of interest; that is, it is used only as a placeholder for the results of a specific query. The name of an anonymous predicate should begin with the underscore ('_') character.

anonymous variable: An unnamed variable, written as an underscore "_", which may be read as "something." If multiple anonymous variables are used in the same expression, they are not assumed to refer to the same individual.

asymmetric: A ring predicate R is asymmetric if and only if, given any x and y, where $R(x, y)$, it cannot be that $R(y, x)$. Example: parenthood.

atom: A formula that applies a predicate to a list of one or more terms, where these terms may be variables or literals. Example: hasGivenName(p,"Terry").

block: A set of LogiQL clauses residing in a workspace originating from a single source file.

clause: A high-level unit of syntax taking the form of either a derivation rule or a constraint.

commit: An action by the execution engine to make permanent the set of changes requested by a transaction.

concrete block: A low-level structuring mechanism for LogiQL source files. Each concrete block corresponds to a single file, and that file contains instructions describing how the block's predicates can be accessed.

conjunction: A formula containing two or more atoms or subformulas separated by commas. The formula is interpreted as true only if all of its atoms are interpreted as true.

constraint: A syntactic unit that is made of two formulas separated by a right arrow ('->'). Also called a *right-arrow rule*. Constraints are used for declarations or to place a restriction on how predicates may be populated with data.

constructor: A one-to-one functional predicate whose value is an entity.

data element: A unit of information managed by a LogiQL program. Data elements are of two types: entity and primitive.

declaration: A syntactic specification of a program predicate.

delta logic: The fact insertions/deletions/upserts and delta rules in a logic program.

delta modifier: One of the symbols '+' (*insert*), '–' (*delete*), and '^' (*upsert*) prefixing a predicate name used to indicate that a change should be made to that predicate's content.

delta predicate: A predicate used to record changes to its associated domain predicate. It is denoted by prepending a delta modifier to the domain predicate.

delta rule: Any rule containing a predicate with a delta modifier.

derivation rule: A clause used to derive new facts from existing facts. Also called a *left-arrow rule* or just a *rule*.

derived entity: An entity whose existence is computed via a derivation rule rather than by being explicitly asserted.

derived-only predicate: A computed predicate whose facts are available for other rules within a transaction but are not stored in the database when the transaction is committed.

disjunction: A formula containing two or more atoms or subformulas separated by semicolons. The formula is interpreted as true only if at least one of the atoms is interpreted as true.

domain: A cohesive topic area, recognized by a community of interested parties and exhibiting a vocabulary understood by that community. Example uses of the term include *problem domain, business domain,* and *application domain*. A domain is sometimes also called a *universe of discourse*.

domain predicate: A predicate specific to the application domain that can be populated with only a finite set of data. Examples: isParentOf is a domain predicate, but the built-in predicate > is not.

EDB predicate: A predicate whose associated facts are explicitly asserted by the user and are stored in the EDB. EDB predicates should be distinguished from IDB and built-in predicates.

entity: An element of the problem domain that you wish to refer to in your program that is not just a simple value. Example: a specific person.

entity type: A set of all possible entities of a given kind in an application domain.

equality constraint: A restriction to ensure that the population of one predicate role must be equal to the population of another, compatible role. Examples: Anyone who has his/her diastolic blood pressure measured also has his/her systolic blood pressure measured, and vice versa. Equality constraints can also be defined for compatible role sequences.

exclusion constraint: A restriction on two roles to ensure that no entity may simultaneously fill both. Example: a person may be male or female, but not both. Exclusion constraints can also be defined for lists of roles.

extensional database: The database of asserted facts with which a program deals. Also called the *EDB*.

fact: In logic, a true assertion about the world being modeled. In a LogiQL program, predicates are *populated* via *fact assertions*, each of which is represented via a tuple of data elements.

fact assertion/retraction: A LogiQL clause with an empty body and a head that contains only delta-modified predicate names. Assertions indicate additions of facts to a predicate, and retractions their removal.

file predicate: A predicate whose contents mirror that of a file. File predicates provide input–output capabilities to LogiQL programs.

final stage: The second part of transaction processing in which installed derivation rules are evaluated.

fixedpoint: A state of the database that remains fixed (unchanged) if its derivation rules are reapplied. Also called *fixpoint*.

formula: A syntactic construct used to build clauses. Typically, a formula combines atoms using *conjunction* or *disjunction* operators.

frequency constraint: A restriction on a predicate role to ensure that, at any given time, the number of occurrences of each instance in the population of that role is a specified positive number, one of a set of such numbers, or within a specified range of such numbers. Example: airline passengers may carry at most two bags or personal items onto a plane. Frequency constraints can also be defined for lists of roles.

functional notation: A notation within LogiQL in which an atom for a functional predicate of arity n is expressed as the predicate name, followed by the first $n-1$ arguments in square brackets, followed by an equals sign "=" and the final argument.

hard constraint: A restriction on the application domain that holds in each possible state of that domain, and hence can never be violated in the domain. In LogiQL, violations of hard constraints result in the termination and rollback of the transaction in which the violation occurred. Hard constraints are also called *alethic* constraints. Any attempt to violate a hard constraint must be rejected. Example: each person was born on at most one date.

head existential: A variable occurring in the head of a rule that does not occur in its body. Such a variable can be used to derive the existence of an entity from its properties rather than by explicitly asserting the entity.

hierarchical syntax: A syntactic mechanism within LogiQL for populating a set of related property predicates.

IDB predicate: A predicate whose associated facts are all derived via rule computations.

IDB rule: A derivation rule in which no predicate name has a delta modifier.

inclusive-or constraint: A restriction on two roles played by instances of a common type to ensure that each instance of that type plays at least one of those roles. Also called a *disjunctive mandatory role constraint*. Example: each person is male or is female. Inclusive-or constraints can also be defined for more than two roles.

initial stage: The first part of transaction processing in which queries are processed and on-demand evaluation is made of inactive blocks.

installation: The process of loading a block into a workspace.

intensional database: The set of facts that are derived from other facts. Also called the IDB.

inverse-functional predicate: A binary predicate whose inverse is functionally determined. Hence, inverse-functional predicates are either one-to-many or one-to-one.

irreflexive: A ring predicate R is irreflexive if and only if, given any x, it cannot be that $R(x, x)$. Example: `isParentOf`.

join: Relating two atoms by matching an argument variable of one atom with an argument variable of the other atom. Also known as an *equi-join*. Example: the following conjunction joins the second role of the `drives` predicate to the first role of the `isOfCarModel` predicate by ensuring that the same car `c` is involved in both: `drives(p,c), isOfCarModel(c,cm)`.

join path: A sequence of atoms, where each subsequent atom is joined to the previous atom by matching an argument variable. Example: `drives(p,c), isOfCarModel(c,cm), hasFuelCapacity (cm,fc)`.

keyspace: The first $n-1$ arguments of a functional predicate of arity n.

library: A compiled LogiQL project.

logic program: A set of blocks residing in a workspace.

mandatory role constraint: For a predicate role that is filled by instances of an entity type, a restriction that each element of that entity type must fill that role in the predicate's population.

many-to-many predicate: A binary predicate where a subject instance may relate to many object instances, and vice versa. Also called an *m:n* (pronounced "m to n") predicate. Many-to-many predicates are used to represent *many-to-many relationships* in a domain.

many-to-one predicate: A binary predicate where many subject instances may relate to the same object instance, but each object instance relates to at most one subject instance. An example of a *functional predicate*.

materialized view: A predicate that is both computed and stored.

metapredicate: A predicate, one of whose arguments is another predicate.

module: An intermediate-level structuring mechanism for the LogiQL source files comprising a directory structure. The directory structure provides a way of naming the module's resources for use by other modules.

namespace: A collection of related predicate names. For legacy code, the predicate names share a common prefix; for code in modules, the files defining the predicates in a namespace reside within a common subdirectory of a properly defined module hierarchy.

one-to-many predicate: A binary predicate where many object instances may be related to the same subject instance.

one-to-one predicate: A binary predicate where each subject instance may relate to at most one object instance, and each object instance relates to at most one subject instance. Also called a *1:1* (pronounced "one to one") *predicate.*

predicate: (1) In logic, a property that may be held by an individual thing or a relationship that may apply to a list of things. (2) In LogiQL a predicate is denoted by a name and is populated by a set of tuples of data elements. All tuples associated with a given predicate name have the same length, called the predicate's *arity.* A predicate with one argument is called a *unary predicate,* a predicate with two arguments is a *binary predicate,* and so on.

predicate signature: The syntactic specification of predicate, comprising its name and followed by a list of its arguments.

primitive type: A class of data elements directly representable by LogiQL. Primitive types include boolean, string, int, float, decimal, and datetime.

project: (1) A high-level structuring mechanism for LogiQL source files comprising a directory structure and a related description file; (2) to compute a projection.

projection: A predicate derived from another predicate by selecting a subset of its roles. A projection can also be constructed from a set of predicates comprising a join path.

property predicate: A predicate used to indicate some property of an entity.

pulse predicate: A predicate that starts empty, may only be asserted to (no retractions), and has its assertions discarded at the end of the transaction. Mainly used to record transitory events such as button clicks.

query: A request to retrieve or derive facts from a database. Conventionally queries often take the form of a rule making use of an anonymous predicate in the rule head.

recursion: The process of defining a concept in terms of a simpler version of itself.

recursive rule: A derivation rule in which a predicate in the head of the rule also appears in the body of the rule. Example: isAncestorOf(x,y) < -isParentOf(x,y) ; isAncestorOf(x,z), isParentOf(z,y).

refmode: The mode or manner in which a single value references an entity of a given type. In LogiQL, a refmode for an entity type takes the form of a 1:1 predicate whose first argument is of that entity type. *Refmode* is a shortened form of the phrase *reference mode*.

ring constraint: A logical restriction on how two type-compatible arguments of a predicate may be populated. Examples: irreflexive, asymmetric, intransitive, and acyclic constraints.

ring predicate: A binary predicate whose two arguments are either of the same type or are based on the same type via subtyping.

role: An argument position within a given predicate signature.

rule: Synonym for *derivation rule.*

rule body: A formula on the right-hand side of the *if* operator ('<-') in a derivation rule.

rule head: A formula on the left-hand side of the *if* operator ('<-') in a derivation rule.

safe rule/query: A derivation rule or query that is guaranteed to return a finite result using a computation that terminates in a finite time.

soft constraint: A restriction on the application domain that ought to be obeyed but may nevertheless be violated. It is the responsibility of a program to detect and handle soft constraint violations. Soft constraints are also called *deontic* constraints. Example: no person may smoke while onboard a public airflight.

stage suffix: A syntactic indicator that can be used to access the state of a predicate at various stages of transaction processing. Allowed suffixes are @init (or @initial), @prev (or @previous), and @final.

subset constraint: A restriction to ensure that the population of one predicate role must be a subset of the population of another, compatible, role. Examples: if a person smokes then that person is cancer prone; If a student passed a course then that student enrolled in that course. Subset constraints can also be defined in terms of lists of compatible roles.

subtype: An entity type B is a subtype of an entity type A if and only if each instance in the population of B must also be in the population of A. If B is a subtype of A, and B ≠ A, then B is a proper subtype of A. Example: *woman* is a proper subtype of *person.*

supertype: An entity type A is a supertype of an entity type B if and only if B is a subtype of A.

transaction: A coherent unit of work in a database management system, computationally independent from other transactions.

transitive: A binary relation R is transitive if and only if, given any arguments x, y, and z, if $R(x,y)$ and $R(y,z)$ then it $R(x,z)$. Example: `isTallerThan`.

transitive closure: The set of all possible relation pairs that can be obtained by one or more applications of a transitive predicate. Example: ancestorhood is the transitive closure of parenthood.

type: A set of related values. In LogiQL, there are two kinds of types: built in (also called *primitive*) and entity.

uniqueness constraint: A restriction on a predicate role to ensure that at any given time, each instance in the population of that role appears there at most once. Uniqueness constraints can also be defined on lists of roles.

upsert modifier: A syntactic prefix ("^") to a functional predicate that requests either to insert a new fact into it if the key of the fact does not already exist, or if the key does designate an existing fact, to alter the fact.

value: A syntactic construct directly expressing the value of a primitive datatype.

value constraint: A restriction on a role in a predicate that specifies what values are allowed to populate that role.

valuespace: In a predicate, the set of roles not part of the predicate's keyspace.

workspace: A database comprising a set of predicate populations and a logic program.

Appendix A: Running Your Programs

L OGIQL PROGRAMS AND THE workspaces they deal with are managed by a command interpreter invoked by issuing the lb command to the operating system's shell. At a high level, these commands interact with a server process responsible for managing one or more workspaces. This includes creating them, adding and removing blocks, installing data, and displaying results.

Each of these commands* takes the following form:

lb *commandName* [*options* | *arguments*]

Options control the execution of the given command, and *arguments* typically supply names of workspaces or files. Not all options are pertinent to all commands.

For example, the simple command lb status tells you whether the server process is running. Normally, when you run this command, you should expect to see the response: Server is 'ON'. If you do not see this, then you should run the command lb services start to get it running.

Note that the lb command and all of its subcommands take the optional -h option that responds with a description of the (sub)command and its options and arguments.

One of the first things you will need to do to run your program is to create a workspace for it. The lb create command is used to do this for you. For example, the command

```
lb create workspaceName
# Create a new workspace with name workspaceName.
```

---

* Examples in this appendix use the bash command language found on Linux.

creates a workspace with name *workspaceName*, which appears in italics to indicate that you can supply a name of your choice for the created workspace. The newly created workspace will be subsequently managed by the lb command. What this means is that the files containing your programs and data are under the control of the server, and you should not expect to see any changes in your current working directory.

There are two options to lb create you might want to use under certain circumstances: (1) lb create --unique creates a workspace with a unique name; that is, you do not have to supply the name. You might use this option if you are running a short test and do not expect to retain the results. (2) lb create --overwrite *workspaceName* reuses an existing name by first ensuring that the old contents of the workspace with the supplied name are deleted.

After you have created the workspace, you will want to add your program to it. This is called *installing* the program in the workspace. Assuming that your program is contained in the file named program.logic, you can accomplish this goal with the following lb command. Note that the suffix on the program name should be ".logic":

```
lb addblock -f program.logic workspaceName
# Add the program in file program.logic to the
# workspace named workspaceName.
```

Complementing the lb addblock subcommand is lb exec. Whereas addblock is used to install your intensional database (IDB) rules, exec is used to alter the extensional database (EDB), typically by asserting new facts. Here is an example of using exec to update *workspaceName* with assertions/retractions taken from the file programData.logic:

```
lb exec -f program.logic workspaceName
# Update the EDB in workspaceName with assertions
# and retractions from the file programData.logic.
```

For both addblock and exec you have the option of including logic on the command line. That is, instead of using the -f *fileName* argument, you can instead include the logic explicitly at the end of the line. If you do this, however, you should be careful to enclose the logic within apostrophes to ensure that the shell does not try to execute your code.

Of course, it does not do you much good to install a program and execute facts unless you can also query the results. There are several ways to do this with the lb command. One way is with the query subcommand. That is, lb query *workspaceName* 'someLogic' executes the query expressed in *someLogic* against the *workspaceName* workspace.

Another way to effect this query is to include it as a *query predicate* in one of the fact files you execute. A query predicate's name begins with an underscore, and its resultant facts are reported to the user rather than being stored into the workspace. For example, if the factData predicate is declared as follows:

```
factData[u, c, v] = fData ->
    Unit(u), Category(c), Version(v), float(fData).
```

then the query predicate

```
_(u, c, f) <- factData[u, c, "Budget"] = f.
```

retrieves those facts from factData for which the Version is "Budget". If this predicate has been defined, then you can use the --print option to lb exec to see the results:

```
lb exec workspaceName -f query.logic --print
```

A third way to see the results of your computation is to use the lb print *workspaceName predicateName* command to print out the facts stored in a predicate. There are two arguments to lb print: *workspaceName* containing the name of your workspace, and *predicateName* naming the predicate you are interested in. The lb print command prints out all of the facts in the named predicate.

The commands described above as well as several other helpful commands are summarized in Table A.1 through Table A.4.

TABLE A.1   Commands for Creating Workspaces

Workspace Commands	
lb create *workspaceName*	Create a workspace with the name *workspaceName*.
lb create --unique	Create a workspace with a (new) unique name.
lb create --overwrite *workspaceName*	Create a workspace *workspaceName*. If one already exists with that name, overwrite it.

TABLE A.2   Commands for Adding Logic

Adding Logic	
`lb addblock -f` *fileName* *workspaceName*	Add the logic contained in file *fileName* into workspace *workspaceName*.
`lb addblock` *workspaceName* `'`*someLogic*`'`	Add the logic expressed explicitly as *someLogic* into workspace *workspaceName*.

TABLE A.3   Commands for Adding and Querying Data

Adding Data and Querying	
`lb exec -f` *fileName* *workspaceName*	Execute the logic in file *fileName* against workspace *workspaceName*.
`lb exec` *workspaceName* `'`*someLogic*`'`	Execute *someLogic* against workspace *workspaceName*.
`lb exec -f` *fileName* *workspaceName* `--print`	Execute logic in file *fileName* against workspace *workspaceName* and display the contents of any anonymous predicates.
`lb query` *workspaceName* `'`*someLogic*`'`	Execute the query expressed in *someLogic* against *workspaceName*.

TABLE A.4   Other Useful Commands

Other Useful Commands and Options	
`lb print` *workspaceName* *predicateName*	Display the contents of predicate *predicateName* in *workspaceName*.
`lb predinfo` *workspaceName* *predicateName*	Display information about predicate *predicateName* contained in *workspaceName*, including its arity, types of its arguments, and other physical and logical properties.
`lb list` *workspaceName*	List the predicates defined in *workspaceName*.
`lb addproject` *workspaceName* *directoryName*	Install a compiled project into the workspace named *workspaceName*. *directoryName* is the name of the directory containing your project file.
`lb delete` *workspaceName*	Delete the workspace named *workspaceName*.
`lb workspaces`	List the currently managed workspaces.
`lb version`	List the version of the runtime engine currently active.
`lb compile file` *fileName*	Compile file *fileName*.
`lb compile project` `[--out-dir` *directoryName*`]` `[--libpath` *path* *projectFileName*`]`	Compile the project whose project file is named *projectFileName*. If `--out-dir` is provided, then place the compiled files into directory *directoryName*. If `--libPath` is provided, then use *path* to find libraries referenced in the project's code.

lb INTERACTIVE

In addition to command-line invocation of lb described above, you can execute the subcommands interactively. If you merely type the command lb by itself, you will see a prompt displayed (lbi >). You can then enter any of the subcommands you need to use (without the lb prefix). That is, if you have a series of commands you would like to execute, running lb interactively in this fashion may be easier than running them from the shell. When you wish to leave interactive mode, you can type exit at the prompt.

A slight variant to the above interactive usage is also available to you. If you have a series of subcommands that you wish to run repeatedly, you can type them into a file (without the lb prefix). Then, you can run the sequence from the shell by entering lb *fileName*, where *fileName* is the name of the file containing them. The subcommands will be executed one after the other, and you should see the results displayed on your screen.

CAVEAT

This glimpse of lb should give you enough information to get started running programs. In so doing, you may be tempted to copy examples from this book. If you do so, be aware that some seemingly innocent text copied from a .pdf file, while looking correct, may actually use illegal characters. For example, the hyphen character ('-'), although looking identical to the hyphen you type to lb or include in a .logic file, is actually represented by different characters in the .pdf file and the command window or editor into which you are typing. You may see an unexpected error message from lb or the execution engine if it detects such a character. For example, if you copy the following line from this appendix:

```
lb exec -f file.logic ws
```

you will see the following error message printed:

```
ERROR. Invalid argument: '-f'
```

To work around this problem, you can either type the text in directly, copy it from one of the included resource files, or edit the pasted text to substitute for the hyphens before executing the command.

Appendix B: Running the LogiQL REPL

THE lb COMMAND IS not the only way to access the LogiQL runtime engine. You can also use the interactive REPL (read-eval-print loop). REPLs exist for many languages and provide an easy-to-use means of learning a language, getting answers to modest language questions, and trying small experiments.

As the name *REPL* indicates, a REPL works by repeatedly taking the following three steps: read in a user request, evaluate its effect on the workspace, and print the results. The commands that it accepts are the same that you can give to the lb including addblock, exec, list, print, and query.

The LogiQL REPL is available for your use through a Web browser at URL http://repl.logicblox.com. (There is also a 30-minute tutorial you can try out available at URL http://developer.logicblox.com/content/docs4/tutorial/repl/section/split.html.) When you visit the REPL Web site, you will see a page like that shown in Figure B.1.

The bottom line in the REPL is a prompt into which you can type or paste your commands. Be aware, however, that when you run the REPL, you are running with a clean workspace, and that when you are done, the contents of the workspace will disappear. If you wish to retain your work so you can continue with it later, you can click the Save button. This will download a file called workspace.db to your Web browser's *Downloads* directory. Later, you can click the Restore button, which will ask you to select one of your downloaded files into the REPL. Also, if at any time you wish to restart, you can click Clear which will place you in a pristine workspace.

As you execute commands, the REPL places its responses on lines beneath the ones on which you entered commands. For example, the screen shot in Figure B.2 shows what the REPL would look like after defining a predicate and loading some data into it.

FIGURE B.1   LogiQL REPL initial view.

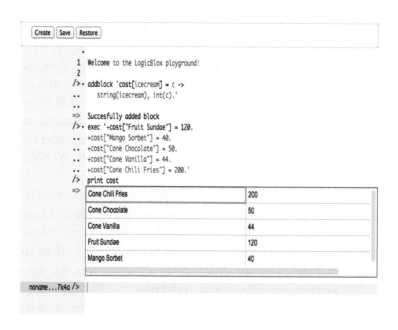

FIGURE B.2   LogiQL REPL with predicate definition and loaded data.

For this example, three commands were entered: addblock added the cost predicate to the workspace, and exec added some facts to the predicate. Then the print command produced a table containing the current contents of the predicate. Note that scrollbars enable navigation if the size of the output is large.

Appendix C: LogiQL Syntax

THIS APPENDIX PROVIDES AN overview of LogiQL's syntax. Its goal is to give a general picture of how LogiQL programs are structured. Hence, some details have been left out and some nuances glossed over. Moreover, you should be aware that even though a program segment is syntactically valid, executing it still may lead to unexpected results or error messages.

The notation used in this appendix is a version of EBNF (Extended Backus Naur Form) in which syntax categories are separated from their definitions via ':: =' and are terminated with a period ('.'). Literal text is surrounded by quotation mark symbols ('"'). Some definitions have alternatives separated by a vertical bar ('|'), and optional constructs are suffixed with a question mark ('?'). Appending an asterisk ('*') to an item indicates zero or more occurrences of that item, and adding a plus sign ('+') indicates one or more occurrences of that item. Finally, parentheses are used to group syntactic elements.

LEXICAL SYNTAX

The lexical syntax of LogiQL is typical of other programming languages. We make special note here only of unusual features:

```
comment ::= "//" text to end of line |
    "/*" text "*/".
identifier ::= (letter | digit | "$" | "?" | "_" |
            ":")+.
```

Identifiers may not begin with digits, and the use of an underscore as the first character of an identifier is interpreted specially by the LogiQL engine. Note also that identifiers may contain embedded colons (':'):

```
integer ::= digit+.
fpnum ::= integer ("." integer)? (exponent)? "f".
```

```
exponent ::= ("e" | "E") ("+" | "-")? integer.
decnum ::= integer (("." integer) | "d" |
                              ("." integer d?)).
string ::= """ text """.
boolean ::= "true" | "false".
```

LogiQL provides a datetime literal, delineated with number signs ('#'):

```
datetime ::= "#" date (time)? (timezone)? "#"
date ::= integer "/" integer "/" integer.
time ::= integer ":" integer (":" integer)?.
timezone ::= text.
```

Strings are contained within paired quotation mark characters ('"') and may contain *escapes* indicating the occurrence of otherwise unrepresentable characters, such as newlines. Escape sequences take one of two forms, both beginning with a backslash character ('\'). In the first form, the remainder of the sequence consists of one of the characters ('"', 'b', 't', 'n', 'f', 'r', '\') standing for, respectively, a quotation mark, a backspace, a tab, a newline, a form feed, a carriage return, or a backslash character. In the second form, the backslash character is followed by a lowercase 'u' (for *Unicode*) and exactly four hexadecimal characters ('0-9,A-F,a-f') that provide the hexadecimal code for the desired Unicode character.

Braces ('{' and '}') may be used for grouping of program elements. In particular, hierarchical assertions and module declarations use braces.

GRAMMAR

A LogiQL program consists of a series of clauses, which can take several forms:

```
program ::= clause*.
clause ::= fact | rule | constraint.
```

The simplest form of clause is called a fact, and it consists of a single formula:

```
fact ::= formula.
```

Facts are used to describe the population of the predicate mentioned in the formula.

Slightly more complex are rules, which look like the following:

```
rule ::= formula "<-" formula.
```

In the case of `rules`, there are two formulas separated by a left-hand arrow. The intent of a `rule` is to say that if the right-hand formula (the body) evaluates to `true`, then so must the left-hand formula (the head).

The third form of `clause` is called a `constraint` in the LogiQL grammar. `Constraints` are used either to declare predicates or to limit the facts that can populate them. Grammatically, there are three forms of constraints:

```
constraint :: = formula "->" formula.
constraint :: = "->" formula.
constraint :: = "!" formula.
```

In the first form, the intent is to say that if the left-hand side evaluates to `true`, then the right-hand side must also evaluate to `true`. In the second form, there is an implicit `true` on the left-hand side. In the third form the right-hand side has an explicit negation, and there is an implicit `true` on the left-hand side and an implicit arrow. If, during execution, any constraint fails to hold, then that constraint is violated, and execution of the transaction containing the constraint is aborted.

Most `formulas` are compound, being formed from smaller `formulas` using some form of punctuation. For example, comma (',') is used to express a conjunctive formula built up from two or more other formulas. Similarly, semicolon (';') is used in disjunctive formulas. A negation formula is denoted by prepending an exclamation point ('!'), and parentheses ('(' and ')') may be used to group `formulas` for readability or to express precedence.

There are three other kinds of `formulas`. The first involves `atoms`, the second involves aggregation functions, and the third involves `exprs` (expressions), possibly separated by `comparators` (comparison operators):

```
formula ::= atom
          | aggregation
          | expr (comparator expr)+
          | formula "," formula
          | formula ";" formula
          | "!" formula
          | "(" formula ")".
```

An `atom` comprises an `identifier` providing a name for a predicate and a parenthesized `arglist` (argument list), where positions in the list correspond to the predicate's roles. `Arglists` are of two forms. The first is a comma-separated list of `exprs`, while the second comprises a single refmode reference. The `identifier` may optionally be preceded by a `deltaop`, indicating that the predicate population is to be changed. Similarly, an optional stage suffix may be appended to the `identifier`, giving the programmer access to interim execution states of the predicate:

```
atom ::= (deltaop)? identifier (size)? (stage)?
     "(" arglist ")".
deltaop ::= "+" | "-" | "*" | "^".
size ::= "[" integer "]".
stage ::= "@" ("prev" | "previous" | "init" |
          "initial" | "final").
arglist ::= (expr ("," expr)*)?
          | identifier ":" (identifier | constant).
comparator ::= "=" | "!=" | "<" | ">" | "< =" | "> = ".
```

Aggregation functions have their own syntax, looking like the following:

```
aggregation ::= "agg<<" identifier "=" atom ">>"
                formula.
```

The final, major element of LogiQL syntax is the `expr`, typically used to denote a value:

```
expr ::= identifier
         | literal
         | expr arithop expr
         | identifier "[" arglist "]"
         | "(" expr ")".
literal ::= string | boolean | fpnum | decnum |
       integer | datetime.
arithop ::= "+" | "-" | "*" | "/".
```

Exprs can take several forms. The simplest `exprs` are either identifiers or `literals`. Other `exprs` are used to indicate functional application if they take the form of an `identifier` followed by an `arglist` in square brackets ('[' and ']'). Still other `exprs` express arithmetic combinations of simpler `exprs`. Finally, as with `formulas`, `exprs` can be grouped by surrounding them with parentheses.

Appendix D:
Built-In Operators
and Predicates

THIS APPENDIX PROVIDES A brief summary of many of the most useful operators and predicates that are pre-defined in LogiQL.

BUILT-IN OPERATORS

Logical Operators

The main logical operators are shown in Table D.1. These are also called *propositional operators* because they operate on propositional expressions to form another proposition. The priority indicates the relative order in which the operators are evaluated unless over-ridden by use of parentheses. Negation has highest priority (1), conjunction has precedence over disjunction, and the arrow operators have lowest priority (4). Expressions inside parentheses are evaluated before operating on them from outside.

For example, the following rules are equivalent:

```
AdultPerson(p) <-
    MalePerson(p), !Boy(p) ; FemalePerson(p), !Girl(p).
AdultPerson(p) <-
    (MalePerson(p), !Boy(p)) ; (FemalePerson(p),
    !Girl(p)).
AdultPerson(p) <-
    (MalePerson(p) ; FemalePerson(p)), !(Boy(p) ;
    Girl(p)).
```

TABLE D.1   Logical Operators

Symbol	Meaning	Priority	Operation Name
!	Not	1	Negation
,	And	2	Conjunction
;	Or	3	Disjunction
->	Implies	4	Implication
<-	If	4	Converse implication

Numeric Operators

Numeric operators, also known as *arithmetic operators*, operate on numeric expressions to return a numeric value. Unary negation ('–') has highest priority, and unary addition is not supported. Multiplication ('*') and division ('/') have precedence over addition and subtraction. Operators with the same priority are evaluated left to right. For example, given the following rules, querying n1 and n2 returns 4 and 2, respectively. LogiQL numeric operators are shown in Table D.2.

```
n1[] = -1+4/2*3-1.    // n1 evaluates to 4.
n2[] = 8/2/2.         // n2 evaluates to 2.
```

When operating on integer expressions, the *division* operator ('/') performs integer division, removing any fraction from the result. To retain the fraction, use the float:divide function instead. For example, given the following rules, if you query the predicate n3 you will get 1 as the result, and if you query the predicate n4 you will get 1.16667:

```
n3[] = 7/(2*3).                  // n3 evaluates to 1.
n4[] = float:divide[7f, 2f*3f].  // n4 evaluates to
                                 // 1.16667.
```

When placed between string expressions, the '+' operator performs string concatenation. For example, given the following code, querying name returns "Albert Einstein":

```
name[] = n -> string(n).
name[] = "Albert" + " " + "Einstein".
```

Comparison Operators

The comparison operators shown in Table D.3, also known as *comparators*, can be used to compare the values of scalar expressions

TABLE D.2   Numeric Operators

Symbol	Meaning	Priority
–	Unary minus	1
*	Multiply	2
/	Divide ·	2
+	Add	3
–	Subtract	3

TABLE D.3   Comparison Operators

Symbol	Meaning
=	Is equal to
! =	Is not equal to
<	Is less than
>	Is greater than
< =	Is less than or equal to
> =	Is greater than or equal to

of primitive types (numbers, `string` and `datetime`). The *ordering comparators* are ('<', '>', '<= ', '>= '). When applied between `strings`, alphabetic ordering is used (e.g., "Alan" < "Ann"). All comparators have the same priority.

An ordering comparator may be immediately followed by another ordering comparator. For example, the following formula is shorthand for the formula below it:

```
0 < = n < 10
0 < = n, n < 10 // Same as above.
```

If n is an integer variable, the formula means that n is a digit (i.e., one of 0, 1, 2, 3, 4, 5, 6, 7, 8, 9).

Precedence

Numeric and string operators have precedence over comparators, which in turn have precedence over logical operators. For example, the following two formulas are equivalent:

```
!2 + 3 > 2 * 3
!((2 + 3) > (2 * 3)) // Same as above.
```

Table D.4 summarizes the overall priorities of the main operators discussed.

TABLE D.4   Precedence of Operators

Symbol	Operator Type	Priority
−	Numeric (unary minus)	1
*, /	Numeric (multiply, divide)	2
+, −	Numeric (add, subtract)	3
+	String (concatenate)	3
=, ! =, <, >, <=, >=	Comparator	4
!	Logical (negation)	5
,	Logical (conjunction)	6
;	Logical (disjunction)	7

BUILT-IN PREDICATES

Numeric Functions

We now summarize many of the most useful built-in predicates in Table D.5. *Numeric functions* take one or more numeric arguments and return a number. Note the use of the square brackets instead of parentheses around the argument(s).

The next three mathematical functions, shown in Table D.6, are trigonometric. The argument of each function is an angle. In the right-angled triangle shown in Figure D.1, the sine of the angle θ is the ratio of the opposite side (a) to the hypotenuse (h)—that is, $sine(\theta) = a/h$. The cosine is the ratio of the adjacent side to the hypotenuse—that is, $cosine(\theta) = b/h$. The tangent is the ratio of the opposite side to the adjacent side—that is, $tan(\theta) = a/b$. The angles of a triangle add up to 180 degrees, which equals θ radians. The value of θ is approximately 3.1416. When using these functions in LogiQL, the angle must be expressed in radians rather than degrees.

The three mathematical functions shown in Table D.7 deal with exponentials and logarithms. Like π, the *exponential constant e* is irrational. (It cannot be expressed as the ratio of two integers.) Its value is the limit of $(1 + 1/n)^n$ as n approaches infinity and is approximately 2.71828. The function e^x is called the *exponential function*. If $e^n = x$, then n is the *natural logarithm* of x, or logarithm of x to base e, which is written as $\log_e (x)$ or simply $\log(x)$. If $10^n = x$, then n is the *common logarithm*, or logarithm to base 10, of x, and is written as $\log_{10}(x)$.

String Functions

String functions take string expressions as arguments. Recall the use of the `string:like(str,pattern)` function for string pattern matching, where *str* is a string expression and *pattern* is a quoted string that may

TABLE D.5 Numeric Functions

Function	Meaning	Examples
abs[x]	Absolute value of x (i.e., x with its sign removed)	abs[3f] = 3f abs[-3f] = 3f
ceil[x]	Ceiling of x (i.e., the smallest floating point integer $> = x$)	ceil[5.0f] = 5f ceil[5.1f] = 6f ceil[5.7f] = 6f
floor[x]	Floor of x (i.e., the greatest floating point integer $< = x$ [a truncation operation])	floor[5.0f] = 5f floor[5.1f] = 5f floor[5.7f] = 5f
pow[x,n]	x to the power n (i.e., $x^0 = 1$ $x^1 = x$, $x^2 = x^*x$, $x^3 = x * x * x$, etc.)	pow[4f, 0f] = 1f pow[4f, 1f] = 4f pow[4f, 2f] = 16f pow[4f, 3f] = 64f
sqrt[x]	Non-negative square root of x (i.e., the non-negative number that returns x when multiplied by itself)	sqrt[4f] = 2f sqrt[16f] = 4f sqrt[5f] = 2.23607f

TABLE D.6 Trigonometric Functions

Function	Meaning	Examples
sin[x]	Sine of angle x (where x is in radians)	sin[0f] = 0f sin[3.1416f/2f] = 1f sin[3.1416f/4f] = 0.707108f
cos[x]	Cosine of x (where x is in radians)	cos[0f] = 1f cos[3.1416f/2f] = 0f cos[3.1416f/4f] = 0.707108f
tan[x]	Tangent of x (where x is in radians)	tan[0f] = 0f tan[3.1416f/3f] = 1.73206f tan[3.1416f/4f] = 1f

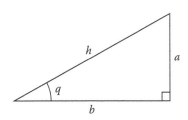

FIGURE D.1 Right triangle used to define trigonometric functions.

TABLE D.7   Exponential and Logarithmic Functions

Function	Meaning	Examples

`exp[x]`	e^x (i.e., e to the power x)	`exp[0f] = 1f`
		`exp[1f] = 2.71828f`
		`exp[2f] = 7.38906f`

`log[x]`	Power to which e must be raised to give x (i.e., n where $e^n = x$)	`log[1f] = 0f`
		`log[2.71828f] = 1f`
		`log[10f] = 2.30259f`

`log10[x]`	Power to which 10 must be raised to give x (i.e., n where $10^n = x$)	`log10[1f] = 0f`
		`log10[2.71828f] = 0.434294f`
		`log10[10f] = 1f`

include an underscore ('_'), as a wildcard denoting any single character and the percentage character ('%'), and as a wildcard for any sequence of zero or more characters. For example, `string:like(cc,"CS%")` is satisfied if cc starts with the characters CS, and `string:like(cc,"__1%")` is satisfied if cc has '1' as its third character.

The `string:substring[s,p,n]` function returns the substring of string s that starts at position p, and is n characters in length. Note that the starting position is numbered from 0, so the first character in the source string is at position 0, the second character is at position 1, and so on. For example:

```
string:substring["ABC", 0, 2] returns "AB".
string:substring["ABCDE", 2, 3] returns "CDE".
```

The `string:replace[s,oldPart,newPart]` function replaces each occurrence in string s of the substring oldPart by newPart. For example:

```
string:replace["ACCA", "C", "B"] returns "ABBA".
string:replace["John Smith", "John", "Ann"] returns "Ann
  Smith".
```

The `string` predicates that we have used in this book are summarized in Table D.8.

Type Conversion Functions

The *type conversion* functions `t1:t2:convert[exp]` are used to convert an expression of type *t1* to type *t2*:

```
int:string:convert[65] returns "65".
string:float:convert["65"] returns 65.
```

TABLE D.8 String Functions

Function	Meaning	Examples
s + t	Catenation of s and t	"ABC" + "DEF" = "ABCDEF"
string:length[s]	Length of string s	string:length[""] = 0 string:length["abc"] = 3
string:like(s,p)	Match string s against pattern p	string:like("ABBCA", "_BB%")
string:lower[s]	Lowercase version of string s	string:lower["ABC"] = "abc"
string:replace[s,op,np]	Replace occurrences of op with np in s	string:replace["ACCA", "C", "B"] = "ABBA"
string:split[s,c,i]	ith segment of s as determined by character c	string:split["A B C", " ", 2] = "C"
string:substring[s,n,l]	Substring of s starting at position n of length l	string:substring["ABCDE", 1, 2] = "BC"
string:upper[s]	Uppercase version of string s	string:upper["abc"] = "ABC"

Aggregation Functions

Aggregation functions operate on a collection of facts and return a single value for some property of the collection considered as a whole. The four most important of these functions are `count`, `total`, `min`, and `max`. These functions are invoked using the following special syntax, where the variable is assigned the result of evaluating the function over those instances of the collection that satisfy *condition*:

```
agg<<v = count()>> condition
agg<<v = f(x)>> conditionOfx // f is one of total, min, max
```

These four functions are summarized in Table D.9 using examples that have been discussed elsewhere in this book.

In addition to the above aggregation functions, the `seq` and `list` functions can be used to produce sorted results:

```
seq<<v = x>> conditionOfx
```

produces values for v in ascending order taken from the values of x produced by *conditionOfx*. Alternatively, `list` works with a pair of functions producing the first and next elements produced by an input condition. Uses of `list` take the following form:

```
first(v1), next(v1, v2) <- list<< >> conditionOfv.
```

`first` and `next` can then be used to navigate through the values produced by the condition in ascending order.

TABLE D.9   Aggregation Functions

Function	Meaning and Example
`count()`	Count of the number of instances where the condition is true, e.g., `nrChildrenOf[p] = n <-` `agg<<n = count()>> isParentOf(p, _).`
`total(x)`	Sum of the values that satisfy the specified condition, e.g., `totalExpenseOfClaim[c] = t <-` `agg<<t = total(e)>> claimItemExpense[c, _] = e.`
`min(x)`	Minimum value of that satisfies the specified condition, e.g., `minIQ[] = n <-` `agg<<n = min(iq)>> iqOf[_] = iq.`
`max(x)`	Maximum value of that satisfies the specified condition, e.g., `maxIQof[g] = n <-` `agg<<n = max(iq)>> iqOf[p] = iq, genderOf[p] = g.`

Range Predicates

The *range population* predicates *numericType*:range(*start, end, increment, x*) are useful for populating a variable *x* of *numericType* with a range of numbers from *start* to *end*, incrementing by *increment*. For example, the following populates rank with all the integers from 0 through 100:

```
int:range(0, 100, 1, rank)
```

datetime Predicates

Several date and time predicates are pre-defined for working with datetime values. A date value may be entered as a #-delimited string in *mm/dd/yyyy* format. For example, #02/15/1946# denotes the date February 15 in the year 1946. Care is needed with datetime data, since the time zone defaults to the time zone of the computer used to enter the data. This can easily result in dates being one day off from what you might expect. This issue can be addressed at least partly by including the name of the time zone (e.g., CET for Central European Time) just before the closing #. You can also include time data in hours, and optionally minutes and seconds, in *hh*, or *hh:mm*, or *hh:mm:ss* format after the year data. For example, #02/15/1946 15:05:40 GMT# denotes the instant that is 3 hours, 5 minutes, and 40 seconds after midday on February 15, 1946, in the Greenwich Mean Time zone.

The following program and data are used to illustrate some of the more useful datetime functions:

```
// Schema
Person(p), hasPersonName(p:n) -> string(n).
birthdateOf[p] = bd -> Person(p), datetime(bd).
deathdateOf[p] = dd -> Person(p), datetime(dd).
birthdateOf[p] = d1, deathdateOf[p] = d2 -> d1 <= d2.

// Data
+birthdateOf["George VI"] = #12/14/1895 GMT#.
+deathdateOf["George VI"] = #02/06/1952 GMT#.
```

The function datetime:format[*dt, formatString*] returns the value of the datetime variable *dt* in the POSIX date-time format specified in *formatString*. The function datetime:formatTZ[*dt, formatString, timezone*] gives you greater control of the output by including the time zone. For example, the following rule may be used to reformat the GMT birthdates from the default "%m/%d/%Y%H:%M:%S" format to the day-month-year format and to ensure that the time zone remains GMT:

```
dmyGMTbirthdateOf [p]  =  datetime:formatTZ [bd,
    "%d/%m/%Y", "GMT"] <- birthdateOf [p] = bd.
```

For the sample data, querying the dmyGMTbirthdateOf predicate returns

```
George VI, 14/12/1895
```

The function datetime:part[*dt,part*] returns the specified part of the datetime value. The part is one of "year", "month", "day", "hour", "minute", "second". For example, the following rule may be used to extract just the birth year from the birthdate. For the data shown, querying the birthYearOf predicate returns 1895:

```
birthYearOf [p] = y <-
    birthdateOf [p] = bd, datetime:part [bd, "year"] = y.
```

The function datetime:partTZ[*dt,part,timezone*] extends this function by including the time zone. For example, if, in the above rule, you replace datetime:part[bd,"year"] by datetime:partTZ[bd,"year","GMT"] you will get the same result, 1895, for the sample data.

The function datetime:offset[*dt1,dt2,unit*] returns the duration of the interval from *d1* to *d2* measured in terms of the number of specified units. The *unit* is specified as one of "years", "months", "days", "hours", "minutes", "seconds". Care is required when using this offset function, as the value returned is based on simple subtraction. For example, recall the following example from the Chapter 1 Consolidation Exercise. To compute the actual age at death, we need to subtract a year from the approximate death age if the day of year of a person's death occurs before the day of year of the person's birth:

```
approxDeathAgeOf [p]  =  n <-
    birthdateOf [p]  =  d1, deathdateOf [p]  =  d2,
    datetime:offset [d1, d2, "years"]  =  n.
```

This appendix has now summarized most of the pre-defined operators, functions, and other predicates that are useful in typical applications. LogiQL includes other built-in predicates not discussed here. For a full list of built-in predicates, issue the following command on an existing workspace: `lb workspace list`.

Appendix E: Summary of Constraints

Table E.1 collects the various constraints described in the book.

TABLE E.1   Constraints

Name	Reference	Definition and Example(s)
Equality constraint	Unit 4.3	A restriction to ensure that the population of one or more predicate roles must be equal to the population of other, compatible roles.
		Example: Patient p has a diastolic blood pressure reading if and only if p has a systolic bp reading.
		`diastolicBPof[p] = _ -> `
		`  systolicBPof[p] = _ .`
		`systolicBPof[p] = _ -> `
		`  diastolicBPof[p] = _ .`
Exclusion constraint	Unit 1.7, Unit 4.3	A restriction on two or more roles (or role lists), to ensure that no tuple may instantiate more than one of those roles (or role lists) at the same time.
		Example: No person authors and reviews the same book.
		`reviews(p, b) -> !authors(p, b).`
		Example involving a join path: Nobody may review a paper authored by someone from the same institute.
		`hasAnAuthorOf(i, ppr) <- `
		`  instituteOf[p] = i,`
		`  authored(p, ppr).`
		`hasAReviewerOf(i, ppr) <- `
		`  instituteOf[p] = i,`
		`  isAssigned(p, ppr).`
		`hasAnAuthorOf(i, ppr) -> `
		`  !hasAReviewerOf(i, ppr).`
Exclusive-or constraint	Unit 2.3	A restriction on two or more roles played by instances of a common type to ensure that each instance of that type plays exactly one of those roles.
		Example: Each person is male or female but not both.
		`Person(p) -> isMale(p) ; isFemale(p).`
		`isMale(p) -> !isFemale(p).`
Frequency constraint (internal or external)	Unit 4.3	A restriction on a list of one or more roles to ensure that at any given time, each instance in the population of that role list appears there a specified number of times.
		Example (internal): Each reviewer is assigned at most three papers to review.
		`positiveNrPapersAssignedTo[r] = n <- `
		`  agg<<n = count()>> isAssigned(r,_).`
		`positiveNrPapersAssignedTo[_] = n -> `
		`  n <= 3.`
		Example (external): No student may enroll more than twice in the same course.

TABLE E.1 (*Continued*)   Constraints

Name	Reference	Definition and Example(s)
| | | ```
nrEnrollmentsFor[s, c] = n <-
  agg<<n = count()>>
  studentInvolvedIn[e] = s,
  courseInvolvedIn[e] = c.
nrEnrollmentsFor[_, _] = n -> n <= 2.
``` |
| Inclusive-or constraint | Unit 2.3 | A restriction on two or more roles played by instances of a common type to ensure that each instance of that type plays at least one of those roles.<br>*Example*: Each valued employee is industrious or intelligent.<br>```
ValuedEmployee(p) ->
  isIndustrious(p) ; isIntelligent(p).
``` |
| Mandatory role constraint | Unit 1.5 | A restriction on a single role of a predicate to ensure that each instance in the population of the role's type must play that role.<br>*Example*: Each person was born on some date.<br>```
Person(p) -> birthdateOf[p] = _ .
``` |
| Ring constraint | Unit 2.5 | One of a class of restrictions on two type-compatible arguments of a predicate. Kinds of ring constraints include irreflexivity, asymmetry, intransitivity, and acyclicity.<br>*Example* (irreflexive): No person is a parent of himself or herself.<br>```
!isParentOf(p, p).
```<br>*Example* (asymmetric): If p1 is a parent of p2 then p2 is not a parent of p1.<br>```
isParentOf(p1, p2) ->
  !isParentOf(p2, p1).
```<br>*Example* (intransitive): If event e1 directly precedes event e2, and e2 directly precedes event e3, then e1 does not directly precede e3.<br>```
directlyPrecedes(e1, e2),
directlyPrecedes(e2, e3) ->
  ! directlyPrecedes(e1, e3).
```<br>*Example* (acyclic): No person is an ancestor of himself or herself, where ancestorhood is derived from parenthood.<br>```
isAncestorOf(p1, p2) <-
  isParentOf(p1, p2) ;
  isParentOf(p1, p3),
  isAncestorOf(p3, p2).
!isAncestorOf(p, p).
``` |

Continued
```

TABLE E.1 (*Continued*)   Constraints

Name	Reference	Definition and Example(s)
Subset constraint	Unit 2.4, Unit 4.3	A restriction to ensure that the population of one or more predicate roles must be a subset of the population of other, compatible roles.
		Example: If student s passed course c then s was enrolled in c.
		`passed(s, c) -> enrolledIn(s, c).`
		Example involving a join path: If person p has a title t that applies to only one gender g, then person p must be of gender g.
		`personTitleOf[p] = pt,`
		`applicableGenderOf[pt] = g ->`
		`  genderOf[p] = g.`
Uniqueness constraint (internal or external)	Unit 2.1 (internal), Unit 2.3 (external)	A restriction on a list of one or more roles to ensure that at any given time, each instance in the population of that role list appears there at most once. If the constrained roles come from the same predicate, the constraint is an internal uniqueness constraint; otherwise, it is an external uniqueness constraint.
		Example (internal uniqueness constraint on first role): Each person has at most one passport number. This constraint is implied by use of functional notation for the predicate declaration.
		`passportNrOf[p] = n ->`
		`  Person(p), string(n).`
		Example (internal uniqueness constraint on second role): Each passport number is held by at most one person.
		`passportNrOf[p1] = n,`
		`passportNrOf[p2] = n ->`
		`  p1 = p2.`
		Example (external uniqueness): Each country and state code combination applies to at most one state.
		`countryOf[s1] = c,`
		`stateCodeOf[s1] = sc,`
		`countryOf[s2] = c,`
		`stateCodeOf[s2] = sc ->`
		`  s1 = s2.`

TABLE E.1 (*Continued*)   Constraints

Name	Reference	Definition and Example(s)

Value constraint	Unit 1.6, Unit 4.3	A restriction on a role that specifies what values can populate that role.
		Example: The possible gender codes are "M" and "F".
		`hasGenderCode(_:gc) ->`
		` gc = "M" ; gc = "F".`
		Example: Product ratings are in the range 1 to 5.
		`productRatingOf[_] = n ->`
		` n >= 1, n <= 5.`

Appendix F: Programming Conventions

THE LOGIQL LANGUAGE AND compiler give a great deal of latitude to programmers to express their ideas. In particular, the choice of names, capitalization, and use of whitespace and comments are relatively unconstrained. Nevertheless, there are some advantages to using uniform conventions: Programs become more readable, errors are more easily detected, and training is facilitated. This appendix describes the set of conventions used in this book. First, a descriptive overview is given, and then summary lists are provided. A short exercise completes the appendix.

OVERVIEW

In this book, we adopted the convention of starting the names of user-defined object types with a capital letter, using a noun phrase to name the type. Typically, these types have been entity types represented by entity predicates (e.g., `Monarch`, `MalePerson`), but we may also use a predicate for a domain-related value type (e.g., `PersonTitle`). In contrast, we started property predicate names with a lowercase letter, using a verb phrase. In both situations, we rendered the remainder of the name in camelCase (e.g., `hasGivenName`), where words after the first are appended, beginning with a capital letter. Remember that LogiQL is case sensitive, so you need to ensure that you use the appropriate case when referencing a predicate. Built-in predicates for types and functions (e.g., `string`, `count`) always start with a lowercase letter.

There are some syntactic rules that must be obeyed. For example, a colon (':') must be used to separate the arguments of a refmode predicate, such as hasGenderCode(g:gc). When declaring functional predicates other than refmode predicates, we must enclose the keyspace arguments in square brackets (e.g., fatherOf[p1]=p2). Predicates that are not functional have their arguments in parentheses, for example, isParentOf(p1,p2).

If a functional predicate is binary, we have often used a *functionOf* style of naming to render a natural reading. For example, the equation genderOf[m]=g (i.e., "the gender of Monarch m is g") reads more naturally than hasGender[m] = g. In some cases, a preposition other than "Of" is more natural (e.g., nrBooksAuthoredBy[p]=n). We have tended to use short names for predicate arguments, often using one or just a few suggestive letters and maybe a digit. Some people like to use more descriptive names for the arguments. For example, instead of isParentOf(p1,p2) they might use isParentOf(parent,child).

In LogiQL, predicates are typed, so each argument of the predicate is constrained in its declaration to belong to a specific, named type. For example, suppose you make the following type declaration for a predicate named runs:

```
runs(p, c) -> Person(p), Company(c).
```

Now suppose that you want to record facts about people running races. If you try to use the same predicate name runs for these facts, you will get an error because the type of the runs predicate would then be ambiguous:

```
runs(p, r) -> Person(p), Race(r). // Error!
```

One way to fix this error is to expand the predicate name to include the type name of the second argument:

```
runsRace(p, r) -> Person(p), Race(r).
```

You could also rename the original runs predicate to runsCompany, but this is not required to resolve the error. Now suppose you also wish to record facts about horses running races. If we add the following declaration, we get another error, because the type of runsRace would be ambiguous:

```
runsRace(h, r) -> Horse(h), Race(r). // Error!
```

One way to fix this error is to expand the predicate name to include the type names of *all* its arguments:

```
horseRunsRace(h, r) -> Horse(h), Race(r).
```

If you wish, you could do this also for the previous predicates, renaming them as personRunsCompany and personRunsRace, although this is not required.

In the above examples, we embedded the type names inside the predicate name simply by concatenation. Another naming style that is often used is to prepend the type names to the rest of the predicate name, using a colon (':') separator. Applying this naming style to all three of the above predicates leads to the predicate names person:company:runs, person:race:runs, and horse:race:runs. The three predicates would then be declared as follows:

```
Person(p), person:company:runs(p, c) -> Company(c).
Person(p), person:race:runs(p, r) -> Race(r).
Horse(h), horse:race:runs(h, r) -> Race(r).
```

This naming style ensures distinct predicate names and facilitates searching for predicates based on the same type(s). It is also convenient for refmode predicates, since these may now be named by prepending the entity type name to a short refmode name. For example, the following declarations

```
Monarch(m), hasMonarchName(m:mn) -> string(mn).
Country(c), hasCountryCode(c:cc) -> string(cc).
State(s), hasStateCode(s:sc) -> string(sc).
```

may be rephrased as follows:

```
Monarch(m), Monarch:name(m:mn) -> string(mn).
Country(c), Country:code(c:cc) -> string(cc).
State(s), State:code(s:sc) -> string(sc).
```

However, in most cases this naming style makes the code longer and less natural to verbalize. For example, compare the following two declarations with their alternatives below:

```
hasGivenName(p, gn) -> Person(p), string(gn).
fatherOf[p1] = p2 -> Person(p1), Person(p2).
```

```
person:string:hasGivenName(p, gn) -> Person(p),
    string(gn).
person:person:hasFather[p1] = p2 -> Person(p1),
    Person(p2).
```

Note that LogiQL allows the same predicate to be declared on multiple subtypes of a common supertype. For example, in the below program isLicensed is constrained to instances of Doctor and Driver, which are overlapping subtypes of Person:

```
Person(p), person:name(p:n) -> string(n).
Driver(d) -> Person(d).
Doctor(d) -> Person(d).
lang:isEntity[`Driver] = true.
lang:isEntity[`Doctor] = true.
isLicensed(d) -> Driver(d).
isLicensed(d) -> Doctor(d).
```

Here, valid arguments to the isLicensed predicate are constrained to be people who are both drivers and doctors (i.e., instances of the intersection of Driver and Doctor). The LogiQL compiler effectively infers Person as a common type for this predicate. If instead you intend that there are two different predicates for being licensed, one for driving an automobile and one for practicing medicine, then you must name these predicates differently:

```
isLicensedToDrive(d) -> Driver(d).
isLicensedToPractiseMedicine(d) -> Doctor(d).
```

USE OF INDENTATION AND WHITESPACE

1. Surround occurrences of arrows, either right arrows ('->') or left arrows ('<-'), with spaces.

2. In executable code, follow commas (',') with a space. For standalone **predicate signatures**, the spaces may be elided (i.e., hasGivenName(p,gn)).

3. When using the functional notation, surround occurrences of equals signs (' = ') with spaces.

4. Surround occurrences of the disjunction operator (';') with spaces.

5. Indent the second and subsequent lines in a rule or constraint four spaces to the right of the first line.

6. Keep individual lines to 80 characters or less.

7. When splitting a rule or constraint across lines, put the left or right arrow at the end of the last line of the head.

COMMENTS

1. Comments in this book that are associated with examples indicate how to verbalize the commented code.

2. LogiQL comment text should be separated from the comment indicators by at least one space.

NAMING AND CAPITALIZATION

1. If any identifier comprises multiple words, capitalize all words after the first.

2. Lowercase letters start the names of non-entity predicates, such as property predicates. These take the form of verbs or verb phrases.

3. Entity type names begin with an uppercase letter and take the form of a noun or a noun phrase.

4. Names for refmode predicates should begin with "has" followed by the entity type name followed by an indicator of the refmode's representation, such as "Name" or "Code."

5. Express a binary functional predicate in the functionOf style, where the name of a property is followed by "Of" or another relevant preposition such as "By".

6. Names of non-functional predicates with two or more arguments can take the form of a verb, possibly adjacent to the types of the arguments. That is, a type might follow the verb, or the verb might be surrounded by two type names.

7. Variable names are typically one or two letters, beginning with a letter descriptive of the type or purpose the variable plays in the rule or constraint. If the rule is so complex that more descriptive names are required of the variables, it may be better to split the rule or constraint into pieces.

8. Underscores should not normally be used in names. Exceptions to this rule are allowed for occurrences of anonymous variables and predicates and to indicate the positions of arguments in verbalizing predicate names, as used, for example, in Unit 4.1.

Exercise 1: Explain what is wrong with the following code, and revise it to avoid the problem:

```
Person(p), person:name(p:n) -> string(n).
Gun(g), gun:serialNr(g:n) -> string(n).
fired(p1, p2) -> Person(p1), Person(p2).
fired(p, g) -> Person(p), Gun(g).
```

ANSWERS TO EXERCISES

Answer to Exercise 1:

The `fired` predicate is declared to have different types that have no common supertype. To fix this, at least one of the `fired` predicates needs to be renamed. To avoid confusion, it's best to rename both. Here is one solution that expands the predicate names to distinguish their meanings:

```
Person(p), person:name(p:n) -> string(n).
Gun(g), gun:serialNr(g:n) -> string(n).
firedPerson(p1, p2) -> Person(p1), Person(p2).
firedGun(p, g) -> Person(p), Gun(g).
```

Here is another solution that prepends the type names with a colon to the original predicate names:

```
Person(p), person:name(p:n) -> string(n).
Gun(g), gun:serialNr(g:n) -> string(n).
person:person:fired(p1, p2) -> Person(p1),
    Person(p2).
person:gun:fired(p, g) -> Person(p), Gun(g).
```

Appendix G: LogiQL and Predicate Logic

L OGIQL IS A PROGRAMMING language capable of computing correct answers for properly formulated problems. It has evolved from efforts to apply formal logical reasoning to databases, and this appendix describes the relationship between logic and LogiQL. In particular, the appendix describes how LogiQL is related to propositional logic and first-order predicate logic.

Propositions are asserted by declarative sentences and are always true or false but not both. In *propositional logic*, atomic propositions are denoted by propositional constants (e.g., R = "It is raining"; S = "It is snowing"). Compound propositions are formed by applying propositional operators to other propositions, using parentheses if needed. For example, using ~ for the negation operator and ∧ for the conjunction operator, we could use the formula ~(R∧S) to denote the proposition that "It is not both raining and snowing." Results about propositional patterns are indicated by using propositional variables (e.g., p, q) to stand for any propositions in general. For example, ~~p is equivalent to p regardless of which proposition is substituted for p.

First-order logic (FOL), also called *first-order predicate logic, predicate calculus, or quantification theory,* extends propositional logic with predicates, quantifiers, and individual constants. In logic, an *individual* is any individual object (entity or value). For a given universe of discourse, specific individuals are denoted by individual constants (e.g., terry), and specific predicates are denoted by predicate constants with their arguments in parentheses, for example, isTallerThan(terry,norma). General results may be stated using individual variables (to range over any individual) and quantifiers. The universal quantifier ∀ means "for each" or "for all." For example, the formula ∀x(~isTallerThan(x,x)) means "for each individual *x*, it is not the case that *x* is taller than *x*" (i.e., nothing is taller than itself). The existential

TABLE G.1   Operator Symbols

Logic Symbol	LogiQL Symbol	Operation Name	English Reading
~	!	Negation	Not; it is not the case that
∧	,	Conjunction	And
∨	;	Inclusive disjunction	Or (inclusive-or)
→	->	Implication	Implies; if … then … ; only if
←	<-	Converse implication	If
∀		Universal quantifier	For all; for each; for every
∃		Existential quantifier	There exists; there is some

quantifier ∃ means "there exists at least one" or "there is some." For example, the following formula may be used to state that "some person is taller than Norma": ∃x(Person(x)∧isTallerThan(x,norma)).

Table G.1 lists basic correspondences between operator symbols in predicate logic and LogiQL.

Both LogiQL and logic use parentheses '()' to group items together, either to list the arguments of a predicate, for example, likes(x,y), or to ensure that a compound expression inside parentheses is evaluated before operating on it from outside. Negation has the highest priority, so it has minimum scope. Hence the following expressions, first in logic and then in LogiQL, mean "p is not tall and p is not male":

~isTall(p) ∧ ~isMale(p)

!isTall(p), !isMale(p)

The following expressions use parentheses to conjoin the atoms before negation is applied, and hence mean "it is not the case that p is both tall and male":

~(isTall(p) ∧ isMale(p))

!(isTall(p), isMale(p))

Logic notations typically also allow square brackets '[]' as delimiters of expressions to be evaluated before connecting them to outside expressions. For example, the first formula above is equivalent to ~[isTall(p)∧ isMale(p)]. However, LogiQL uses square brackets to delimit the arguments of a function term (e.g., fatherOf[p1]=p2).

The logic formulas in this appendix do not assume any precedence among the binary operators. In LogiQL, however, the *and* operator has priority over the *or* operator, which itself has priority over the *implication* operators. Hence, each of the following formulas may be read as "*p* either is male and tall, or is female and short":

```
[isMale(p) ∧ isTall(p)] ∨ [isFemale(p) ∧ isShort(p)]

isMale(p), isTall(p) ; isFemale(p), isShort(p)
```

The semantics of the five propositional operators shown above are provided by the following truth tables, where p and q denote propositions, and 1 and 0 denote the truth values True and False, respectively. First, the negation operator reverses the truth value of its argument, so negating a true proposition results in a false proposition, and negating a false proposition results in a true proposition. This is shown in Table G.2.

A conjunction is true if and only if all of its conjuncts are true. An inclusive disjunction is true if and only if at least one of its disjuncts is true. A material implication p→q is true unless its antecedent p is true and its consequent q is false. Hence, p→q evaluates to true if p is false, and the same is true of q←p (Table G.3). Later we discuss some differences between the implication operators of logic and the *arrow* operators of LogiQL.

Over a finite domain, universal quantification is equivalent to the conjunction of its instantiations, and existential quantification is equivalent

TABLE G.2   Truth Table for Negation Operator

p	~p
1	0
0	1

TABLE G.3   Truth Table for Binary Logical Operators

p	q	p∧q	p∨q	p→q	p←q
1	1	1	1	1	1
1	0	0	1	0	1
0	1	0	1	1	0
0	0	0	0	1	1

to the disjunction of its instantiations. For example, if the domain of individuals is $\{a,b,c\}$ and $\Phi(x)$ is a FOL formula referring to x, then $\forall x \Phi(x)$ is equivalent to $\Phi(a) \land \Phi(b) \land \Phi(c)$, and $\exists x \Phi(x)$ is equivalent to $\Phi(a) \lor \Phi(b) \lor \Phi(c)$.

In first-order logic, predicates and quantifiers range over individuals only. In logic, a specific individual may be denoted by an individual literal (e.g., 2) or by a function term (e.g., `sqrt(4)`). In LogiQL, function terms are indicated with square brackets (e.g., `squareRootOf[4]`). In logic, individual variables are usually denoted by letters at the end of the alphabet, possibly subscripted (e.g., x, y, z, x_1, x_2). In LogiQL, individual variables typically start with one or more letters, and may include certain other characters such as digits, underscores, and colons (e.g., p, c, `person1`, `car2`).

In a classical Datalog rule, head variables are understood to be universally quantified, and variables that occur only in the body are assumed to be existentially quantified. For example, the following predicate logic formula for grandparenthood is equivalent to the LogiQL rule below it. Note that our logic notation allows a quantifier to be followed by a list of individual variables; hence, $\forall x, y$ is shorthand for $\forall x \forall y$.

```
∀x,y[isGrandparentOf(x, y) ← ∃z(isParentOf(x, z) ∧
    isParentOf(z, y))]
```

```
iGrandparentOf(x, y) <- isParentOf(x, z),
    isParentOf(z, y).
```

In LogiQL, the anonymous variable ('_') is used as shorthand for an existentially quantified variable that is not used elsewhere in the rule. For example, the following predicate logic formula and LogiQL rule each mean that "*p* is a driver if *p* drives something":

```
∀p[Driver(p) ← ∃x(drives(p, x))]
```

```
Driver(p) <- drives(p, _).
```

In LogiQL, all predicates are typed, so the types of their arguments are known. For example, each of the following declarations restricts the `speaks` predicate to range over (person, language) pairs:

```
∀x,y[speaks(x, y) → Person(x) ∧ Language(y)]
```

```
speaks(p, lang) -> Person(p), Language(lang).
```

In LogiQL, if a variable that occurs only in the body of a rule lies in the scope of a *negation* operator, its implicit existential quantifier is assumed to be placed after the *negation* operator. This is the case for both named and anonymous variables. Hence, it might appear that the two following formulas are equivalent, each meaning "*p* is illiterate in Asian languages if *p* is a person who does not speak something that is Asian":

```
∀p[AsianLanguageIlliterate(p) ←
    (Person(p) ∧ ~∃l(speaks(p, l) ∧ isAsian(l)))]

AsianLanguageIlliterate(p) <- Person(p),
  !(speaks(p, l), isAsian(l)).
```

Unfortunately, LogiQL does not support negations in this form. Instead, the same formula can be expressed using two rules as follows:

```
∀p[AsianLanguageIlliterate(p) ←
    (Person(p) ∧ ~∃l(speaks(p, l) ∧ isAsian(l)))]

AsianLanguageLiterate(p) <- speaks(p, l), isAsian(l).
AsianLanguageIlliterate(p) <- Person(p),
    !AsianLanguageLiterate(p).
```

In the above logic formula, the quantification ∀p has scope over the rest of the formula, and the quantification ∃l has scope over the conjunction after it. Each occurrence of the variable *p* is *bound* to the universal quantifier, and each occurrence of the variable *l* is bound to the existential quantifier. Binding multiple occurrences of the same variable to the same quantifier ensures that when the formula is instantiated, each of those occurrences of the variable is replaced by the same instance.

As an example with a negated, anonymous variable, the following formulas each mean that "a non-driver is a person who does not drive anything":

```
∀p[NonDriver(p) ← (Person(p) ∧ ~∃x(drives(p, x)))]

NonDriver(p) <- Person(p), !drives(p, _).
```

The following formulas each mean that "*p* is strictly fasting if *p* is a person who does not drink anything and does not eat anything." The first existential quantification ∃x has scope over just eats(p,x). Both occurrences of the x variable in ∃x(eats(p,x)) are bound to the first ∃ quantifier. The second existential quantification ∃x has scope over just drinks(p,x). Both occurrences of the x variable in ∃x(drinks(p,x)) are bound to the second ∃ quantifier. The five occurrences of p in the whole formula are bound to the same universal quantifier. Hence, when the formula is instantiated, each p must be replaced by the same item, but the item replacing the x in eats(p,x) may differ from the item replacing the x in drinks(p,x). Similarly, the two anonymous variables in the LogiQL formula are not required to denote the same individual thing:

```
∀p[isStrictlyFastingy(p) ←
    (Person(p) ∧ ~∃x(eats(p, x)) ∧ ~∃x(drinks(p, x)))]

isStrictlyFasting(p) <- Person(p), !eats(p, _),
    !drinks(p, _).
```

In the context of just the NonDriver rule body (Person(p) ∧~∃x (drives(p,x))), only the variable x is bound. Within that body, the variable p is said to be *free* or *unbound*, even though in the context of the whole rule it is bound to the universal quantifier.

Recall the following safety condition discussed in Unit 3.2.

> **SC2:** *Each named variable appearing in the scope of a negation within the body of a rule must also appear in a positive context in that rule body.*

Another way of thinking about this safety condition is that variables that are free in the body of the rule must occur in a positive context as the argument of a domain predicate or a domain equality. In the LogiQL formulation of the AsianLanguageIlliterate and NonDriver rules given above, the body variables x and _ occur in a negative context but do not violate SC2 because they are not free in the body. (They are bound to the implicit existential quantifier.) Understanding this may help make sense of error messages from the LogiQL compiler concerning unbound variables in unsafe rules.

In LogiQL, many entity types are declared using a refmode for their reference scheme. For example, the following declaration indicates that Country is an entity type whose instances are referenced by country codes, which are represented by character strings:

```
Country(c), hasCountryCode(c:cc) -> string(cc).
```

This declaration is equivalent to the following set of logical formulas. The last three formulas capture the injective (mandatory, 1:1) nature of the refmode predicate:

```
∀x[Country(x) → Entity(x)]
∀x,y[hasCountryCode(x, y) → (Country(x) ∧ string(y))]
∀x[Country(x) → y(hasCountryCode(x, y))]
∀x,y₁,y₂[(hasCountryCode(x, y₁) ∧
      hasCountryCode(x, y₂)) → y₁ = y₂]
∀x,x₁,y₂[(hasCountryCode(x₁, y) ∧
      hasCountryCode(x₂, y)) → x₁ = x2]
```

In LogiQL, facts are asserted using delta rules with a '+' modifier. For example, given the refmode declaration above for Country, the following code may be used to assert that there is a country that has the country code "AU":

```
+Country("AU").
```

This is actually just convenient shorthand for the following longer assertion, whose expansion can be inferred from the refmode declaration:

```
+Country(c), +hasCountryCode(c:"AU").
```

This is equivalent to the following assertion in logic:

```
∃x[Country(x) ∧ hasCountryCode(x, "AU")]
```

Internally, LogiQL identifies entities by the combination of an auto-generated number (e.g., 0, 1, 2, etc.) and their type (e.g., Country, Person). However, refmodes provide a far more convenient way for humans to identify entities in natural communication.

LogiQL allows entities with refmodes to be referenced simply by their reference values in other contexts as well, since the compiler can always use the refmode declaration to infer the relevant expansion. For example, given the following declaration

```
countryNameOf[c] = cn -> Country(c), string(cn).
```

the following code can be used to add the country name of Australia:

```
+countryNameOf["AU"] = "Australia".
```

This is equivalent to the following assertion in logic:

```
∃x[hasCountryCode(x, "AU") ∧
   hasCountryName(x, "Australia")]
```

Given the refmode declaration above, the assertion "+Country("AU")" is now implied, so there is now no need to explicitly assert it.

In logic, a *sentence* is a well-formed formula with no free variables, and every sentence expresses a proposition, and hence is either true or false. A collection of items is said to be monotonically increasing if over time it either remains constant or has new items added. A system built on classical logic is *monotonic* (more precisely, *monotonic increasing*) because you can add more sentences to it, but you can't retract any sentence. In contrast, LogiQL supports retraction by use of delta predicates with the retraction modifier ('-'). Consider, for example, the following delta rule:

```
-Country("AP").
```

Rather than simply expressing the proposition that there is no country with the country code "AP," this is a command to retract the fact (if any) that there is a country with the country code "AP" (if no such fact is present, no action is taken). Hence, if the previous state of the extensional database (EDB) included the fact Country("AP"), execution of the above delta rule would remove this fact from the EDB. Hence, use of retraction rules makes LogiQL *non-monotonic* (i.e., facts may be removed from its EDB). The capability of retraction is often needed in practical information systems, either to remove a fact that is no longer true or of interest, or to correct a mistaken entry.

Although delta rules to simply insert an atom could be viewed as merely asserting propositions, all other delta rules must be viewed as action rules, and if they include the *left-arrow* operator they are either event–action rules, condition-action rules, or event-condition-action rules.

In logic, the formula p(x)→q(x) is equivalent to the formula q(x)←p(x). However, in LogiQL, p(x)->q(x) is not equivalent to q(x)<-p(x). This is because in LogiQL, right-arrow rules are treated as *constraints* on the EDB, while left-arrow rules are treated as *derivation rules* for inferring new facts. Consider, for example, the following program and data, which are accessible along with sample queries in the files Pass.logic and PassData.logic:

```
// Schema
Person(p), hasPersonName(p:pn) -> string(pn).
Gender(g), hasGenderCode(g:gc) -> string(gc).
```

```
genderOf[p] = g -> Person(p), Gender(g).
hasGenderCode(_:gc) -> gc = "M" ; gc = "F".
Person(p) -> genderOf[p] = _.
isIndustrious(p) -> Person(p).
isIntelligent(p) -> Person(p).
passes(p) -> Person(p).
fails(p) -> Person(p).
passes(p) <- isIndustrious(p) ; isIntelligent(p).
fails(p) <- Person(p), !passes(p).

// Data
+genderOf["Adam"] = "M", +isIndustrious("Adam"),
+genderOf["Eve"] = "F", +isIntelligent("Eve").
+genderOf["Bob"] = "M".
```

Since persons and genders have refmodes, facts about them may be entered in the abbreviated form shown, using just their refmode values to identify them. For example, genderOf["Adam"]="M" expands internally to the equivalent of the following logic:

$$\exists x,y[genderOf(x) = y \land hasPersonName(x, "Adam") \land$$
$$hasGenderCode(y, "M")]$$

The value constraint on hasGenderCode of the program ensures that its second argument is populated only with the values "M" and "F". Any update attempt to use a different gender code will be rejected by the system. Similarly, the constraint on Person ensures that any attempt to add persons without their gender will be rejected.

In contrast, the derivation rules at the end of the program are used to draw inferences. If a person is asserted to be either industrious or intelligent, then the system infers that he/she passes. For the data shown, querying the passes predicate returns "Adam" and "Eve". The second derivation rule is used to infer that a person fails if he/she is not known (either by assertion or inference) to pass. For the data shown, querying the fails predicate returns Bob.

Classical logic adopts the *open-world assumption*, allowing that some facts may simply be unknown. So the absence of a fact does not imply that it is false. However, in logic, you can directly assert that some proposition is false simply by negating it. For example, in logic you could assert that there is no country with the ISO two-letter country code "AP" as follows:

$$\sim\exists x(hasCountryCode(x, "AP"))$$

LogiQL derivation rules with a negation in their body apply the *closed-world assumption*. This approach assumes all relevant facts are known, so the failure to find the fact that Bob passes (either by inspecting the EDB or by inferring new facts from the derivation rules) is interpreted to mean that Bob does not pass. This *negation as failure* semantics differs from classical logic, where the open-world assumption entails that it is unknown whether Bob passes, and consequently, it cannot be inferred that Bob fails.

Thus, LogiQL's inferencing capabilities allow some conclusions to be drawn that do not follow from classical logic. But first-order logic allows many kinds of inferences to be made that are not possible in LogiQL. For example, in propositional logic, the argument of the form p→r, q→s, p∨q, and therefore, r∨s can be trivially shown to be valid using a truth table. However, LogiQL does not allow disjunctions in fact assertions or in the heads of LogiQL rules, so it cannot support disjunctive inferences.

LogiQL also forbids negations in the head of derivation rules and has other restrictions such as the safety conditions considered in Chapter 3. Although these restrictions limit the power of LogiQL, they guarantee that legal programs in LogiQL will always execute in a finite time. In contrast, first-order logic is undecidable, meaning that there are some forms of argument that cannot be evaluated in a finite time.

As discussed in Chapter 4, LogiQL extends classical Datalog by allowing head existentials. Recall the following example, where `presidentOf` is used as a constructor to derive the existence of a country's president from the existence of the country:

```
President(p) ->.
presidentOf[c] = p -> Country(c), President(p).
lang:constructor(`presidentOf).
President(p), presidentOf[c] = p <- Country(c).
```

The final line of code is equivalent to the following logic formulation:

$$\forall x[\exists y(President(y) \land presidentOf(x) = y) \leftarrow Country(x)]$$

The existential quantifier in the rule head is implicit in the LogiQL formulation. The rule may be verbalized as "For each country, there is a president who is the president of that country."

Appendix H:
LogiQL and SQL

SQL IS A STANDARD language used for defining, manipulating, and querying relational databases. This appendix provides a brief discussion of how basic queries conveyed in SQL may be expressed in LogiQL.

Consider the following relational database, which includes two relational tables (Tables H.1 and H.2) describing countries in 2011. The country table lists the ISO two-letter code, name, and population of various countries. For discussion purposes, the population of Finland (5,396,292) is omitted simply to illustrate SQL's use of a null value to indicate that a data value is missing (e.g., because it is unknown or inapplicable). To save space, only a small number of countries are included. For those countries that have presidents, the president table lists the name, country, gender, and birth year of those presidents. Australia, Canada, and the United Kingdom have prime ministers instead of presidents, so they are not included in the president table.

Throughout the database, countries are standardly identified by their country codes. The entries in the first two columns of the tables are necessarily unique, so each of these columns is a *candidate key* for its table. The country table has *countryCode* as its *primary key* and *countryName* as an alternate key.

The president table has *presidentName* as its primary key, and *countryCode* as an alternate key. Note that the *countryCode* column appears in both tables. In fact, the *countryCode* column in the president table serves as a foreign key constraint ensuring that each country code in the president table also appears in the country table. A *foreign key* is a column, or list of columns, within a table, that is not the primary key, but the foreign key entries must also occur in a candidate key of some table.

TABLE H.1   Country Codes and Populations

countryCode	countryName	Population
AU	Australia	22,778,975
CA	Canada	34,482,779
DE	Germany	81,729,000
FI	Finland	
FR	France	65,300,000
GB	United Kingdom	62,300,000
IN	India	1,210,193,422
US	United States	312,702,000

TABLE H.2   Genders and Birth Years of Presidents

presidentName	countryCode	Gender	birthYear
Christian Wulff	DE	M	1959
Tarja Halonen	FI	F	1943
Nicolas Sarkozy	FR	M	1955
Pratibha Patil	IN	F	1934
Barack Obama	US	M	1961

Each row entry of a relational table is an ordered *n*-tuple of values, or *tuple* for short. Each tuple represents one or more atomic facts. For example, the first row of the country table stores the fact that the country with the code "AU" has the name "Australia," and also stores the fact that the country with the code AU has a population of 22,778,975. In contrast, LogiQL uses a separate predicate to store each kind of atomic fact. This enables the data to be stored without using *nulls*. For example, instead of setting the population of Finland to be null, LogiQL simply does not store a population fact for Finland. The schema for the sample relational database described above may be set out in LogiQL as follows. For simplicity, years and populations are modeled simply as numbers:

```
Country(c), hasCountryCode(c:cc) -> string(cc).
President(p), hasPresidentName(p:pn) -> string(pn).
Gender(g), hasGenderCode(g:gc) -> string(gc).
countryNameOf[c] = cn -> Country(c), string(cn).
populationOf[c] = n -> Country(c), int(n).
countryOf[p] = c -> President(p), Country(c).
genderOf[p] = g -> President(p), Gender(g).
birthyearOf[p] = y -> President(p), int](y).
```

```
countryTable(c, cn, ns) -> Country(c), string(cn),
    string(ns).
isPairedWith(mp, fp) -> President(mp), President(fp).
isHighlyPopulated(c) -> Country(c).
hasGenderCode(_:gc) -> gc = "M" ; gc = "F".
Country(c) -> countryNameOf[c] = _.
President(p) -> countryOf[p] = _, genderOf[p] = _,
    birthyearOf[p] = _.
```

If you ever wish to display LogiQL data in the form of a relational table, you can use a rule or query to conjoin the relevant facts into a single tuple. If the relational tuple includes a null, you can check for instances where the relevant fact does not exist and then display an empty string to represent the null. If the data type for a nullable column is not string, you can use a conversion function to coerce the data type to be string. For example, the following rule may be used to derive a predicate which displays like the relational country table:

```
countryTable(c, cn, ns) -> Country(c), string(cn),
    string(ns).
countryTable(c, cn, ns) <- countryNameOf[c] = cn,
    ((populationOf[c] = n, ns = int:string:convert[n]);
    (!populationOf[c] = _, ns = "")).
// Show the country code, country name, and a
// population string for each country. If the country
// population is recorded,display it,otherwise
// display an empty string for the population
```

The above program, together with the data, a derivation rule and query to display the relational tables, and some later queries, are accessible in the files SQL1.logic and SQL1Data.logic.

SQL is based partly on two formal notations called the relational algebra and the relational calculus. To construct SQL queries, you make use of several operations that have their historical roots in these notations. Relational *selection* is the operation of selecting those rows from a relation (which may be either asserted, or derived from other relations) that satisfy a specified condition. In SQL, this is achieved by including the condition in a **where**-clause. Relational *projection* is the operation of choosing just those columns of interest from a relation. In SQL, this is achieved by including the source relation(s) in a **from**-clause and the relevant columns in a **select**-list. For example, a query to list the names and birth years of the female presidents may be formulated in SQL:

```
select presidentName, birthyear
from President
where gender = 'F'
```

When run, this query returns the result displayed in Table H.3.

Relational algebra and LogiQL are both *set-oriented* languages. What this means is that a given tuple can appear at most once in a table. SQL, on the other hand, is *bag oriented*. This means that duplicate tuples are allowed. For example, the result of the following query to list the genders of presidents includes multiple occurrences of each gender code:

```
select gender
from President
```

The result of executing the query is shown in Table H.4.

SQL includes a **distinct** option to convert bags to sets, so the following query returns only a single occurrence of each gender. The same result is obtained from the LogiQL query: _(g) <- genderOf[_]=g.

```
select distinct gender
from President
```

TABLE H.3 Names and Birth Years of Female Presidents

presidentName	birth Year
Tarja Halonen	1943
Pranab Mukherje	1935

TABLE H.4 Genders (Only) of Presidents in SQL

Gender
M
F
M
F
M

The result of executing the query is shown in Table H.5.

SQL includes various relational operators for *joining* multiple relations into a single relation. The most expansive of these is the **cross join** operator, which outputs the *Cartesian product* of the input relations. Given any two sets A and B, the *Cartesian product A × B* is the set of all ordered pairs (*x, y*) where *x* belongs to A and *y* belongs to B. If A and B are relations, *x* and *y* are tuples.

For example, the following query lists all the possible ways of pairing a male president with a female president. Here **as**-clauses are used to introduce aliases for the president table (MP, male president; FP, female president). The aliases enable the table to be cross joined to itself (pairing each president with each president) before the **where**-clause condition filters out the unwanted rows from the Cartesian product. The aliases are necessary to distinguish the two occurrences of the president table in forming the join:

```
select MP.presidentName, FP.presidentName
from President as MP
    cross join President as FP
where MP.gender = 'M'
    and FP.gender = 'F'
```

The result of executing the query is shown in Table H.6.

TABLE H.5   Genders (Only) of Presidents in LogiQL

Gender
M
F

TABLE H.6   Male–Female Presidential Pairings

MP.presidentName	FP.presidentName
Christian Wulff	Tarja Halonen
Christian Wulff	Pratibha Patil
Nicolas Sarkozy	Tarja Halonen
Nicolas Sarkozy	Pratibha Patil
Barack Obama	Tarja Halonen
Barack Obama	Pratibha Patil

The following LogiQL rule computes the same set of ordered pairs:

```
isPairedWith(mp, fp) -> President(mp), President(fp).
isPairedWith(mp, fp) <- genderOf[mp] = "M",
    genderOf[fp] = "F".
// Pair each male president with each female president.
```

If we remove the **where**-clause from the previous SQL query, the full Cartesian product would be listed, pairing each of the five presidents with each president, resulting in 25 rows. The equivalent computation in LogiQL is shown below. Notice how much simpler the LogiQL code is compared with the SQL code:

```
isPairedWith(p1, p2) -> President(p1), President(p2).
isPairedWith(p1, p2) <- President(p1), President(p2).
// Pair each president with each president.
```

Now suppose that we wish to list each president as well as the ISO code and name of the country of which he/she is president. If you look back at the relational tables, you'll see that the relevant country codes are listed in both tables, but the presidents are listed in only the president table, while the country names are listed only in the country table.

The query may be formulated by forming the *natural join* of the two tables (matching rows in the country table with rows in the president table that have the same value for country code) and then projecting on the three required columns from the join result. In the SQL standard, this query may be formulated as shown below, using the **natural join** operator:

```
select presidentName, countryCode, countryName
from President natural join Country
```

Although included in the SQL standard since 1992, many commercial SQL dialects do not yet support this syntax. In this case, the query may be reformulated as a *conditional inner join* as follows. Here the join condition is stated in an **on**-clause, and the *countryCode* columns must be qualified by prepending their table name:

```
select presidentName, President.countryCode,
    countryName
from President join Country
on President.countryCode = Country.countryCode
```

The result of executing the query is shown in Table H.7.

The same results may be formulated in LogiQL:

```
result(p, c, cn) -> President(p), Country(c),
    string(cn).
result(p, c, cn) <- countryOf[p] = c,
    countryNameOf[c] = cn.
```

Notice that the join is achieved simply by using the same variable c in each conjunct. This ensures that the c value in countryNameOf[c]=cn matches the c value in countryOf[p]=c for each (p,c,cn) triple that satisfies the body condition.

$A \cup B$, the union of sets A and B, is the set of all elements that belong to either A or B. SQL includes the **union** operator to form the *union* of two compatible relations. As an example, consider the following two *m:n* relations, shown in Tables H.8 and H.9. Notice that their populations are properly compatible. A corresponding LogiQL schema is set out below the tables:

```
Person(p), hasPersonName(p:pn) -> string(pn).
Food(f), hasFoodName(f:fn) -> string(fn).
eats(p, f) -> Person(p), Food(f).
likes(p, f) -> Person(p), Food(f).
```

TABLE H.7   President Names, Country Codes, and Country Names

presidentName	countryCode	countryName
Christian Wulff	DE	Germany
Tarja Halonen	FI	Finland
Nicolas Sarkozy	FR	France
Pratibha Patil	IN	India
Barack Obama	US	United States

TABLE H.8   Eats Relation

personName	foodName
Spencer	Pizza
Spencer	Spinach
Spencer	Raisins
Terry	Mangoes
Terry	Pizza
Terry	Vegemite

TABLE H.9   Likes Relation

personName	foodName
Spencer	Pizza
Spencer	Raisins
Terry	Chocolate
Terry	Mangoes
Terry	Pizza

Since the types of the *Eats* and *Likes* relations are compatible, it is meaningful to construct their union. The following SQL query may be used to list who eats or likes what foods:

```
select personName, foodName
from Eats
union
select personName, foodName
from Likes
```

The result of executing the query is shown in Table H.10.

The following, disjunctive LogiQL query returns the same set of ordered pairs. In general, unions may be formulated in LogiQL by using the *inclusive-or* operator (';'). Again, the LogiQL query is simpler than the corresponding SQL query. The program, data, and query are accessible in the files SQL2.logic and SQLData.logic:

```
_(p, f) <- eats(p, f) ; likes(p, f).
```

Returning to our country and president tables, suppose we want to list the presidents of those countries that have a population of at least 100 million people. Although we need to access both tables to determine the answer, the final projection comes from just the president table. Hence, even though we could formulate the query using a join, it is also possible to formulate the query in SQL without a join by using a *subquery*:

```
select presidentName
from President
where countryCode in
(select countryName
 from Country
 where population > = 100000000)
```

TABLE H.10   Union of
Eats and Likes Relations

personName	foodName
Spencer	Pizza
Spencer	Spinach
Spencer	Raisins
Terry	Chocolate
Terry	Mangoes
Terry	Pizza
Terry	Vegemite

TABLE H.11   Presidents of
Highly Populated Countries

presidentName
Pratibha Patil
Barack Obama

The result of executing the query is shown in Table H.11.

Here the bracketed **select**-statement is a subquery to derive which countries have a population above 100 million. This subquery returns the set {'IN', 'US'}, and this intermediate result is used to transform the outer query into **select** *presidentName* **from** president **where** *countryCode* **in** {'IN', 'US'}, which is then run to return the final result.

In LogiQL the subquery to compute the highly populated countries may be specified as a derivation rule such as

```
isHighlyPopulated(c) -> Country(c).
isHighlyPopulated(c) <- populationOf[c] > = 100000000.
```

That computed predicate may then be referenced in the final query to return the presidents of highly populated countries. This code is included in the file SQL1.logic:

```
_(p) <- countryOf[p] = c, isHighlyPopulated(c).
```

SQL provides several aggregation functions, including **count, sum, min**, and **max** which roughly correspond, respectively, to the count, total, min, and max functions in LogiQL. SQL's **avg** function for computing averages may be emulated in LogiQL by dividing the sum computed by the total function by the number of elements computed by the count function.

SQL's **count** function may be applied to a single column, but when its argument is specified as an asterisk it counts all the rows in the specified bag or set. For example, the following SQL query may be used to count the number of female presidents:

```
select count(*) from President
where gender = 'F'
```

Result: 2

In LogiQL, we could derive this result using the following derivation rule:

```
nrFemalePresidents[] = n -> int(n).
nrFemalePresidents[] = n <-
    agg<<n = count()>> President(p), genderOf[p] = "F".
```

SQL's syntax for aggregation functions is usually simpler than that of LogiQL. The following SQL query may be used to list the name of the country (or countries) with the maximum population. Since China was omitted from our data, the query returns India:

```
select countryName from Country
where population =
    (select max(population) from Country)
```

Result: India

In LogiQL, the maximum population may be derived as follows:

```
maxPopulation[] = n -> int(n).
maxPopulation[] = n <- agg<<n = max(pop)>>
    populationOf[_] = pop.
```

The name of the country with the maximum population may now be listed using the following query:

```
_(cn) <- countryNameOf[c] = cn, populationOf[c] =
    maxPopulation[].
```

SQL includes a **group by** clause for partitioning a table into groups of rows, where each row in a specific group has the same value(s) for the specified grouping criterion/criteria. This may then be used to list properties that apply to each group as a whole, so the final query result has at most one row for each group. For example, the following SQL query lists the number of presidents for each gender, as well as the minimum birth year for each gender:

```
select gender, count(*), min(birthyear)
from President
group by gender
```

Result:

```
F 2 1934
M 3 1955
```

When executed, the **from**-clause chooses the president table, and then the **group by** clause partitions the president table into two groups, one for each gender, as depicted below. The **select**-clause is then executed to list for each gender the count of all the rows in its group and the minimum birth year in its group.

The result of executing the query is shown in Table H.12.

In LogiQL, the grouping criterion is used as an argument to the derived functions, and thus,

```
nrOfPresidentsOf[g] = n -> Gender(g), int(n).
nrOfPresidentsOf[g] = n <- agg<<n = count()>>
   genderOf[_] = g .
// Computes the number of presidents for each gender.
minBirthYearOf[g] = n -> Gender(g), int(n).
minBirthYearOf[g] = n <-
    agg<<n = min(y)>> genderOf[p] = g ,
    birthyearOf[p] = y.
// Computes the minimum birth year for each gender.
```

TABLE H.12   Illustration of Group by Clause

presidentName	countryCode	Gender	birthYear
Tarja Halonen	FI	F	1943
Pratibha Patil	IN	F	1934
Christian Wulff	DE	M	1959
Nicolas Sarkozy	FR	M	1955
Barack Obama	US	M	1961

The following query may now be used to return the required result:

```
_(g, np, mby) <-
   nrOfPresidentsOf[g] = np,
   minBirthYearOf[g] = mby.
```

The program, data, and query codes for the above grouping examples are accessible as SQL3.logic and SQL3Data.logic.

Now consider Table H.13. This table records, for each item, region, and quarter, the number of items sold in that region during that quarter. To save space, we include just two items and two regions, and limit the quarters to a single year. The key of this table is itemCode, region, and quarter. To help with later discussion, the table is displayed as partitioned into four groups, where all rows in any specific group share the same item and region.

The LogiQL schema for this table may be set out as follows;

```
Item(i), hasItemCode(i:c) -> string(c).
Region(r), hasRegionName(r:rn) -> string(rn).
Quarter(q), hasQuarterNr(q:qn) -> int(qn).
nrSoldOf_In_In_[i, r, q] = n -> Item(i), Region(r),
    Quarter(q), int(n).
hasRegionName(_:rn) -> rn = "East" ; rn = "West".
hasQuarterNr(_:qn) -> qn > = 1, qn <= 4.
```

TABLE H.13   Product Sales Report

itemCode	Region	Quarter	Number Sold
BBB	East	1	50
BBB	East	2	100
BBB	East	3	100
BBB	East	4	150
BBB	West	1	100
BBB	West	2	150
BBB	West	3	200
BBB	West	4	250
DL	East	1	20
DL	East	2	30
DL	East	3	40
DL	East	4	50
DL	West	1	50
DL	West	2	100
DL	West	3	100
DL	West	4	150

Now suppose we wish to list for each item and region the total number of items sold over all quarters. The query groups by multiple criteria, in this case item and region. The SQL query may be formulated as follows, yielding the result shown:

```
select itemCode, region sum(nrSold)
from Sale
group by itemCode, region
```

Result:

```
BBB    East    400
BBB    West    700
DL     East    140
DL     West    400
```

In LogiQL, sums are computed by the total function. To sum over the quarters for each item–region combination, we include the two grouping criteria as the arguments of the required function, which may be computed using the following derivation rule:

```
totalNrSoldOf_In_[i, r] = n -> string(i), string(r),
    int(n).
totalNrSoldOf_In_[i, r] = n <-
    agg<<n = total(qty)>>
    nrSoldOf_In_In_[i, r, _] = qty.
// Computes for each item and region combination
// the total number of items sold.
```

Querying the totalNrSoldOf_In_ predicate now gives the same result set as output by the SQL query. The program, data, and query code for the above grouping example are accessible as SQL4.logic and SQL4Data.logic.

Appendix I: Testing Your Programs

THIS APPENDIX DESCRIBES THE `lb unit` unit-testing framework. An important part of constructing programs in any language is testing them, and one purpose of this appendix is to get you thinking about constructing tests as you write your programs.

The `lb unit` is invoked by typing `lb unit args`, where `args` is used to indicate the tests you want to run and other options you can supply. Individual tests can be run by using the `--test` *fileName(s)* option, where *fileName(s)* gives the name of the file(s) containing the tests that you want to run.

You can also organize your tests into *suites*, collections of related tests. Similar to the above, you would use the `--suite` *suiteName(s)* option to run suite(s) of tests. Each of them names a directory containing a set of test files to execute. You can even run a series of suites by using the `--suiteDir` *suiteDirectory(ies)* option. In this case, `lb unit` will recursively execute the tests in each of the named directories.

Regardless of how you invoke `lb unit`, it first runs any user-specified setup instructions common to the tests in the directory containing them. The instructions are placed in a file named `setUp.lb`. Similarly, after the tests are run, `lb unit` runs the instructions in the file `tearDown.lb`. Note that all test script files should use the `.lb` suffix.

`setUp.lb`, `tearDown.lb`, and your test files comprise two types of content: LogiQL code and instructions in the form accepted by the `lb` command. (See Appendix A.) For example, here is the setup file as found in the `setUp.lb` file in the resource directory for this appendix:

```
create --unique
```

This instruction tells lb unit to create a new workspace with a made up and unique name. Alternatively, instead of --unique, you can specify a name for the workspace, such as ws.

Similarly, tearDown.lb contains the following line:

```
close --destroy
```

which closes and removes the workspace used in the tests.

Besides opening and closing workspaces, lb unit instructions can load LogiQL code blocks and data. For example, say we wanted to make sure that a simple declaration like the following had no problems. The following instruction could be used to do this:

```
addblock 'Monarch(m), hasMonarchName(m:s) ->
  string(s).'
exec --file b.logic
```

addblock is the lb command for adding declarations, rules, and constraints to a workspace. The LogiQL code is contained within apostrophes to prevent inadvertent interpretation by the shell from which you execute lb unit. In this example, the addblock transaction adds the declarations of Monarch and hasMonarchName to the workspace created with setUp. lb. The second transaction above shows an alternative way to include information in a test. The --file option to exec requests that lb unit obtain information from a file b.logic, which contains the following content:

```
+Monarch("George VI").
```

Note the suffix .logic should be used for files containing only LogiQL statements.

Of course, the above two transactions do not comprise a very interesting test. If they were executed by lb unit, the compiler and runtime would check for simple errors, such as syntax problems. While this can be valuable information, normally, you will want to determine that the program actually computes the intended output. One way to make this check is to define a new predicate and populate it with the output expected. Then the two predicates (the original one and the new one) can be compared.

The following test, based on chapter1/tests/CE1/q1c.lb, illustrates this technique. It assumes the same setUp.lb and tearDown. lb files as shown above. The test's main purpose is to check whether the computation expressed in the `foreignMonarch` predicate derives the expected answers. Here is the first part of the test providing declarations, constraints, derivation rules, and basic data:

```
addblock '
  Monarch(m), hasMonarchName(m:s) -> string(s).
  Country(c), hasCountryCode(c:cc) -> string(cc).
  wasBornIn[m] = c -> Monarch(m), Country(c).
  Monarch(m) -> wasBornIn[m] = _ .
  foreignMonarch(m) -> Monarch(m).
  foreignMonarch(m) <- wasBornIn[m] = c, c ! = "GB".
'
```

```
exec '
  +wasBornIn["Anne"] = "GB".
  +wasBornIn["George I"] = "DE".
  +wasBornIn["George II"] = "DE".
  +wasBornIn["George III"] = "GB".
  +wasBornIn["George IV"] = "GB".
  +wasBornIn["William IV"] = "GB".
  +wasBornIn["Victoria"] = "GB".
  +wasBornIn["Edward VII"] = "GB".
  +wasBornIn["George V"] = "GB".
  +wasBornIn["Edward VIII"] = "GB".
  +wasBornIn["George VI"] = "GB".
  +wasBornIn["Elizabeth II"] = "GB".
'
```

Based upon the above declarations and the derivation rule for `foreign-Monarch`, you would expect the derived answers to be "George I" and "George II". In order to make this check, you can express these expectations by introducing a new predicate, as shown in the following code segments:

```
addblock 'foreignMonarch:expected(m) -> Monarch(m).'
```

The segment defines a new predicate named `foreignMonarch:expected`. The name is conventionally constructed from the name of the predicate being checked, `foreignMonarch`, and the suffix, `expected`, separated by a colon (':').

You can now populate the new predicate with the facts you expect to be contained in the `foreignMonarch` predicate: that is, that George I and George II were not born in Great Britain:

```
exec '
  +foreignMonarch:expected("George II").
  +foreignMonarch:expected("George I").
'
```

If the code above is correct, you would expect the two predicates, `foreignMonarch` and `foreignMonarch:expected`, to be identical. The final segment of the test comprises two constraints that make this check:

```
addblock '
  foreignMonarch:expected(m) -> foreignMonarch(m).
  foreignMonarch(m) -> foreignMonarch:expected(m).
'
```

The first constraint expresses the expectation that all of our predicted answers were, in fact, derived. The second checks that no other outputs were produced.

There is some flexibility into which transactions the various statements are placed. For example, the declaration of `foreignMonarch` could have been placed with the declarations for `Monarch` and `hasMonarchName` in the first transaction above. Also, the first of the two constraints in the last segment could have been placed there. Stylistically, however, we recommend that you place your testing code separate from and after the code being tested. Note however, we could not have put the second constraint with the declarations in the first transaction. Can you see why?

If you place the second constraint in any transaction before the `foreignMonarch:expected` facts were asserted, the test would fail, even if the underlying code was correct. This is because at the moment when the transaction containing the constraints completed, there would, in fact, be two `foreignMonarch` facts for which there were not yet `foreignMonarch:expected` facts, violating the second constraint. The code for this example can be found in the file `example.lb`.

Information about other `lb unit` options can be found by executing `lb unit --help`.

Appendix J: Improving Your Program's Performance

T HIS APPENDIX PROVIDES A brief summary of some ways to help improve the performance of your LogiQL programs.

DERIVED-ONLY PREDICATES

By default, predicates computed via rules are treated as materialized views, so their fact populations are stored for use in later transactions. This is typically better because it allows updates to be computed incrementally (e.g., computing a bank account balance from the latest update to the previous balance is much faster than calculating the balance each time by processing all the updates on the account that have occurred since the account was opened).

However, it is sometimes useful to fully re-evaluate a derived predicate, making its result available for other rules within the current transaction, but not installing its result in the database when the transaction is committed. Such *derived-only predicates* are declared using the metapredicate setting `lang:derivationType['`]="Derived"`.

Derived-only predicates are useful for defining a complex computation, which could potentially result in an infinite set of facts, for reuse elsewhere in the transaction in a context that finitely constrains its arguments. Recall the following example discussed in Unit 4.5:

```
Mass(m), hasKgValue(m:kg) -> float(kg).
Energy(e), hasJouleValue(e:j) -> float(j).
cSquared[m] = e -> Mass(m), Energy(e).
```

```
cSquared[m] = e <- m * pow[300000000f, 2f] = e.
lang:derivationType[`cSquared] = "Derived".
isHighEnergySource(m) -> Mass(m).
isHighEnergySource(m) <- Mass(m), cSquared[m] >
    pow[10f, 18f].
isVeryHighEnergySource(m) -> Mass(m).
isVeryHighEnergySource(m) <- Mass(m), cSquared[m] >
    pow[10f, 19f].
```

The cSquared rule would normally be treated as unsafe, because there are infinitely many values of m and e that satisfy it. However, because cSquared is a derived-only predicate, its values are computed only in the context of the other rules that use them, and those rule bodies restrict m to the finite set of values asserted for the domain predicate Mass(m). The following performance tip summarizes appropriate usage.

> **PT1:** *Use the default setting (derived-and-stored) for computed predicates whenever incremental computation is desired (the typical situation). If you wish to reuse a computation with potentially infinite results within other rules in the same transaction that finitely constrain it, then declare the predicate derived-only.*

Unguarded Delta Rules

Recall how in Exercise 5B of Chapter 3 grandparent facts were added using an intentional database (IDB) rule. Here isGrandparentOf is declared instead as an extensional database (EDB) predicate to allow direct assertions about grandparenthood when we do not know at least one of the parenthood facts whose combination would imply it. The delta rules automatically add grandparent facts when relevant parenthood facts are added:

```
Person(p), hasPersonName(p:pn) -> string(pn).
isParentOf(p1, p2) -> Person(p1), Person(p2).
isGrandparentOf(p1, p2) -> Person(p1), Person(p2).
+isGrandparentOf(p1, p2) <- +isParentOf(p1, p3),
    isParentOf(p3, p2).
+isGrandparentOf(p1, p2) <- isParentOf(p1, p3),
    +isParentOf(p3, p2).
```

Executed delta rules are evaluated before the installed delta rules, so the relevant parenthood facts are already there when the installed delta rules are run. For the same reason, the single installed delta rule below expresses the same result as the combination of rules above:

```
+isGrandparentOf(p1, p2) <- isParentOf(p1, p3),
    isParentOf(p3, p2). // Error!
```

This rule would derive all applicable grandparenthood facts on every transaction, in contrast to the guarded delta rules in the first version that derive the relevant grandparenthood facts only when a relevant parenthood fact is added. However, this delta rule generates an error message because its rule body does not include a delta or pulse predicate that provides a condition, or *guard*, that must be satisfied before the rule is executed. Such a delta rule is said to be *unguarded*. If they were allowed, unguarded delta rules would be evaluated on every transaction. Apart from the extra expense incurred by such redundant computation, unguarded delta rules might lead to predicate locking problems that can potentially disable programs that are intended to be concurrent.

Problems can also occur if a delta rule to be executed at a stage other than `initial` references a negated atom from an earlier stage.

PT2: *Avoid unguarded delta rules (i.e., delta rules in which the rule body contains no delta predicate or pulse predicate condition that is required for the rule to be evaluated).*

FOLDING DISJUNCTIONS

Consider the following program, which includes a derivation rule to select a short list of applicants to be interviewed for a technical position:

```
Applicant(a), hasApplicantNr(a:n) -> int(n).
Language(la), hasLanguageName(la:n) -> string(n).
hasIndustryExperience(a) -> Applicant(a).
isFluentIn(a, la) -> Applicant(a), Language(la).
nrPublicationsOf[a] = n -> Applicant(a), int(n).
Discipline(d), hasDisciplineName(d:n) -> string(n).
hasPhDIn(a, d) -> Applicant(a), Discipline(d).
isShortListed(a) -> Applicant(a).
```

```
isShortListed(a) <-
    hasIndustryExperience(a), isFluentIn(a, "English"),
    nrPublicationsOf[a] >= 20,
    (hasPhDIn(a, "Computer Science") ;
    hasPhDIn(a, "Logic")).
```

The derivation rule includes a conjunction of conditions to be satisfied (industrial experience, fluency in English, and at least 20 publications), as well as a disjunction of conditions to be satisfied (must have a Ph.D. in either computer science or logic).

Although this program works, internally the LogiQL engine transforms the derivation rule into the following, disjunction-free rules, in order to execute it:

```
isShortListed(a) <-
    hasIndustryExperience(a), isFluentIn(a, "English"),
    nrPublicationsOf[a] >= 20,
    hasPhDIn(a, "Computer Science").

isShortListed(a) <-
    hasIndustryExperience(a), isFluentIn(a, "English"),
    nrPublicationsOf[a] >= 20,
    hasPhDIn(a, "Logic").
```

Each of the transformed rules includes the original conjunction of three conditions, as well as one of the original disjuncts. Hence, the conjunction in the original rule has to be processed twice, once for each original disjunct. If the original conjunction is complex or the number of disjuncts is high, this kind of duplication of effort can significantly impact performance. In such cases, it is better to specify one rule to compute just the disjunction (known as "*folding* the disjunction"), and then use that computed predicate instead of the disjunction in a second rule. For the current example, this leads to the following reformulation:

```
hasRelevantPhD(a) <-
    hasPhDIn(a, "Computer Science") ;
    hasPhDIn(a, "Logic").
isShortListed(a) <-
    hasIndustryExperience(a), isFluentIn(a, "English"),
    nrPublicationsOf[a] >= 20, hasRelevantPhD(a).
```

With this approach, the conjunction is computed once only, leading to better performance. For some more complicated disjunctions, folding cannot be done (e.g., if a disjunct negates over a variable that is positively bound only outside the disjunction). However, where it can be done, folding disjunctions often improves performance.

> **PT3:** *If the rule body includes a complex conjunction as well as a disjunction, consider folding the disjunction to a separate rule.*

DISJOINT PREDICATE RULES

Unit 2.6 used the following example code to compute the number of children that a Person has:

```
nrChildrenOf[p] = 0 <- Person(p), !isParentOf(p, _).
nrChildrenOf[p] = positiveNrChildrenOf[p] <-
    isParentOf(p, _).
// The number of children of p = 0
// if p is a person who is not a parent of someone ,
// else it's the positive number of children of p .
```

Notice that there are two rules for nrChildrenOf. Because nrChildren Of is a functional predicate, there is a danger that the two rules will produce different values for a given argument Person. To make sure this does not happen, the execution engine must specifically check for violations. For these two rules, however, we know that a given argument Person can only satisfy one of the two rules. Hence, in principle, the check need never be made.

Fortunately, LogiQL has a way for you to let the execution engine know that at most one of these possibilities could ever hold. To do this, you should make use of the lang:isDisjoint metapredicate:

```
lang:isDisjoint[`nrChildrenOf] = true.
// The two rules for nrChildrenOf return mutually
// exclusive results.
```

Notice that the predicate nrChildrenOf serves as argument of the metapredicate lang:isDisjoint. Although this metapredicate is not needed to get the right result, it can improve performance by notifying the compiler that the result sets returned individually by the two rules for nrChildrenOf are mutually exclusive. Since each of the two individual result sets is known to be functional, disjointedness between them implies that the overall result set is also functional. Hence, the LogiQL execution engine does not need to perform a separate check to ensure that this functional dependency is satisfied.

> **PT4:** *If multiple rule bodies defining the same functional predicate can never be applied to the same argument, use the* `lang:isDisjoint` *metapredicate to avoid making unnecessary functional dependency violation checks.*

Index